The Performance of Performance Standards

The Performance of Performance Standards

James J. Heckman
Carolyn J. Heinrich
Pascal Courty
Gerald Marschke
Jeffrey Smith
Editors

2011

W.E. Upjohn Institute for Employment Research
Kalamazoo, Michigan

Library of Congress Cataloging-in-Publication Data

The performance of performance standards / James J. Heckman . . . [et al.], editors.
p. cm.
Includes bibliographical references and index.
ISBN-13: 978-0-88099-292-3 (pbk. : alk. paper)
ISBN-10: 0-88099-292-1 (pbk. : alk. paper)
ISBN-13: 978-0-88099-294-7 (hardcover : alk. paper)
ISBN-10: 0-88099-294-8 (hardcover : alk. paper)
1. Government productivity. 2. Performance standards. 3. Civil service—Personnel management. I. Heckman, James J. (James Joseph)
JF1525.P67P476 2011
352.6'7—dc22

2011007877

W.E. Upjohn Institute for Employment Research
300 S. Westnedge Avenue
Kalamazoo, Michigan 49007-4686

Cover design by Alcorn Publication Design.
Index prepared by Diane Worden.
Printed in the United States of America.
Printed on recycled paper.

Contents

1
Performance Standards and the Potential to Improve Government Performance

James J. Heckman
Carolyn J. Heinrich
Jeffrey Smith

A number of recently implemented reforms to public sector incentive systems have sought to reorient them toward a focus on measuring *results* and inducing public agencies to become more efficient, responsive, and accountable to the public. They share at least two features. The first is a system of performance measures and standards designed to create clear expectations for government performance and to assess results. A second feature is a means for rewarding individuals, teams, or entire organizations for achievement relative to the established performance goals, primarily through budgetary allocations. By clearly defining goals and developing explicit rewards for their attainment, these systems have aimed to replicate, in a nonmarket setting, the incentive structures, competition, and resulting high performance and efficiency of private markets (Light 2005).

Among its first steps in advancing these reforms, the Obama administration has required federal agencies to identify a limited number of high-priority performance goals for which performance trends will be tracked, and through its new Open Government initiative, it will make these data publicly available and promote the use of new methods in the analysis of them. The government is also now compelling the private sector to provide more information on its performance for transparency and accountability (beyond longer-standing areas of public scrutiny such as health care and the environment), and has devised incentives for cooperation and penalties for withholding information (Cukier 2010). For example, it is now possible for the public to get statistics on job-related deaths that name employers and to see restaurants' health inspection scores online.

As the use of performance measurement and incentive systems has expanded in the public sector, so has the number of studies calling attention to their problems and unintended effects (Bevan and Hood 2006; Brooks 2000; Courty and Marschke 2004; Heckman and Smith 2004; Heinrich 2004, 2007; Heinrich and Marschke 2010; Koning and Heinrich 2010; Propper and Wilson 2003; Radin 2000; Smith 1995; General Accounting Office [GAO] 2002). Performance standards systems and bonuses are (or have been) used in Food Stamps (now the Supplemental Nutrition Assistance Program) and welfare-to-work programs, employment and training programs, public school accountability systems under No Child Left Behind, child welfare agencies and child support enforcement programs, Medicaid and SCHIP programs, and other social programs, although not without some degree of controversy and ongoing challenges in their design and implementation. The development of performance incentive systems in public bureaucracies also continues to advance in Europe, led by Great Britain's early exploration, and with some governments (such as Australia and the Netherlands) now implementing incentive systems with fully (100 percent) performance-contingent pay/contracting arrangements (Finn 2008; Struyven and Steurs 2005).

While the broad introduction of incentive systems in many government agencies is new, U.S. employment and training programs have used both performance standards and monetary bonuses for over two decades. Klerman (2005, p. 347) describes the Job Training Partnership Act (JTPA)/Workforce Investment Act (WIA) performance measurement system as one of the "most mature implementations of performance-based management." It is also one of the most studied systems, in part because of the randomized experimental evaluation of the JTPA program that produced important information for assessing the performance of these performance standards systems in measuring program impacts (Bloom et al. 1993; Dickinson et al. 1988; Heckman, Heinrich, and Smith 2002; Heckman, LaLonde, and Smith 1999; Orr et al. 1995). Policymakers have looked to the results of these studies to guide changes to these systems in employment and training programs and to also inform the design and operation of performance standards systems in other government programs.

At the same time, one of our motivations for assembling the research presented in this book is that despite decades of study and practice, some of the important lessons that have been learned are not reflected in the current design and implementation of performance standards systems. Bevan and Hood (2006), for example, describe the development and use of performance targets in the English public health care system, along with the perverse incentives they generated, as "hitting the target and missing the point."[1] And despite the long tenure of performance standards in U.S. employment and training programs, a 2002 GAO report (p. 14) confirms the persistence of gaming responses that influence who gets access to program services as well as service intensity, concluding that "the need to meet performance levels may be the driving factor in deciding who receives WIA-funded services at the local level."

It may be that some of the more rigorous empirical evidence from past studies has not been effectively communicated or penetrated policymaking and public management circles deeply enough.[2] Or, as Heckman, Heinrich, and Smith comment in Chapter 3, it may be that policymakers who have mandated such systems (and administrators involved in their implementation) have not fully appreciated the challenges of designing a performance management system that generates incentives for improving program impacts. Research in this area has also continued to evolve, with advances in theoretical conceptions, modeling, and data, and of course, changes in the incentive systems over time have facilitated analysis of their implications for performance standards system design and functioning. The chapters included in this volume embody a number of these important advancements, and yet our primary aim is to make the lessons of our research clear to those who design and implement these incentive systems in the public sector.

The nine chapters that follow use U.S. employment and training programs as a "laboratory" for investigation. They draw extensively from the data and experiences of the earlier JTPA performance standards system, both because of its longer tenure and the availability of experimental data. Using a variety of data sources on these incentives systems, the authors of these chapters explore how performance standards and incentives affect the behavior of public managers and agency employees, their approaches to service delivery, and ultimately, the outcomes for participants. Both the JTPA and WIA programs have allowed state and local administrators and their governing boards substantial discretion, within broad limits, to determine performance goals, standards, and bonus systems. This administrative flexibility is reflected in the range of incentive systems that have been implemented by different states and by the same states over time. It is this variation that serves as the grist for our empirical mill and is used to extract general lessons that can be applied on a wider scale to both existing and newly developing performance incentive systems.

KEY QUESTIONS AND CHARACTERISTICS OF PERFORMANCE STANDARDS SYSTEMS IN U.S. EMPLOYMENT AND TRAINING PROGRAMS

While investigating formal incentive structures and organizational behavior within U.S. employment and training programs, the authors in this volume address the following six fundamental questions:

1) How do performance standards and measures operate to include or exclude individuals with different characteristics in these programs?
2) How do performance standards and measures affect the types of services offered?
3) How do the processes for setting standards and weights for performance goals and for recognizing and rewarding performance affect system incentives and bureaucratic responses?
4) Are the performance standards, measures, and incentives effective in motivating bureaucratic behavior toward the achievement of program goals?
5) Do short-term outcome measures used in the performance standards systems predict long-term impacts of the programs on participants?
6) What general lessons can be learned from a study of these performance standards systems and the variation in the rules governing their administration over time?

In the next chapter, the JTPA and WIA performance standards systems are described in greater detail. Below, we briefly list four key features of the programs that are pertinent to understanding the contributions of this volume. We follow with an overview of the chapters and their salient findings.

1) Federal job training programs (formerly JTPA and currently WIA) are highly decentralized. Local level governing boards include local business officials along with other government, community, and labor leaders. States control most aspects of the performance standards system that guides training activities, including determining the rules that govern how outcome measures count and how performance awards are made.
2) Workforce development programs generate relatively easily measured outcomes such as employment, wages, completion of education programs, enrollment in the military, and continued schooling. More difficult to assess, however, is the value added produced by the programs, which, as we show, does not necessarily correlate strongly with shorter-term outcome measures.
3) Most performance standards have been formulated in terms of *levels* of achievement, rather than in terms of achievement *gains* resulting from program participation. This practice gives rise to the potential for "cream skimming," which results when centers enroll persons who are likely to have high outcome levels rather than those whose outcomes would improve most through participation in the program.
4) Training centers (or states under WIA) that meet or exceed their performance standards typically receive budgetary rewards. Training centers have shown, however, that they can manipulate the performance standards system in ways that improve measured performance but may not contribute to value-added or individual gains. The ability of program managers and staff to manipulate the data used to monitor them poses a major challenge to the successful design of performance standards systems.

OVERVIEW OF THE CHAPTERS AND THEIR RELATIONSHIP TO PREVIOUS RESEARCH

The studies in this volume take advantage of data that are superior in scope and detail to some of the data used in the existing literature or available on a regular basis for assessing program performance. The research described in Chapters 4, 6, 8, and 9 benefitted from detailed longitudinal, microlevel data that were collected in the National JTPA Study (NJS) and through other administrative data sources. The NJS data also include information on JTPA-eligible nonparticipants in four experimental sites. These data have two important advantages over samples of eligible populations constructed from large public-use data sets: 1) they are collected from eligible nonparticipants residing in the same geographical area as participants, and 2) the data are gathered using the same survey instruments as those used for participants.

In addition, the authors collect and analyze complete information about state-level variation in the JTPA and WIA performance standards systems. Chapters 4 and 5 show that state incentive systems are highly complex and differ widely across states and over time within states. They are not easily characterized by small dimensional summary measures as used in previous studies (see, for example, Anderson, Burkhauser, and Raymond [1993] and Dickinson et al. [1988]). This wealth of data is very helpful in assessing the implications of changes and differences in performance standard regimes, and a variety of analytical strategies are applied to learn from these data.

Before addressing the key questions listed above, the contributing authors provide some basic information in Chapter 2 about the design and implementation of the JTPA and WIA programs to aid our readers' understanding of the research that follows. Chapter 2 describes the origins and organizational structure of these programs, eligibility rules and the types of services made available to participants, details of the performance measures, and other aspects of these performance standards systems' design. Chapter 2 also highlights some of the changes in these systems over time, particularly in the shift from JTPA to WIA.

In Chapter 3, James Heckman, Carolyn Heinrich, and Jeffrey Smith set up a formal model of a performance standards system that theoretically frames many of the fundamental questions and issues that are addressed in this book. For example, their model demonstrates how the JTPA and WIA program goals to promote equity and efficiency interact with a performance standards system based on short-term outcome measures. As such, they show that whether or not cream skimming is at odds with equity or efficiency (or both) is an empirical question that depends on the relationship between the benefits of program services and the location of trainees in the skill distribution of applicants. Importantly, the broad conceptual framework that they develop provides a foundation for future investigation about when (and if) performance standards systems in active labor market programs will increase labor market impacts, and when (and if) they are more likely to have unintended consequences due to responses by program staff to the incentives they provide.

In Chapter 4, Courty and Marschke describe the structure of the JTPA performance standards system and highlight important details that go into developing a performance-contingent budgeting scheme. They describe the performance measures upon which awards were contingent, the nature of the awards, and how performance awards were computed in JTPA; they also show how crucial the handling of these details can be to the success of performance funding. Courty and Marschke find that interstate differences in the implementation of the performance incentives system grew over time, reflecting the substantial discretion federal authorities gave to state and local agencies in its management. Their findings suggest that the objectives of states' incentive systems increasingly diverged from the original federal ones, leading to some unintended consequences.

Courty, Heinrich, and Marschke draw from the information economics, contract theory, and public administration literatures to derive theoretical implications for the establishment of appropriate benchmark levels of performance (i.e., performance standards) in Chapter 5. They then assess alternative methods that are commonly used to construct performance standards and evaluate their application in the JTPA and WIA systems. They find evidence that performance measurement system designers have attempted to "level the playing field" over time to provide equivalent performance incentives across states and localities. However, they also identify some negative dynamic properties of the JTPA and WIA performance measurement systems. The dynamics of performance benchmarking, and the politically motivated ambition to demonstrate continuous performance improvement, likely introduced inefficiencies and generated incentives to influence performance in ways other than increasing effort. These potentially harmful behaviors include selecting trainees according to observed characteristics associated with their labor market success, limiting the availability of more intensive training services and demonstrating lower performance early on to allow for performance improvements over time.

In Chapter 6, Heckman and Smith present a detailed, step-by-step analysis of the process by which individuals become participants in employment and training programs. Using data from the JTPA system, the goal of their analysis is to determine the sources of demographic disparities in participation rates and to isolate the roles of personal information, program eligibility rules, and administrative discretion in determining the probability of program participation. Disparities arising from voluntary decisions not to participate by informed persons raise different policy concerns from disparities arising from inequitable administrative practices or bureaucratic treatment. Models for the determination of eligibility, awareness of the program, and application and acceptance into the program are estimated. Bureaucratic discretion is assumed to play the major role in the final stage of the process. The evidence reported in this chapter indicates that while cream skimming is an important feature of the JTPA program, program eligibility rules, the personal choices of potential participants, and informational constraints are also important determinants of demographic disparities in JTPA participation.

Another important lesson from the incentive literature is that explicit incentives may elicit unintended and dysfunctional responses, also known as gaming responses. In Chapter 7, Courty and Marschke present a comprehensive overview of the literature on dysfunctional responses and develop a theoretical framework to classify the various dysfunctional responses that have been identified in practice. They distinguish three types of dysfunctional responses: 1) accounting manipulations that have no impact on the organization, 2) gaming responses that boost performance outcomes but have a negative impact on the organization, and 3) marginal misallocations that have positive impacts but are suboptimal because alternative allocations would have a higher impact. They then summarize the empirical evidence of dysfunctional responses in the JTPA system and assess the extent to which such responses may impede the effective functioning of performance measurement systems.

A widely cited GAO report (1991) claims that the JTPA performance standard system produced inequities by encouraging frequent routing of minorities and women into the least productive training activities and by denying them training altogether. The GAO alleges that training centers' pursuit of incentive payments and recognition for high performance has a perverse effect on participant selection as well as on trainees' access to services. In Chapter 8, through an extensive analysis of a JTPA training center in Illinois, Heinrich shows that bureaucratic decisions involving the selection of participants and their assignments to JTPA program services are frequently interdependent. She combines case-study and econometric approaches to investigate the screening decisions made by program staff and the influence of performance standards on these decisions. Heinrich finds evidence that these frontline staff cream-skim in making their enrollment and treatment-assignment decisions, and she also documents how shifts in federal policy fostered a movement away from more costly but higher value-added services toward less costly services. In the face of declining JTPA budgets, it appears that bureaucrats sought to preserve their client load and maintain low costs by offering cheaper but less cost-effective services. The resulting effect, most likely unintended, is that bureaucrats cut service quality to keep program costs low and maintain service quantity.

In Chapter 9, Heckman, Heinrich, and Smith use data from the NJS to examine the relationship between the short-run performance measures used in the JTPA performance standards system, such as employment and wages at termination from the program (or 13 weeks after termination), and experimental estimates of the impact or value added of the program on employment and earnings. In most cases, the data reveal a very weak relationship between the short-run measures and the long-run impacts. In fact, this relationship is often perverse, so that higher short-run measures are associated with lower long-term impacts from training. The JTPA performance standards system was, and the current WIA system is, based on measures that are not highly correlated with the gains from the program. Thus, evidence presented in the other chapters that the performance standards system "works" in the sense that it motivates bureaucrats to achieve certain standards does not imply that the performance standards system leads training centers to choose the combination of persons served and services offered that maximizes total gains obtained from the program.

In Chapter 10, Heckman, Heinrich, and Smith summarize three main lessons of the volume regarding the effectiveness of performance standards in public organizations and the need for further research. First, organizations respond to incentives, but sometimes the responses are perverse. In the first iteration of an incentive system's design, well-meaning designers of the performance standards system are unlikely to anticipate the shrewd responses of program administrators and frontline workers to system incentives, or the many possible ways they might influence measured performance without necessarily adding to (or possibly even detracting from) program value or impact. For example, individuals' access to program services and the nature and duration of the services participants receive are sometimes adversely affected by bureaucrats' responses to the performance incentives.

Second, the short-term outcome measures that continue to be used in the WIA performance standards system are only weakly related to the true long-run impacts of the program on earnings and employment. Measures of changes in earnings were tried under WIA but were discontinued, and the U.S. Department of Labor (USDOL) continues with measures of entry into unsubsidized employment, retention in unsubsidized employment six months after entry into the employment, and earnings levels six months after entry into the employment. Researchers and policymakers have yet to identify performance measures that will promote key, long-term program objectives while simultaneously generating more readily available performance information for ongoing program management.

Third, the importance of the cream skimming issue has been overstated in popular discussions. In the provision of employment and training services, the trade-off between efficiency and equity is modest at best. Personal choices and informational constraints play an important role in accounting for demographic differences in program participation among those eligible, while the effect of administrative discretion in accounting for demographic disparities among the eligible population is relatively limited. Chapter 10 includes a brief discussion of some policy implications of these findings.

In his book *The Dynamics of Performance Management*, Donald Moynihan (2008, pp. 4–5) argues that performance management reforms have become so central to recent public management agendas that it "is only a slight exaggeration to say that we are betting the future of governance on the use of performance information." Clearly, the design and implementation of performance standards and incentive systems in the public sector will continue to be a dynamic pursuit, and it is our hope that the lessons distilled in this volume will have a role in shaping and speeding their evolution and the improvement of government performance.

Notes

1. In the effort to achieve hospital accident and emergency waiting time targets, hospitals cancelled operations and required patients to wait in ambulance queues outside the hospital until they were confident the patients could be seen within the targeted (four-hour) time. Bevan and Hood also find discrepancies between official reported levels of performance and those from independent surveys of patients.
2. Or, it may be the case that some of the fundamental lessons from studies to date have been ignored or deferred in pursuit of other objectives (political or otherwise); see, for example, Radin (2000).

References

Anderson, Kathryn, Richard Burkhauser, and J. Raymond. 1993. "The Effect of Creaming on Placement Rates under the Job Training Partnership Act." *Industrial and Labor Relations Review* 46(4): 613–624.

Bevan, Gwyn, and Christopher Hood. 2006. "What's Measured Is What Matters: Targets and Gaming in the English Public Health Care System." *Public Administration* 84(3): 517–538.

Bloom, Howard, Larry Orr, George Cave, Steve Bell, and Fred Doolittle. 1993. *The National JTPA Study: Title IIA Impacts on Earnings and Employment at 18 Months*. Bethesda, MD: Abt Associates.

Brooks, Arthur C. 2000. "The Use and Misuse of Adjusted Performance Measures." *Journal of Policy Analysis Management* 19(2): 323–329.

Courty, Pascal, and Gerald Marschke. 2004. "An Empirical Investigation of Gaming Responses to Performance Incentives." *Journal of Labor Economics* 22(1): 23–56.

Cukier, Kenneth. 2010. "Data, Data Everywhere." *Economist* 394(8671): 1–18.

Dickinson, Katherine, Richard West, Deborah Kogan, David Drury, Marlene Franks, Laura Schlichtmann, and Mary Vencill. 1988. *Evaluation of the Effects of JTPA Performance Standards on Clients, Services, and Costs.*

Research Report No. 88–16. Washington, DC: National Commission for Employment Policy.

Finn, D. 2008. *The British "Welfare Market": Lessons from Contracting Out Welfare to Work Programmes in Australia and the Netherlands*. York, UK: Joseph Rowntree Foundation. http://www.jrf.org.uk/sites/files/jrf/2306-welfare-unemployment-services.pdf (accessed June 10, 2010).

General Accounting Office (GAO). 1991. *Job Training Partnership Act: Racial and Gender Disparities in Services*. Report to the Chairman, Legislation and National Security Subcommittee, Committee on Government Operations, House of Representatives. HRD-91-148. Washington, DC: GAO.

———. 2002. *Improvements Needed in Performance Measures to Provide a More Accurate Picture of WIA's Effectiveness*. Report to Congressional Requesters. GAO-02-275. Washington, DC: GAO.

Heckman, James, Carolyn Heinrich, and Jeffrey Smith. 2002. "The Performance of Performance Standards." *Journal of Human Resources* 37(4): 778–811.

Heckman, James, Robert LaLonde, and Jeffrey Smith. 1999. "The Economics and Econometrics of Active Labor Market Programs." In *Handbook of Labor Economics,* Vol. 3A, Orley Ashenfelter and David Card, eds. Amsterdam: North Holland, pp. 1865–2097.

Heckman, James, and Jeffrey Smith. 2004. "The Determinants of Participation in a Social Program: Evidence from a Prototypical Job Training Program." *Journal of Labor Economics* 22(4): 243–298.

Heinrich, Carolyn J. 2004. "Improving Public-Sector Performance Management: One Step Forward, Two Steps Back?" *Public Finance and Management* 4(3): 317–351.

———. 2007. "False or Fitting Recognition? The Use of High Performance Bonuses in Motivating Organizational Achievements." *Journal of Policy Analysis and Management* 26(2): 281–304.

Heinrich, Carolyn J., and Gerald R. Marschke. 2010. "Incentives and Their Dynamics in Public Sector Performance Management Systems." *Journal of Policy Analysis and Management* 29(1): 183–208.

Klerman, Jacob Alex. 2005. "Measuring Performance." In *High Performance Government: Structure, Leadership, Incentives*, Robert Klitgaard and Paul C. Light, eds. Santa Monica, CA: RAND Corporation, pp. 343–380.

Koning, Pierre, and Carolyn J. Heinrich. 2010. "Cream Skimming, Parking, and Other Intended and Unintended Effects of Performance-Based Contracting in Social Welfare Services." IZA Discussion Paper No. 4801. Bonn, Germany: IZA.

Light, Paul C. 2005. *The Four Pillars of High Performance.* New York: McGraw Hill.

Moynihan, Donald. 2008. *The Dynamics of Performance Management: Constructing Information and Reform*. Washington, DC: Georgetown University Press.

Orr, Larry, Howard Bloom, Stephen Bell, Winston Lin, George Cave, and Fred Doolittle. 1995. *The National JTPA Study: Impacts, Benefits, and Costs of Title IIA*. Bethesda, MD: Abt Associates.

Propper, Carol, and Deborah Wilson. 2003. "The Use and Usefulness of Performance Measures in the Public Sector." *Oxford Review of Economic Policy* 19(2): 250–267.

Radin, Beryl. 2000. "The Government Performance and Results Act: Square Pegs in Round Holes?" *Journal of Public Administration Research and Theory* 10(1): 11–35.

Smith, Peter. 1995. "On the Unintended Consequences of Publishing Performance Data in the Public Sector." *International Journal of Public Administration* 18(2–3): 277–310.

Struyven, L., and G. Steurs. 2005. "Design and Redesign of a Quasi-Market for the Reintegration of Jobseekers: Empirical Evidence from Australia and the Netherlands." *Journal of European Social Policy* 15(3): 211–229.

2
U.S. Employment and Training Programs and Performance Standards System Design

Pascal Courty
Carolyn J. Heinrich
Gerald Marschke
Jeffrey Smith

Prior to the recession that began in 2007, public expenditures on employment and training services were declining. For example, in fiscal year 2007, the total U.S. federal government appropriations for WIA programs—youth employment, adult job training, dislocated worker assistance, Job Corps, and other national activities—was $4.4 billion, down 18 percent from fiscal year 2005. Within the WIA program, the number of adults receiving training was likewise declining appreciably relative to its predecessor, JTPA (Frank and Minoff 2005). Furthermore, the JTPA program had substantially reduced the size and scope of federal public employment and training programs relative to its predecessors, the Manpower Development and Training Act (MDTA) and the Comprehensive Employment and Training Act (CETA).

In 2009, the Obama administration reversed these trends of diminishing public expenditures on employment and training. The American Recovery and Reinvestment Act (ARRA) injected an unprecedented level of funding (an addition of more than $3.5 billion) into the public workforce development system and associated employment and training programs.[1] This infusion of resources to aid unemployed and underemployed workers nearly doubled U.S. federal government funding for WIA programs and rejuvenated public interest in improving the effectiveness of the workforce development system.

This book focuses on the two most recent workforce development programs, JTPA and WIA. JTPA is widely known for having introduced outcomes-based performance standards to public employment and training programs (in 1982). WIA has retained the basic structure of its predecessor while making important operational changes in the performance standards system (in 2000).[2] This chapter aims to provide basic information about U.S. employment and training programs to aid our readers in understanding the research and analyses presented in this book. In the following sections, essential features of these programs are described, including their origins and organizational structures, eligibility rules and the types of services made available to participants, and the design of the performance standards systems.

ORIGINS AND ORGANIZATIONAL STRUCTURE OF JTPA AND WIA

During the period in which it operated, JTPA constituted the largest federal employment and training program for disadvantaged U.S. workers. The act mandated the provision of employment and training services to "those who can benefit from, and are most in need of, such opportunities." It also required that the basic return on training investments "be measured by the increased employment and earnings of participants and the reduction in welfare dependency" (U.S. Congress 1982). Designed in the Reagan era of New Federalism, JTPA was distinguished by a more decentralized administrative structure that included a larger role for the private sector; a performance standards system developed to measure program outcomes, increase local-level accountability, and encourage more efficient program management; and lower program costs per participant, in part due to elimination of public service employment and participant stipend components. Dickinson et al. (1988), LaLonde (1995), and O'Leary, Straits, and Wandner (2004) provide more detail on the history of employment and training programs in the United States.

The original titles of the JTPA legislation established four different programs.[3] Title IIA authorized the largest of these programs to serve economically disadvantaged youths and adults, accounting for the majority of JTPA client enrollments and training expenditures.[4] The primary services provided under JTPA Title IIA—vocational training, on-the-job training, basic/remedial education, job search assistance, work experience, and other services such as counseling and assessment, job-readiness activities, and case management—continue to be available in WIA, although training priorities and service access have changed. While amendments to JTPA had shifted service provision away from low-cost job search activities and toward more intensive (e.g., classroom) training, WIA made important changes to refocus the program toward assessment and job search assistance services that are made available to a broader population. WIA, enacted in 1998, officially superseded the JTPA program in July 2000. See O'Shea and King (2001) for a comprehensive discussion of the WIA provisions and changes, Social Policy Research Associates (2004) for a comprehensive report on WIA implementation.

In both JTPA and WIA, responsibility for the interpretation and implementation of program provisions was delegated to the USDOL. The USDOL communicates some specific policy directives to states, but the interpretation of many critical provisions and the major responsibility for program administration and service delivery lie with state and local job training agencies. Under JTPA, the distinct (nonoverlapping and exhaustive) program jurisdictions were known as service delivery areas; in WIA, they are called workforce investment areas.

Federal funding for these programs is allocated to states in proportion to measures of economic need, e.g., the number of unemployed and economically disadvantaged individuals residing within them.[5] And although states are required to expend the recent federal stimulus funding by the end of June 2011, the Obama administration encouraged them to spend the funds in "transformational efforts" to realize the "full capacity" of the system to innovate and improve the effectiveness of workforce development programs (USDOL 2009a).

The organizational forms of the job training centers and their approaches to service delivery have varied across states and localities under both JTPA and WIA.[6] Some job training centers are public entities at the state, county, or municipal government level, and others are private, not-for-profit, or for-profit organizations. Under WIA, states are required to establish a State Workforce Investment Board, including the governor, members of the state legislature, and representatives of business, labor, educational entities, economic development agencies, and community-based organizations. A major responsibility of the board is to develop a state plan that outlines a five-year strategy for the statewide workforce investment system. At the local level, all job training centers are directed and supervised by a board of representatives from business, labor, the community, and local elected officials, known formerly as Private Industry Councils under JTPA and currently as Workforce Investment Boards under WIA. These boards determine who is served, the types of services made available, and who should provide the services (within the limitations of the statute).

The particular structure of local program administration depends on a number of factors, including the size of the job training jurisdiction and its population, urban versus rural location, local political configurations, and state-level administrative policies. In the JTPA program, some agencies provided training services directly to eligible clients, while a majority contracted with independent service provider organizations to select participants and deliver program services (see Dickinson et al. 1988). Workforce Investment Boards in the current program are required to operate at least one One-Stop Career Center in their service area, with the objective of colocating programs of the USDOL, Department of Education, Department of Health and Human Services, and Department of Housing and Urban Development (e.g., employment services, unemployment insurance, vocational rehabilitation, adult education, welfare-to-work, and postsecondary vocational education). The local boards develop and enter into a "memorandum of understanding" with the One-Stop partners that specifies the services to be provided through the One-Stop delivery system, how the service and operating costs of the system will be funded, and methods for referral of customers between the One-Stop operator and the partners.

WIA also uses a form of vouchers for some participants, called individual training accounts (ITAs), which allows them to purchase training services directly from certified providers, a provision intended to increase "customer choice" over the JTPA approach of using subcontracted providers. Implementation of ITAs varies on several dimensions, including how the amount of the ITAs (or customers' spending) is determined, whether counseling in the use of the ITAs is required or voluntary, and how much local staff restrict customers' training choices. D'Amico and Salzman (2004), Decker and Perez-Johnson (2004), and McConnell et al. (2006) provide more detail on ITAs and also describe an experimental evaluation of alternative ITA implementations.

The research presented in the subsequent chapters of this book conveys how critical these structures and processes are (as well as the allocation of authority and discretion within them) in determining service access and program effectiveness.

PROGRAM ELIGIBILITY AND SERVICES

Although JTPA and WIA differ considerably in their eligibility criteria, they have in common the voluntary nature of program participation. The JTPA Title IIA program was more narrowly focused on serving the disadvantaged, requiring 90 percent of all enrollees to be disadvantaged and minimum levels of service to particular segments of the population, including youths, high school dropouts, and welfare recipients.[7] At the same time, Devine and Heckman (1996) show that the federal eligibility rules defined a fairly broad JTPA-eligible population, and local job training centers retained discretion to enroll noneconomically disadvantaged persons who satisfied other "hardship" criteria defined in the act (e.g., displaced homemakers, persons with limited English proficiency, etc.) for the other 10 percent of their participant populations. Because annual program funding levels afforded services to less than 3 percent of the JTPA-eligible population (Heckman and Smith 1999), state and local administrative entities had considerable leeway in identifying specific target groups and developing additional participant selection criteria within the eligibility guidelines (i.e., being eligible did not guarantee one the opportunity to participate).

Under WIA, the most basic "core" services—outreach, intake/assessment, job search assistance/placement, and labor market information—are made available to the general public with no qualifying criteria/eligibility requirements. The USDOL does not require monitoring and tracking of participants using the self-directed core services or non-WIA services at the One-Stop centers, but rather only those participants who receive substantial staff assistance in the WIA programs. Individuals' access to intensive or training services (e.g., comprehensive assessment and case management, vocational, or on-the-job training) proceeds sequentially if they are "unemployed and are unable to obtain employment through core services provided" (WIA, Section 134 3.A.i).

However, as Eberts, O'Leary, and DeRango (2002) note, the USDOL offers little guidance to One-Stop center workers on how to identify the needs of this broader target population and how to refer customers to the various levels of service in a cost-effective manner. Wandner (2002) nicely summarizes the differences in JTPA and WIA "service referral principles," and argues that there is a greater need for the use of targeting tools under WIA to aid frontline staff in determining appropriate service levels for customers.

PERFORMANCE STANDARDS SYSTEM DESIGN

Under both JTPA and WIA, the performance standards system is designed to reward job training centers or state workforce development programs, respectively, that achieve performance goals with incentive (budgetary) awards and external recognition. The USDOL, state job training agencies, and local job training centers have together defined and enforced these incentive policies.

The federal government is primarily involved in defining the basic structure of the performance standards system in public employment and training programs. These responsibilities of the USDOL include defining mandatory performance measures to be used by states and local areas, setting state accounting and reporting rules, and monitoring, rewarding, and/or sanctioning job training center performance. Table 2.1 shows the performance measures currently in effect under WIA and also indicates which of these are new to WIA (i.e., were not used in JTPA). Though the majority of these measures are common to JTPA and WIA, there were a number of changes made in JTPA that shifted the focal point of performance measurement from enrollees' labor market status at the time of program completion to three months after termination from the program. Under WIA, the follow-up period has been extended to six months after program completion. Chapter 4 includes additional discussion of the evolution of the performance measures under JTPA.

States are also now required to calculate performance outcomes using Unemployment Insurance (UI) data. An earlier GAO report (2002) indicated that some states were experiencing difficulties in getting access to these records and developing or modifying data systems to produce this information. The USDOL has since been working to promote data exchange between states via the Wage Record Interchange System (WRIS), which specifically facilitates the exchange of wage data for the purpose of assessing and reporting on state and local employment and training program and provider performance. As of August 2009, all states were participating in the WRIS.[8]

Performance standards are the numerical goals that job training centers must achieve to become eligible for incentive awards and to avoid sanctions. In JTPA, the USDOL exercised greater authority in the determination of performance standard levels (or targets). It established expected performance levels in JTPA using a regression-based model with national departure points. States could use the optional Labor Department adjustment model or develop their own adjustment procedures, although state-developed procedures and adjustments had to conform to the department's parameters (Social Policy Research Associates 1999). A majority of states adopted the optional USDOL adjustment model and used the USDOL-provided performance standards worksheets to determine performance targets, although sometimes with modifications. Chapters 4 and 5 present additional information about how performance standards were adjusted under the JTPA program.

Under WIA, states negotiate with the USDOL and local service delivery areas to establish performance targets, using estimates based on historical data that are similarly intended to take into account differences in economic conditions, participant characteristics, and services delivered. Since performance data were collected in JTPA, more than half of the states used these baseline data to determine appropriate levels for the WIA-negotiated performance standards or to inform negotiations with local workforce development officials. The informal process of making these adjustments during negotiations in WIA contrasts noticeably with the standardized regression-based approach used by states under JTPA. States' own reports of procedures used to determine WIA performance standards suggest that there is substantially greater discretion and variation in both the processes and types of information used to establish the state-level standards (Heinrich 2004). The pretext for making this change to a system of negotiated standards was to promote "shared accountability," described as one of the "guiding principles" of WIA (USDOL 2001, p. 8).[9]

Table 2.1 Performance Measures—JTPA and WIA

Performance measure	Description
Adults	
Entered employment rate	The percentage of adults who obtained a job by the end of the first quarter after program exit (excluding participants employed at registration).
Employment retention rate at 6 months	Of adults who had a job in the first quarter after exit, percentage with a job in the third quarter after exit.
Average earnings change in 6 months	Of those who had a job in the first quarter after exit, the postprogram earnings increases relative to preprogram earnings.
Employment and credential rate[a]	Of those adults who received WIA training services, the percentage who were employed in the first quarter after exit and received a credential by the end of the third quarter after exit.
Dislocated workers	
Entered employment rate	The percentage of dislocated workers who obtained a job by the end of the first quarter after program exit (excluding those employed at registration).
Employment retention rate at 6 months	Of those who had a job in the first quarter after exit, the percentage of dislocated workers who have a job in the third quarter after exit.
Earnings replacement rate in 6 months	Of those who had a job in the first quarter after exit, the percentage of preprogram earnings that are earned postprogram.
Employment and credential rate[a]	Of those dislocated workers who received WIA training services, the percentage who were employed in the first quarter after exit and received a credential by the end of the third quarter after exit.
Older youths (19–21)	
Entered employment rate	The percentage of older youths who were not enrolled in postsecondary education or advanced training in the first quarter after program exit and obtained a job by the end of the first quarter after exit (excluding those employed at registration).

Employment retention rate at 6 months	Of those who had a job in the first quarter after exit and were not enrolled in postsecondary education or advanced training in the third quarter after program exit, the percentage of older youths who have a job in the third quarter after exit.
Average earnings change in 6 months	Of those who had a job in the first quarter after exit and were not enrolled in postsecondary education or advanced training, the postprogram earnings increases relative to preprogram earnings.
Older youths employment/education/ training and credential rate[a]	The percentage of older youths who are in employment, postsecondary education, or advanced training in the first quarter after exit and received a credential by the end of the third quarter after exit.
Younger youths	
Retention rate	In employment, postsecondary education, advanced training, apprenticeships in third quarter after exit.
Skill attainment rate	Attain at least two goals relating to basic skills, work readiness, skill attainment, entered employment and skill training.
Diploma rate	Earn a secondary school diploma or its recognized equivalent (GED).
Customer satisfaction	
Participant satisfaction[a]	The average of three statewide survey questions, rated 1 to 10 (1 = very dissatisfied to 10 = very satisfied), asking if participants were satisfied with services, if services met customer expectations, and how the services compared to the "ideal set" of services.
Employer satisfaction[a]	The average of three statewide survey questions, rated 1 to 10 (1 = very dissatisfied to 10 = very satisfied), asking if employers were satisfied with services, if services met customer expectations, and how the services compared to the "ideal set" of services.

[a]New to WIA.

In JTPA, 6 percent of the federal government's JTPA appropriation to states was designated for performance incentive awards to local job training centers. Some states made the incentive awards for job training centers dependent on their performance relative to other service delivery areas. Other states defined a maximum incentive payment for each job training center, with the fraction awarded depending on the difference between the center's measured performance and the state standards. Until recently in the WIA program, the Secretary of Labor awarded incentive grants to states that achieve at least 80 percent of their negotiated performance levels on each performance measure and at least a 100 percent cumulative program area score for each of the program areas (adults, dislocated workers, and youths) and the customer satisfaction measures.[10] States were required to apply for the incentive grants and may receive a minimum grant award of $750,000, up to a maximum amount of $3,000,000 (conditional on the availability of funds), for use in innovative programs. States that did not meet their performance goals for two consecutive years may be sanctioned with a 5 percent reduction in their WIA grants. In addition to the monetary incentives and penalties under JTPA and WIA, states have also recognized high performers and innovative programs with special nonmonctary awards. In general, the performance standards system serves as the primary means for federal- and state-level monitoring and motivation of local job training center operations and performance.

SUMMARY

The goal of this chapter is to provide the basic information essential to understanding the more in-depth and rigorous analyses of the performance standards systems in U.S. employment and training programs that follow in this book. The subsequent chapters delve into the complexities and challenges of operating an efficient, informative, and accurate performance standards system, and the implications of basic program design elements—i.e., legislative objectives, organizational structures, accountability requirements, reporting relationships, and funding—for the effective functioning of a performance standards system. And importantly, the research presented in this book also addresses the implications of these systems for the programs' outcomes and impacts on participants' employment and earnings. The majority of the following chapters focus primarily on JTPA, in part because it was the longest running public sector employment and training program in the United States and has had the longest history of any public sector program with an outcomes-based performance standard system; in part because of the unique data available from the experimental evaluation of the JTPA program; and in part because it is similar enough to yield important lessons for current WIA programs and their future adaptations.

Notes

1. "Agency Reported Data," Recovery.gov, accessed February 22, 2010, http://www.recovery.gov/Transparency/agency/reporting/agency_reporting3.aspx?agency_code=16&dt=02/12/2010.
2. According to Franklin and Ripley (1984, pp. 176–177), performance standards were under development for JTPA's predecessor, CETA, but were not implemented prior to CETA's replacement by JTPA.
3. Title IIB authorized a summer youth program, Title III funded a program for dislocated workers, and Title IV governed various federally administered programs. Title I of the act described JTPA's administrative structures, and Title V contained amendments and miscellaneous provisions relating to the interaction between JTPA and other programs such as the former Aid to Families with Dependent Children.
4. In the early 1990s, Title IIA was split, and a new Title IIC was created specifically for economically disadvantaged youth, while IIA was reauthorized to serve adults only.
5. In both the JTPA and WIA programs, one-third of the funds received by states depends on the relative number of unemployed individuals in the state; another third depends on the relative excess number of unemployed individuals (over 4.5 percent), and the final third depends on the number of economically disadvantaged persons (as defined by the act).
6. The term *job training center* is used interchangeably with service delivery area and workforce investment area in this book.
7. Section 4.8 of JTPA specifically defined economic "disadvantage" and was the basis from which the program eligibility criteria were derived. An individual was eligible for JTPA services if 1) the person or another member of his or her family received cash public assistance; 2) the person's family income did not exceed the higher of the poverty level, or 70 percent of the lower living standard level; 3) the person was a handicapped adult whose own income met these criteria even though his/her family income may not have; 4) the person was eligible for food stamps

sometime during the six months prior to applying to JTPA; or 5) the person (a youth applicant) was a foster child.

8. "WRIS Membership, August 7, 2009," accessed March 4, 2010, http://www.doleta.gov/performance/pfdocs/WRIS_MAP_08_07_09.pdf.
9. The USDOL is currently testing regression models for the WIA performance standards with the goal of returning to a system of regression-based adjustments beginning in July 2011 (USDOL 2009b).
10. For example, if a state negotiates a 70 percent adult entered employment rate standard and then achieves actual entered employment rate performance of 75 percent, it will have a score of 107 percent for that measure. If it does less well on its adult employment retention rate, say, achieving 60 percent instead of the 62 percent standard, its score of only 96.8 percent on this measure will be offset by its exceptional achievement on the entered employment rate measure (or possibly one of the other two adult measures as well). Among the four adult performance measures, the cumulative score must be 100 percent (determined "by simple or weighted averaging").

References

D'Amico, Ron, and Jeffrey Salzman. 2004. *An Evaluation of the Individual Training Account/Eligible Training Provider Demonstration.* Social Policy Research Associates final interim report to the USDOL-ETA. Oakland, CA: Social Policy Research Associates.

Decker, Paul, and Irma Perez-Johnson. 2004. "Individual Training Accounts, Eligible Training Provider Lists, and Consumer Report Systems." In *Job Training Policy in the United States,* Christopher O'Leary, Robert Straits, and Stephen Wandner, eds. Kalamazoo, MI: W.E. Upjohn Institute for Employment Research, pp. 177–209.

Devine, Theresa, and James Heckman. 1996. "The Structure and Consequences of Eligibility Rules for a Social Program." In *Research in Labor Economics,* Vol. 15, Solomon Polachek, ed. Greenwich, CT: JAI Press, pp. 111–170.

Dickinson, Katherine, Richard West, Deborah Kogan, David Drury, Marlene Franks, Laura Schlichtmann, and Mary Vencill. 1988. *Evaluation of the Effects of JTPA Performance Standards on Clients, Services, and Costs.* Research Report No. 88-16. Washington, DC: National Commission for Employment Policy.

Eberts, Randall, Christopher O'Leary, and Kelly DeRango. 2002. "A Frontline Decision Support System for One-Stop Centers." In *Targeting Employment Services*, Randall Eberts, Christopher O'Leary, and Stephen Wandner, eds. Kalamazoo, MI: W.E. Upjohn Institute for Employment Research, pp. 337–379.

Frank, Abbey, and Elisa Minoff. 2005. "Declining Share of Adults Receiving Training under WIA Are Low-Income or Disadvantaged." Washington, DC: Center for Law and Social Policy.

Franklin, Grace, and Randall Ripley. 1984. *CETA: Politics and Policy 1973–1982*. Knoxville, TN: University of Tennessee Press.

General Accounting Office (GAO). 2002. *Improvements Needed in Performance Measures to Provide a More Accurate Picture of WIA's Effectiveness*. Report to Congressional Requesters. GAO-02-275. Washington, DC: GAO.

Heckman, James, and Jeffrey Smith. 1999. "The Pre-Programme Earnings Dip and the Determinants of Participation in a Social Programme: Implications for Simple Programme Evaluation Strategies." *Economic Journal* 109(457): 313–348.

Heinrich, Carolyn. 2004. "Improving Public-Sector Performance Management: One Step Forward, Two Steps Back?" *Public Finance and Management* 4(3): 317–351.

LaLonde, Robert. 1995. "The Promise of Public Sector–Sponsored Training Programs." *Journal of Economic Perspectives* 9(2): 149–168.

McConnell, Sheena, Paul Decker, and Irma Perez-Johnson. 2006. "The Role of Counseling in Voucher Programs: Findings from the Individual Training Account Experiment." Unpublished manuscript. Mathematica Policy Research, Princeton, NJ.

O'Leary, Christopher, Robert Straits, and Stephen Wandner. 2004. "U.S. Job Training: Types, Participants, and History." In *Job Training Policy in the United States,* Christopher O'Leary, Robert Straits, and Stephen Wandner, eds. Kalamazoo, MI: W.E. Upjohn Institute for Employment Research, pp. 1–20.

O'Shea, Daniel, and Christopher King. 2001. *The Workforce Investment Act of 1998: Restructuring Workforce Development Initiatives in States and Localities*. Albany, NY: Nelson A. Rockefeller Institute of Government.

Social Policy Research Associates. 1999. *Guide to Performance Standards for the Job Training Partnership Act for Program Years 1998 and 1999*. Report prepared for USDOL-ETA, Office of Policy Development, Evaluation and Research. Oakland, CA: SPRA.

———. 2004. *The Workforce Investment Act after Five Years: Results from the National Evaluation of the Implementation of WIA*. Report prepared for the USDOL-ETA, Office of Policy Development, Evaluation and Research. Oakland, CA: SPRA.

U.S. Congress. 1982. *Job Training Partnership Act*. Public Law 97-300, 29 U.S.C.§ 1501, Sections 141(c) and 106(a). Washington, DC: U.S. Government Printing Office.

U.S. Department of Labor (USDOL). 2001. *2002 Annual Performance Plan for Committee on Appropriations*. Washington, DC: USDOL, Employment and Training Administration.

———. 2009a. "Training and Employment Guidance Letter 13-08." Washington, DC: USDOL, Employment and Training Administration.

———. 2009b. "Training and Employment Guidance Letter 21-09." Washington, DC: USDOL, Employment and Training Administration.

Wandner, Stephen. 2002. "Targeting Employment Services under the Workforce Investment Act." In *Targeting Employment Services*, Randall Eberts, Christopher O'Leary, and Stephen Wandner, eds. Kalamazoo, MI: W.E. Upjohn Institute for Employment Research, pp. 1–25.

3
A Formal Model of a Performance Incentive System

James J. Heckman
Carolyn J. Heinrich
Jeffrey Smith

This chapter presents a model of training center behavior in an environment that includes a generic performance management system for active labor market programs (ALMPs), such as those funded under JTPA and WIA in the United States. The model builds on the work of Heckman, Heinrich, and Smith (2002) and provides more intuition and discussion of the model and its implications, along with some useful extensions.[1] Additionally, our model offers an essential conceptual context for the detailed analyses of the JTPA and WIA programs that follow in the remaining chapters of this volume.

The model we develop assumes that training (or workforce development) centers seek to maximize the present discounted value of earnings (or employment) impacts from the services they provide, as well as, potentially, goals related to the characteristics of participants and to the effort levels exerted by program staff.[2] The JTPA and WIA programs both have formally stated equity (service to particular subgroups) and efficiency (improving labor market outcomes relative to what would have occurred without the program) goals. Our model demonstrates how these objectives interact with a performance standards system based on short-term outcome measures, and we discuss in detail why all of the performance standards systems we know of rely on performance measures based on outcome levels measured in the short term rather than on impacts ("value added") over the long run. The use of short-term outcomes as performance measures has the potential to misdirect activity by focusing training center attention on criteria only loosely (or even perversely) related to long-run net benefits, long-run equity criteria, or both. For example, if program activities encourage further training and schooling, they may reduce employment and earnings in the short run but raise them in the long run.

Most discussions of performance standards focus on cream skimming, sometimes defined as selecting persons into a program who would have done well without it. Anderson et al. (1992) and Barnow (1992) represent early examples of this literature, while Courty, Kim, and Marschke (forthcoming) provide an important recent contribution. In the context of a system of performance standards, cream skimming occurs when training centers serve individuals who will increase their measured performance rather than basing service provision decisions on individuals' expected long-run benefits from participation. In this chapter, we provide a concise formal definition of cream skimming in terms of our model notation, show how performance standards based on participant outcomes in the short run encourage it, and discuss the conditions under which it does or does not lead centers away from the goal of maximizing discounted impacts.

The model we introduce allows responses to performance standards in terms of who gets selected into the program from among the eligible population and how program resources get allocated among participants, as well as strategic responses that seek to increase measured performance conditional on actual performance, such as those considered in Chapter 7. More generally, this model provides a clear conceptual framework within which to think about when (and if) performance standards systems in ALMPs will increase the labor market impacts they produce, and when (and if) they will have unintended consequences due to responses by program staff to the sometimes misguided incentives they provide.

A MODEL OF TRAINING CENTER CHOICES

Training centers face three choices in each period: 1) how many people to train, 2) which particular people to train, and 3) how many resources to devote to each trainee. In the current WIA program, access to "core" workforce development services (such as labor market information and job search assistance) is universal, but access to more intensive levels of service (such as comprehensive assessment and case management, vocational training, and subsidized on-the-job training) still involves some degree of selection by caseworkers in light of the available training resources for individual clients and services (see Social Policy Research Associates [2004] for more institutional details on WIA). Thus, in the WIA context, our model applies to these more intensive services. Adding a requirement that all eligible individuals receive some very small level of service would not change any of the basic results from the model.

For simplicity, we assume that training centers face a completely new cohort of potential trainees in each period; this avoids potential complications associated with training centers making choices about when to serve particular people. More generally, we assume that training centers operate in a "stationary" environment, which means that the center's decision rules do not change over time. Put differently, if a center faces the same set of potential trainees, the same technology for producing trainee outcomes, and the same budget constraint in two different periods, it will make exactly the same choices in those two periods. We assume that the set of potential trainees and the technology stay the same, and, in later sections, that the budget varies only as a result of performance awards.

We ignore the individual application decision in our model and simply assume that the training center can choose to serve any or all of the eligible individuals in each cohort (given its budget constraint). In so doing, we abstract from center choices regarding marketing, outreach, contractor selection, and other factors that might affect who applies to the program, even though the presence or details of a performance standards system might affect these choices.

We also assume that individuals participate or not in the first period of their adult lives, which we denote age zero, and that training takes exactly one period for all trainees. Thus, we implicitly ignore individual choices regarding the timing of training.[3] Each individual has two potential outcomes at each age: a benchmark (or untreated) outcome that arises if the individual does not participate (at age zero), and a treated outcome that arises if the individual does participate (at age zero). In terms of the usual notation, we denote the participant outcomes by $Y_a^1, a = 0,\ldots, A$, where A is the final period of the person's life, and denote the nonparticipant outcomes by $Y_a^0, a = 0,\ldots, A$. The per-period treatment effect equals $Y_a^1 - Y_a^0 = \Delta_a$. The treatment effect can be negative in the short run if, for example, program participation leads to additional schooling or distracts the individual from useful job search.[4] We abstract from potential general equilibrium effects in our discussion.[5] In the language of the treatment effects literature, we make the stable unit treatment value assumption (SUTVA), which means that the treated and untreated outcomes just defined do not depend on who participates or on how many individuals participate.

To allow our analysis to fit into a standard cost-benefit framework, let Y denote earnings; we can easily generalize the model to include employment or education outcomes. The net (of costs) present value of the program impacts (hereinafter just "net impacts") measured at time zero for participant i then equals

$$(3.1) \quad PV_i = \sum_{a=0}^{A} \frac{\Delta_{ai}}{(1+r)^a} - c_i ,$$

where c_i denotes the costs associated with participant i. We assume that (Δ_a, c) varies among individuals but the interest rate r does not.[6]

The model assumes that training centers can apply different amounts of input, e, to each participant. In the context of JTPA or WIA (or similar programs), the input variable represents the value of staff time and the direct costs of the services provided. The inputs affect the outcomes experienced by participants. In particular, input e yields

$$(3.2) \quad Y_a^1 = f(Y_a^0, e),$$

at cost $c(e)$, where $c(0) = 0$. The total cost for participant i is given by $c_i = c_i(e_i) + k$, where k denotes a per-participant fixed cost. Note that we allow both the amount of the inputs and the marginal cost of the inputs to vary among participants.

By choosing to model a continuous input e, we abstract from reality on two important dimensions. First, most of the services provided by ALMPs come in discrete chunks of a particular type. For example, JTPA offered, and WIA currently offers, classroom training in occupational skills, job search assistance, and subsidized on-the-job training at private firms, among other services. Classroom training consists of various types of courses, each aimed at a particular occupation and each having a specific duration. The other service types vary in a similar way. Representing this complex mix of discrete services by a continuous input simplifies our model considerably, but at the cost of abstracting from the potential impact of performance standards not only on the amount of services provided but on their type and duration. For example, Heinrich (1999), Barnow and Gubits (2002), and D'Amico and Salzman (2004) (and many others) have argued that a focus on short-term outcomes in performance standards pushes training centers toward providing shorter, less-intensive services such as job search assistance to a larger number of trainees. Second, we ignore the fact that inputs often get allocated to participants dynamically in response to their experiences in particular treatments and in response to their labor market outcomes. For example, at the end of a classroom training course, participants with a job lined up do not receive job search assistance, while those without a job lined up often do. Our simplifying assumption means that our model also fails to capture any effects of performance standards on this dynamic service allocation process.

Given these assumptions, training centers have several degrees of freedom in regard to whom to serve and how many inputs to devote to each participant. First, for a fixed set of inputs, a training center can choose to serve individuals with different (Δ_a, c) combinations. Second, holding the set of participants fixed, the training center can choose the inputs it provides to each participant, which has the effect of changing their potential outcomes given participation (and, necessarily, changing their impacts of participation as well). Third, a training center can choose the number of participants by trading off between the fixed cost k and the variable input cost $c_i(e_i)$.

If the training center maximizes the ex post present value of the net earnings impacts realized by its trainees, it solves a constrained optimization problem. Maximizing the present value of the net impacts corresponds to a social goal of efficiency in the economic sense; it means making the economic "pie" as large as possible while ignoring equity concerns other than those implicit in the program's eligibility rules. In the absence of a budget constraint, the center would simply find the e that maximizes the present value of net impacts for each participant:

$$\text{(3.3)} \quad \hat{e} = \arg\max_{e} \sum_{a=0}^{A} \frac{(Y_a^1 - Y_a^0)}{(1+r)^a} - c(e) - k.$$

In the real world, and in our model, training centers operate under a budget constraint. Let B denote the center budget in each period. With a budget constraint, centers face a trade-off between serving more clients and devoting more inputs to each client. Let $\{1,...,I\}$ be the index set of eligible individuals; put differently, label each eligible person with a number from 1 to I. Person i has associated variable costs $c_i(e_i)$ and fixed cost k. We assume that technology (3.2) is common across persons although this assumption can easily be relaxed.

The training center solves its maximization problem in two steps. In the first step, for each possible set of trainees $S \subseteq \{1,...,I\}$ in the current cohort it determines the optimal choice of inputs to devote to each member of the set. Formally, for each possible set S, the center solves the problem

$$(3.4) \quad \max_{e_i, i \in S} \sum_{i \in S} \left[\sum_{a=0}^{A} \frac{\left(Y_{a,i}^1 - Y_{a,i}^0\right)}{\left(1+r\right)^a} - c_i\left(e_i\right) - k \right],$$

subject to Equation (3.2), and

$$(3.5) \quad B \geq \sum_{i \in S} \left(c_i(e_i) + k\right).$$

For LaGrange multiplier λ attached to the constraint in (3.5), solving the optimization problem produces the first order condition

$$(3.6) \quad \sum_{a=0}^{A} \left[\frac{\partial f\left(Y_{i,a}^0, e_i\right)}{\partial e_i} \right] \frac{1}{\left(1+r\right)^a} = \lambda \frac{\partial c_i\left(e_i\right)}{\partial e_i}$$

for each observation $i \in S$. Condition (3.6) represents the standard efficiency condition for e_i which sets marginal benefit equal to marginal cost. In the absence of a budget constraint, $\lambda = 1$ at an interior optimum. In general, $\lambda \geq 1$, reflecting the scarcity of the resources available to the center, and the center invests less in each person than it would in the absence of resource constraints.[7]

The second step to solving the overall optimization problem for each cohort consists of comparing the optimal value of the present value of net impacts for each subset S and choosing the subset S^* that has the highest one. Formally, write the maximized present value implied by the solution to the constrained optimization problem in Equation (3.4) as $\psi(S,B)$, where this notation shows the dependence of the optimum on both the set S of participants selected and the available budget B. The center chooses the optimal S, which we denote by S^*, so that

$$\psi(S^*,B) = \arg\max_S \psi(S,B).$$[8]

Implementing this ex post optimal solution requires information that both the centers and (to a lesser extent) the individuals themselves do not possess at the time of participation. In particular, they do not know future values of (Y_a^1, Y_a^0), although they may have other information useful for predicting these values. For example, most ALMPs collect information on observable characteristics associated with outcomes from prospective participants, and some may also have access to administrative data on past labor market outcomes.

The available evidence suggests the difficulty of forecasting future Δ_a. In particular, Bell and Orr (2002) show that caseworkers do a very poor job of predicting Δ_a in a program that provides job training to welfare recipients, and Lechner and Smith (2007) show that Swiss caseworkers also do not perform well at this task. Carneiro, Hansen, and Heckman (2003) demonstrate that individuals cannot forecast most of the variation in the earnings impact associated with attending college.

Let J_i denote the center's information set for individual i. Taking into account the lack of complete information, the criterion for *ex ante* optimality for each S becomes

$$\text{(3.7)} \quad \underset{e_i}{\text{Max}} \sum_{i \in S} \left\{ \left[\sum_{a=0}^{A} \frac{E\left(Y_{a,i}^1 - Y_{a,i}^0 \mid J_i\right)}{\left(1+r\right)^a} \right] - c_i(e_i) - k \right\},$$

subject to Equation (3.2), Equation (3.5), and the individual-specific information sets $\{J_i\}_{i \in S}$. For each $S, \{J_i\}_{i \in S}$, B, and r, we may write the solution to this present value maximization problem as $\psi\left(S,B,J\right)$, where $J = \{J_1,\ldots,J_I\}$. The training center seeks to maximize this criterion with respect to S, so that

$$\psi\left(S^*,B,J\right) = \arg\max_S \psi\left(S,B,J\right).$$

In this model, training centers adjust at three margins: 1) which eligible individuals become trainees (in WIA, which participants receive intense services), 2) the amount of inputs devoted to each trainee, and 3) the number of trainees. While the exact trade-offs depend on the specifications of the technology for producing outcomes in Equation (3.2), the marginal cost functions, and the level of fixed costs k, a set of intuitive comparative static results follow directly from the model. For example, increasing the slope of the marginal cost function $c(e)$, all else equal, leads centers to increase the number of participants and to serve each one less intensively. Increases in the fixed cost k have the opposite effect, reducing the number of participants and increasing the amount of resources devoted to each one. Individuals with higher marginal costs—i.e., larger values of $c_i'(e_i)$—will, all else equal, receive fewer inputs. Increasing the amount of complementarity between the untreated outcome and the costs in the production function in Equation (3.2) leads centers to devote relatively more inputs to participants with good untreated outcomes. Increases in the budget lead, in general, to both more participants and more inputs per participant. Finally, in a stationary environment, the training center makes the same decision in every period.[9]

MOTIVATING PERFORMANCE STANDARDS

The model in the preceding section assumes that training centers maximize the net present value of impacts and nothing else. In fact, training centers exist in a political context and they employ caseworkers and managers who care about outcomes other than just the maximization of the present value of net impacts. Consider the politicians first. Politicians care about what training centers do. In particular, they care not only about present value maximization but also about other aspects of who, and how many, get served. For example, politicians may care about the absolute number of participants, based on the view that each participant will feel that he or she has received something from the politician, and so, perhaps, will vote accordingly. Politicians may also care about serving members of particular groups whose leaders support them or about serving highly visible individuals, such as those who lose their jobs when a major plant closes; see, e.g., Heinrich (1999) on the role of politics in JTPA contract award decisions.

We can summarize politicians' preferences by the utility function $U_P[\psi(S),N(S),Q(S)]$, where $\psi(S)$ denotes the expected present value of net impacts for participant cohort S (with the other arguments suppressed for simplicity), and $N(S)$ denotes the number of participants ($\leq I$) served in cohort S. $Q(S)$ denotes other qualities of the persons served such as demographic characteristics or their untreated outcomes, with the latter motivated by a desire to serve those least well off in the absence of the program due to equity concerns.

Training center staff members also care about aspects of their work other than just present value maximization. For example, as discussed in Heckman, Smith, and Taber (1996), caseworkers may prefer to serve the most disadvantaged (those with the lowest benchmark outcomes Y_a^0) or members of particular subgroups among the eligible. At the same time, they may prefer to serve fewer individuals than present value maximization would imply if, for example, they get utility from getting to know their clients in depth. Abstracting for simplicity from the fact that training center managers (some of them future politicians) may have different preferences than the line workers they manage, we can summarize the training center utility function by $U_T[\psi(S),N(S),Q(S)]$.

Given either utility function, we can define a constrained optimization problem similar to that defined in the preceding section. The problem consists of maximizing the utility function subject to the technology for producing participant outcomes in Equation (3.2) and the budget constraint in Equation (3.5) through choices about how many people to serve, which ones to serve, and how to allocate the inputs among those served. The equilibrium from this modified optimization problem will differ in simple and intuitive ways from that obtained under present value maximization in the preceding section. For example, if we consider maximizing the training center's utility and if the training center gets disutility from a larger number of participants, then the resulting number of participants will not exceed that chosen under present value maximization. If the training center gets utility from serving some particular group, say unemployed musicians, then it will serve more of them (or at least no fewer of them) under utility maximization than under present value maximization, and so on.

In this setting, performance standards have no role to play, even if the training center has imperfect information about potential outcomes, so long as the utility functions of the politicians and the training center are similar enough (e.g., one is a linear transformation of the other) that they would reach the same solution to the *ex ante* utility maximization problem just described. A role for performance standards emerges when the two utility functions imply different choices. In that event, politicians may want to provide additional incentives to training centers in a way that makes their choices closer to those implied by the politicians' utility function. For example, if the training centers dislike having more participants at the margin and politicians like having more participants at the margin, then politicians will want to introduce performance standards in a way that rewards centers for having more participants.

In one view, this situation, in which the politicians set up the local training centers, which then deliver services within the context of broad rules, represents a classic principal-agent problem. The politicians would like the training centers to choose an optimum that corresponds to their own utility, rather than that of the center staff. See the insightful survey in Dixit (2002) and the references cited therein (as well as the other papers in the related special issue of the *Journal of Human Resources*) for further elaboration of this point.

Politicians can bring center behavior in line with their own preferences in two basic ways.[10] One obvious way consists of specifying the rules governing center behavior so narrowly as to leave center staff with little discretion to do otherwise than as specified by program rules.[11] The fundamental problem with this approach in the context of ALMPs arises from the complexity of the task at hand and the large amount of (often tacit) local knowledge, in the sense of Hayek (1945), required for the task. Most training centers under JTPA and now under WIA serve individuals with quite heterogeneous desires and abilities by matching them with a (wide) variety of services provided either directly by the center or a service provider under contract. Attempting to prespecify the matches between participants and services would require either numbing levels of regulatory detail or a false simplicity that would likely seriously degrade the quality of the resulting matches. Performance standards represent an alternative to micromanagement by the politicians via program regulations. Here politicians define the goals they seek by defining the performance measures and the "reward functions" (described in Chapters 4 and 5 for the JTPA program) that link observed performance to rewards and punishments. In so doing, they allow centers to continue using their local knowledge in choosing whom to serve and how to serve them, while at the same time directing the application of this knowledge toward the politicians' own goals.

An alternative view from a principal-agent perspective assumes that politicians and training centers share the same preferences about whom to serve and how to serve them, but differ in their desired level of training center effort. Put simply, politicians would like training center staff to work very hard, while training center staff would like to consume some on-the-job leisure. This view links to the literature on piece rates, performance-based compensation for CEOs, and other types of incentives often found in private firms; this literature focuses almost exclusively on methods for tying remuneration to measured output as a means to increase unobserved effort (see Prendergast [1999] for an able survey, Lazear [1995] for a book-length treatment, and Chapter 5 for additional discussion in our context). We could incorporate this view into our model by breaking inputs e into two components, one representing staff effort and the other representing other inputs. The sum of staff effort would then enter negatively into the training center utility function, capturing the negative direct effect of staff effort; at the same time, staff effort would have an indirect positive effect on center utility through its effect on the present value of net impacts.

A third view of performance standards emphasizes the information they provide rather than their role in solving (or attempting to solve) one or the other of the principal-agent problems just described. In this view—discussed, for example, in Smith (2004)—performance standards represent quick and dirty impact evaluations. They provide valuable feedback to training center managers and staff (and to politicians) about their progress at meeting equity and efficiency goals—feedback that, as Lechner and Smith (2007) note, training centers often otherwise never receive, because they rarely interact with those they serve after they serve them. Because the feedback comes quickly, it allows rapid responses to changes in performance due to changes in program operation, local economic conditions, or other factors. Our model does not capture this role for performance standards in a formal way; doing so would substantially complicate the model, as it would need to incorporate training center learning in response to the information provided by the performance measures. We note in Chapter 9 some implications of thinking about performance measures in this way for the interpretation of the evidence on the correlation between performance measures and program impacts. Rather obviously, if performance measures exist to proxy long-run impacts, their correlation with those impacts becomes the paramount measure of their value.

All three views about the role of performance standards appear in the literature; in our view, all three have empirical relevance. In this chapter, we focus our model mainly on the first of the three roles; generalizing our analysis to include the second is straightforward.

PERFORMANCE MEASURES IN PRACTICE

In practice, most performance measures *M* consist of participant outcomes in the short run. The focus on the short run stems from the desire to provide prompt feedback to program managers and politicians. Feedback that arrives years after the corresponding actions by program staff does little to either motivate or inform. The focus on observed outcomes (i.e., did the participant get a job soon after finishing the program?) rather than estimated impacts (i.e., did the participant do well in the labor market relative to what would have transpired had he or she not participated?) has several motivations. First, evaluations (experimental or nonexperimental) that seek to estimate impacts by estimating the counterfactual outcomes of participants take a long time, typically on the order of years, to carry out. Even short-run impact estimates require considerable time to collect and prepare the necessary outcome data on participants (and, if required, a comparison group) for use in econometric analyses. Second, performance measures based on impacts often generate controversy, either because of uncertainty about the econometric method utilized, in the case of nonexperimental methods, or politically, in the case of random assignment. Finally, performance measures based on outcome levels generally cost much less to produce than measures based on impacts. As the literature on evaluating active labor market programs makes clear (see, e.g., Heckman, LaLonde, and Smith 1999), impact evaluation poses demanding technical problems that typically require the assistance of expensive experts and make the process difficult to automate. In contrast, measuring outcomes presents much simpler problems and, once established, becomes a routine data collection and processing exercise. Costs matter, because an expensive performance management system, even if it accomplishes something, may not accomplish enough to justify the expense.

The most common performance measure consists of employment rates in the period immediately following program participation. In terms of our notation, we can represent this measure as

$$(3.8)\quad M(S_0) = \frac{1}{N(S_0)} \sum_{i \in S_0} 1(Y_{1,i}^1 > 0) = \frac{1}{N(S_0)} \sum_{i \in S_0} E_{1,i}^1 ,$$

where the first subscript on $Y_{1,i}^1$ denotes age 1, the 0 subscript on S_0 indicates the current cohort of trainees; $1(\cdot)$ denotes the indicator function, which takes a value of 1 when its argument holds and a value of 0 when it does not; and $E_{1,i}^1 = 1(Y_{1,i}^1 > 0)$ is a dummy variable for employment (defined here as positive earnings) at age 1 (the first period after participation). A slightly different formulation captures measures such as those in JTPA and WIA that consider wages or earnings conditional on employment. For example, in our notation, a measure based on earnings conditional on employment becomes

$$M(S_0) = \frac{1}{\sum_{i \in S_0} 1(Y_{1,i}^1 > 0)} \sum_{i \in S_0} 1(Y_{1,i}^1 > 0) Y_{1,i}^1 = \frac{1}{\sum_{i \in S_0} 1(Y_{1,i}^1 > 0)} \sum_{i \in S_0} E_{1,i}^1 Y_{1,i}^1 .$$

In this performance measure, the indicator function serves to condition the average on the set of participants with positive wages or earnings.

As described in Chapters 2 and 4, not all performance measures focus on labor market outcomes. Some capture the receipt of various educational credentials, such as the GED, or, in the WIA program, customer satisfaction measures based on surveys (where customers include both participants and the firms that might hire them). Smith, Whalley, and Wilcox (2010a,b) discuss and provide evidence on the value of such participant self-evaluation measures. For many years, the WIA performance standards system also included a measure based on before-after earnings changes, which took advantage of thc well-known preprogram dip in mean earnings among participants to produce the (highly misleading) appearance of large program impacts. Heckman and Smith (1999) document the dip using the National JTPA Study data and show its implications for, among others, the before-after estimator of program impacts. Incorporating any or all of these alternative performance measures into our model requires no conceptual innovations.

REWARD FUNCTIONS IN THE MODEL

The reward function $R(M)$ links observed performance on the performance measures to rewards and (much more rarely) punishments for training centers. In most performance systems for ALMPs around the world, rewards come informally, through praise and recognition. In contrast, Chapter 4 documents that rewards in the JTPA performance standards system took the form of budgetary increments determined by formal rules. The WIA system lies somewhere in between, with monetary bonuses awarded to states that were probably more consequential for the recognition they accord than the funds they provide (see, for example, Heinrich [2007]).

The simplest system assigns a discrete reward R to centers meeting a defined standard in terms of observed performance. In terms of our notation, this implies the reward function

$$(3.9) \qquad R(M(S)) = \begin{cases} R \text{ if } M(S) > \tau; \\ 0 \text{ otherwise.} \end{cases}$$

Here τ denotes some fixed level of attainment on the performance measure, such as 60 percent of former participants employed in the period after training. Training centers that exceed that level get the reward and those that fall below it do not. As noted in Chapter 4, many more complicated reward functions exist (or have existed) in practice, including functions that reward relative rather than absolute performance, functions that require certain levels of performance on multiple measures, and functions that reward marginal improvements in performance above τ. Extending our model to incorporate such reward functions is straightforward.

For nonbudgetary rewards, it makes sense to put the reward function directly in the training center utility function, as in

$U_T[\psi(S),N(S),Q(S),R(M)]$ where we leave the dependence of M on training center choices regarding whom to serve (S) and how to allocate the inputs e among those they serve implicit. Almost by definition, we assume a positive partial derivative.

In the case of budgetary rewards, things become a bit more complicated. In that case, as in the JTPA and WIA programs, recognition remains part of the reward for good performance, and thus it makes sense to keep the reward function in the utility function. At the same time, receiving a budgetary reward changes the underlying choice problem in the next period by allowing the center to serve more individuals, to direct more inputs to those it would have served in any case, or both. Exactly how the additional budget affects choices depends in part on whether individuals served with the reward money count toward measured performance in the following period. If they do not, this allows centers to focus on satisfying their preferences regarding $Q(S)$ with the reward money; for example, they might devote additional attention to the "hard to serve" among their eligible population. In the JTPA and WIA systems, individuals served with reward money do not, in fact, count toward measured performance; nonetheless, later in this chapter we assume for simplicity in our discussions of dynamics that they do, so that we can simply add the reward money R to the original budget B and proceed as before.

THE EFFECT OF PERFORMANCE STANDARDS ON CENTER BEHAVIOR: CREAM SKIMMING

This section outlines the implications of our model for center behavior in the presence of a performance standards system that uses the mean earnings (including the zeros) of participants at age "1" (i.e., in the period after program participation) as the performance measure and includes a reward function that increases in measured performance. To make things even simpler, in this section we suppose that training center utility depends only on the present value of net impacts and the reward, corresponding to the utility function $U_T[\psi(S),R(M)]$.

Adding the basic performance management system just described to the model changes all of the first order conditions. In each case, when choosing how many to serve, whom to serve, and how to allocate inputs, the training center now considers the effect of the choice on both $\psi(S)$ and $R(M)$. Thus, when it evaluates a potential participant, instead of just considering their expected discounted stream of net impacts, the center also considers their expected earnings in the period immediately following participation. A potential participant who wants to enroll in, say, a two-year vocational training program after getting a GED with the help of the program becomes less attractive in the presence of the performance standards system laid out in the preceding paragraph. On the other hand, a potential participant who will find a job with high earnings one or two weeks earlier with the program's help but otherwise derives no benefit from it becomes more attractive. This new emphasis on short-term outcomes in choosing whom to serve and how to allocate inputs leads to the common criticism that performance standards systems generate cream skimming (see, e.g., Barnow and Smith [2004]; Radin [2006]; Trutko et al. [2005]; GAO [2002]).

Before turning to a discussion of the effects of cream skimming on the efficiency and equity of training center operation, we now formally define cream skimming. The policy literature often defines cream skimming rather casually to mean serving the least "hard to serve" among the eligible population. In terms of our model's notation, the simple performance system described above creates an incentive to serve persons with high values of $Y_{1,i}^{1}$, regardless of whether that high value results from a high value of $Y_{1,i}^{0}$ or a high value of $\Delta_{1,i}$.

The existing literature is vague about whether cream skimming should be defined in terms of $Y_{1,i}^{1}$ or $Y_{1,i}^{0}$. Our model, and the logic of performance measurement systems more generally, suggests a definition in terms of $Y_{1,i}^{1}$, as it is $Y_{1,i}^{1}$ that the performance standards incentivize training centers to take account of in their decisions.[12] Of course, given the evidence in Bell and Orr (2002) that caseworkers do reasonably well at forecasting $Y_{0,i}^{1}$ and reasonably poorly at forecasting $\Delta_{1,i}$, as well as the evidence in Heckman, Smith, and Clements (1997) that, at least for the JTPA program, most of the variance in $Y_{1,i}^{1}$ corresponds to variance in $Y_{1,i}^{0}$ (or, put differently, the variance of $\Delta_{1,i}$ is small relative to that of $Y_{1,i}^{0}$), the distinction may not matter much empirically.[13]

We now consider the implications of cream skimming for program equity and efficiency in the context of our model. To keep the discussion simple, for the purposes of this section we make the simplifying assumption that untreated outcomes do not vary with age, so that $Y_{0,i}^{a} = Y_{0,i}$ for all "a." This assumption allows us to summarize equity concerns in a single number, where we define equity as serving those with the lowest values of $Y_{0,i}$ among the eligible.

Consider first an important special case. As noted in Heckman (1992); Heckman, Smith, and Clements (1997); and Djebbari and Smith (2008), conventional models of program evaluation assume that $Y_{a,i}^{1}$ and $Y_{a,i}^{0}$ differ by a constant, so that $\Delta_{a,i} = Y_{a,i}^{1} - Y_{a,i}^{0} = \Delta_{a}$ for all i. Put differently, they assume that everyone has the same impact of treatment—the so-called common effect model.[14] In the common effect world, a high $Y_{1,i}^{1}$ goes hand in glove with a high $Y_{1,i}^{0}$, and picking persons with a high $Y_{1,i}^{0}$ helps toward satisfying Equation (3.8). In the context of our model, the common effect assumption simplifies the production function in Equation (3.2) to

$$(3.2') \quad Y_{a}^{1} = f(Y_{a}^{0}, e) = Y_{a}^{0} + \Delta_{a},$$

which removes the input choice decision from the problem (and with it the variable cost portion of the cost function).

Assuming equal fixed costs for all trainees, training centers in a common effect world serve only the individuals at the top of the distribution of untreated outcomes among the eligible. In this world, the discounted stream of impacts does not depend on who gets served, leaving the center free to maximize their measured performance. Thus, in the common effect world, our simple performance standards system has no effect on economic efficiency but very unattractive equity effects.

A mild generalization of the common effect world illustrates another important point. Suppose that all individuals share the same discounted sum of impacts

$$\Delta_{d,i} = \left[\sum_{a=0}^{A} \frac{\left(Y_{a,i}^{1} - Y_{a,i}^{0} \right)}{(1+r)^{a}} \right],$$

but that the timing of the impacts varies. To keep things very simple, suppose that one random half of the eligibles have impacts of zero in periods 0 and 1, the period of participation and the period just after, while the other random half has impacts of zero in period 0 but positive impacts in period 1 and all future periods, with the impacts just a bit smaller than those in the first group so that the discounted sum comes out the same. Training centers will now prefer, at the margin and to the extent that they can identify them, the individuals with the earlier impacts. Put differently, given the same value of $Y^0_{1,i}$, an individual with a positive impact the period following participation adds more to a center's measured performance than an individual with no positive impacts until the second period after participation. Thus, performance measures based on outcomes in period 1 encourage the provision of services that yield quick improvements in outcomes relative to later improvements in outcomes, even conditional on the same discounted sum. At the margin, the center would even trade off some of the discounted impacts to get a larger impact in the period of performance measurement, an incentive that those who complain about an overemphasis on low-intensity "work first" strategies clearly have in mind.

Another simple model inspired by Heckman, Smith, and Clements (1997) assumes independence between impacts and untreated outcomes, while continuing to assume no variable inputs and constant fixed costs. The production function becomes

$$(3.2') \quad Y^1_{a,i} = f(Y^0_{a,i}, e) = Y^0_{a,i} + \Delta_{a,i},$$

with $\Delta_{a,i}$ independent of $Y^0_{a,i}$ for $a = 1, \ldots, A$. In this world, in the absence of performance standards the training centers rank individuals by their discounted impacts and start serving individuals from the top, continuing down the distribution until the budget runs out from paying fixed costs. In contrast, adding in our simple performance standards system makes the problem two-dimensional, with centers now serving those individuals with good present values of impacts and good outcomes in the period following participation, whether due to a large impact or to a good untreated outcome (or both) in that period. As in the common effect model, the introduction of performance standards leads centers to move toward serving individuals who, on average, have better outcomes in the untreated state. Thus, once again, it has problematic equity effects. In this model, the performance standards clearly reduce efficiency, as centers will now, at the margin, implicitly trade off discounted impacts for good untreated outcomes in the period of performance measurement.

Finally, consider the same simple world as in the previous example, with production function (3.2') and so on, but assume that impacts and untreated outcomes have rank correlation γ. We have already considered the case of independence, which implies a rank correlation of zero. With a positive rank correlation equal to one, training center behavior does not change at all with the introduction of performance standards because, given our simplifying assumptions, the same individuals have both the largest impacts and the largest outcomes in the period following participation. More generally, with a positive rank correlation of less than one, we expect relatively small reductions in both the equity and efficiency associated with training center choices. This is because some individuals with good discounted impacts but bad outcomes in period 1 get dropped in favor of individuals with good untreated outcomes in period 1 but smaller discounted impacts; at the same time, most individuals either participate or not both with and without the performance standards. In contrast, with a negative rank correlation, the introduction of performance standards should lead to greater losses on both dimensions, as there is more scope for training centers to trade off impacts and outcomes. A negative correlation implies more individuals below the cutoff (in terms of discounted impacts in a world without performance standards) with high values of the untreated outcome, who can therefore add substantially to measured performance in the world with the performance standards.

If we now undo some of our simplifying assumptions by restoring variation in untreated outcomes over time and in marginal inputs costs, the model becomes much more complicated but the same intuition applies. In general, if we start from a situation where training centers care only about discounted net impacts, adding performance standards to the model reduces efficiency. The common effect case constitutes an interesting but empirically irrelevant exception. The effects on equity depend on the correlation between impacts and untreated outcomes in the period of performance measurement. With no correlation or a positive correlation, performance standards lead to cream skimming, implying negative equity effects.

The final relaxation of our assumptions occurs when we return to assuming that the training center utility function includes not just discounted impacts and performance rewards but also trainee characteristics and the number of trainees. With this utility function as the starting point, it becomes possible to describe cases in which performance standards increase efficiency. For example, if frontline workers have the "social worker mentality" described in Heckman, Smith, and Taber (1996) and prefer to serve those with the lowest untreated outcomes, and if impacts have a positive correlation with untreated outcomes as suggested in Heckman, Smith, and Clements (1997), then performance standards based on short-term outcomes may increase efficiency compared to the status quo, even though they reduce efficiency relative to the case of net impact maximization.

In the end, the effect of introducing performance standards on efficiency becomes an empirical question, as it depends on the relationship between impacts and untreated outcomes, on the relationship between short-run and long-run impacts, and on the extent to which training centers pursue objectives other than maximizing discounted impacts in a world without performance standards. Chapter 6 considers how to measure cream skimming and discusses the available empirical evidence. Chapter 9, as well as Heckman, Smith, and Clements (1997), considers the relationship between outcomes and impacts. Hotz, Imbens, and Klerman (2006); Lechner, Miquel, and Wunsch (2004); and Dyke et al. (2006) (among others) consider the relationship between short-run and long-run impacts.

STRATEGIC RESPONSES TO PERFORMANCE STANDARDS

Until now, we have not considered strategic responses of the sort documented in Chapters 7 and 8 in our model. This section considers "static" strategic responses related to measurement; we consider dynamic responses related to the manipulation of termination dates later on in the chapter after introducing the dynamic version of our model. The static responses we have in mind include the strategic enrollment decisions in the JTPA program documented in Doolittle and Traeger (1990) and the apparent manipulation of the telephone surveys originally used to measure employment shortly after termination in the JTPA program, which the USDOL sought to end with stricter procedural directives.[15] In regard to the former, only individuals formally enrolled in JTPA (or, in WIA, those receiving more than core services), count for the performance measures. The evidence makes it clear that, in the early years of JTPA prior to the tightening of the rules on enrollment, training centers sometimes provided services to individuals but did not formally enroll them until their prospects for contributing positively to the center's measured performance looked good. In regard to the latter, until response rate requirements appeared (and then, later, administrative data replaced telephone surveys for this outcome), centers appeared to selectively survey their recent terminees with the goal of maximizing their measured performance.

A simple extension of the model to incorporate this strategic behavior begins by making a distinction between actual performance and measured performance. Actual performance, denoted by $M(S)$, consists of what the performance measure would equal if measured by a neutral outsider objectively applying program rules, while measured performance, denoted by $M^*(S)$, consists of performance as measured and reported by the training center. Now assume that centers can incur some cost to improve their measured performance. Formally, let

$$M^*(S) = g[M(S), c_s],$$

where c_s denotes the cost of manipulating the measured performance numbers in terms of both staff time and effort and the present value of any political fallout from doing so. Further assume positive first derivatives, as well as a negative second derivative with respect to c_s, so that additional costs increase measured performance but at a decreasing rate. This production function will likely differ among training centers depending on the types of services they provide and the honesty of their staff (which affects their psychic costs of strategic behavior and thus the compensation they must receive for engaging in it). For example, under JTPA, centers that specialized in job search assistance and subsidized on-the-job training at private firms, both of which provide clear signals of likely success at obtaining employment, may have had an easier time manipulating enrollment decisions than centers that provided more classroom training, where employment outcomes typically do not get realized until course completion but where payments to providers may have necessitated enrollment.

Incorporating these costs into the model by replacing actual performance in the reward function with measured performance as determined by this production function adds an additional first order condition to the solution of the training center optimization problem. Training centers now select c_s to balance the marginal benefits and marginal costs of altering their measured performance relative to their actual performance. Because their actual performance enters the production function for measured performance and the cross-partial of the production function need not equal zero, and because centers will choose to spend real resources on manipulating their measured performance, the possibility of strategic misrepresentation also alters centers' actual performance.

PERFORMANCE STANDARDS AND BUDGETARY DYNAMICS IN A TWO-PERIOD MODEL

We now consider the dynamics that arise in our model when training centers receive budgetary rewards for performance (as with the bonus awards under WIA). In particular, assume that reward R augments the center budget for the next cohort of trainees but cannot be used as direct bonuses to center administrators or line workers. The possibility of receiving a budgetary reward directs attention toward the short-run goal of maximizing performance on $M(S_0)$, and may or may not serve to maximize the present value of net impacts $\psi(S,B,J)$ for the current cohort of participants. We begin with an analysis of a model for a training center that serves only two cohorts of trainees, with the first served in period 0 and the second served in period 1. This simple model provides a useful point of departure for the more complicated model we analyze in the next section.

In this context, the incentives provided by performance standards create a new intertemporal dynamic. Decisions by the center today affect the quality and quantity of participants in the first period as well as the resources available to the center to serve the second period cohort. In addition to this intertemporal connection, the center's decision problem changes in character because center performance $M(S_0)$ is a random variable as of date 0. Thus, when making decisions in period 1, the center faces a fixed budget B for period 1 but a stochastic budget for period 2, call it $\tilde{B}$, with the budgetary uncertainty resolved only after the center chooses S_0 and e in the first period and the resulting labor market outcomes for the first period participants are revealed.

Assuming a simple reward function that pays out B for performance above a threshold earnings target, we can write

$$\tilde{B} = \begin{cases} B \text{ if } M(S_0) < \tau; \\ B + R \text{ if } M(S_0) \geq \tau. \end{cases}$$

In this simplified two-cohort model, the center picks S_0 to maximize

$$\text{(3.10)} \quad U\left[\psi(S_0, B, J), N(S_0), Q(S_0)\right]$$
$$+ \frac{1}{1+\rho} \Pr\left[M(S_0) \geq \tau \mid S_0\right] \max_{S_1^1} U\left[\psi(S_1^1, B+R, J), N(S_1^1), Q(S_1^1)\right]$$
$$+ \frac{1}{1+\rho} \Pr\left[M(S_0) < \tau \mid S_0\right] \max_{S_1^0} U\left[\psi(S_1^0, B, J), N(S_1^0), Q(S_1^0)\right],$$

where $1/(1+\rho)$ is a discount rate, S_1^1 denotes the participants selected in the second period if $M(S_0) \geq \tau$, and S_1^0 denotes the participants selected in the second period if $M(S_0) < \tau$.

Centers can solve this maximization problem in two stages. For the second period cohort, there are two possible states, corresponding to whether the first cohort succeeds or fails relative to the performance standards. In the first stage, the center solves the second period optimization problem for both possible budgets. Given these optimal values, in the second stage it picks S_0 and e_0 to maximize the criterion Equation (3.10) given the values for the second period selected in the first stage. Heuristically, if S_0 were a continuous variable, and Equation (3.10) were differentiable in S_0, the first order condition for S_0 would be

$$0 = \frac{\partial U\left[\psi(S_0, B, J), N(S_0), Q(S_0), R(S_0)\right]}{\partial S_0} + \frac{\partial \Pr\left[M(S_0) \geq \tau \mid S_0\right]}{\partial S_0}$$
$$\Big\{\max_{S_1^1} U\left[\psi(S_1^1, B+R, J), N(S_1^1), Q(S_1^1), R(M\{S_1^1\})\right]$$
$$- \max_{S_1^0} U\left[\psi(S_1^0, B, J), N(S_1^0), Q(S_1^0), R(M\{S_1^0\})\right]\Big\}.$$

The first term reflects the value of S_0 in raising the current utility of the training center. The second term captures the dynamic effect of budgetary rewards, which link current period performance to future period utility. This effect equals the marginal effect of S_0 on the probability of winning the award times the increase in center utility from winning.[16] Of course, the actual solution is more complicated because the criterion is not differentiable in S_0. A similar condition holds for the choice of inputs e_0 in the first period. As the two-cohort model includes, by definition, no third cohort, the center's second period choices have no intertemporal aspect.

In this two-cohort model, performance standards may distort center choices in two ways. The first consists of the static distortions already discussed. The second results from the intertemporal linkage induced by the budgetary rewards. For certain values of the parameters, the center may choose to trade off first period utility for second period utility by distorting its first period choices so as to obtain the performance reward and thereby a larger budget in the second period. This scenario becomes more likely as the reward increases and $\rho > 0$ decreases, because both of these increase the value in the first period of having a larger budget to spend in the second period. The substantive importance of this scenario also depends on having a sufficiently small positive (or even negative) correlation between the performance measure and discounted impacts. As discussed above, if discounted impacts have a large positive correlation with the performance measure, the center does not face much of a trade-off between the two.

PERFORMANCE STANDARDS AND BUDGETARY DYNAMICS IN A STATIONARY ENVIRONMENT

This simple two-cohort model abstracts from the fact that training centers serve multiple cohorts over many time periods. In this section, we examine our model under the extreme (but analytically simple) assumption that training centers operate forever in a stationary environment; that is, other than the potentially time-varying budget induced by the performance system, the key aspects of the center's decision problem, such as the distribution of eligibles, the budget constraint in

Equation (3.5), and the production function for treated outcomes in Equation (3.2), all remain the same.

In each period, training centers can be in one of two states: 1) in receipt of a bonus R, so that they have budget $B+R$ to spend in the current period, or 2) without the bonus, so that they have budget B. The budget in each period depends on the center's choices regarding S and e in the preceding period. As the model assumes a stationary environment and only two states of the world, the centers face what the technical literature calls a Markovian decision problem. In this type of decision problem, the center's optimal decision depends only on which of the two budget states it occupies in the current period; as a result, the choices S and e require subscripts for the state of the world but not for the time period.

Let V_0 denote the center's value function with budget B in the current period, and let V_1 denote the value function for a center budget $B + R$ in the current period. Then,

$$V_0 = \arg\max_S U\left[\psi(S,B,J),N(S),Q(S)\right] + \frac{1}{1+\rho}\Pr\left[M(S) \geq \tau\right]V_1$$
$$+\frac{1}{1+\rho}\Pr\left[M(S) < \tau\right]V_0.$$

Similarly, we have

$$V_1 = \arg\max_S U\left[\psi(S,B+R,J),N(S),Q(S)\right]$$
$$+\frac{1}{1+\rho}\Pr\left[M(S) \geq \tau\right]V_1 + \frac{1}{1+\rho}\Pr\left[M(S) < \tau\right]V_0 .$$

It follows from the usual assumptions about the utility function that $V_1 > V_0$; in other words, centers prefer to have more resources available. The optimal choice of S depends on the rewards, the preferences, and the constraints facing centers.

We now present some intuitive analysis of some of the effects of the incentives induced by the performance standards in our simple dynamic model. First, let P^{01} indicate the probability of not receiving a reward in one period and receiving one in the next period and let P^{11} indicate the probability of receiving a reward in two consecutive periods. As having more resources makes it easier to attain all center objectives, including meeting the performance standards, it follows that $P^{11} > P^{01}$. Performance standards with budgetary rewards impart a value to incumbency.

Second, the analysis of the two-period model carries over in part in this more general setting. With sufficiently large R, sufficiently small ρ, and sufficiently misdirected performance incentives (incentives not aligned with maximizing the present value of net impacts), centers may sacrifice utility in the current period in order to obtain the budgetary reward and thereby increase their utility in the next period.

Third, consider the special case of centers that, in the absence of the performance standards, care only about maximizing the present value of net impacts (and thus not about $N(S)$ or $Q(S)$). For certain values of the parameters, such centers may divert resources away from that goal in low budget (nonreward) periods. They will do so in order to get the budgetary reward in the following period, which can then be spent on generating a larger total discounted stream of net impacts than would period-by-period net impact maximization.

Fourth, continuing with the same special case, with a sufficiently low probability of attaining the reward threshold and a sufficiently high reward R, the introduction of performance standards can lower the aggregate net impacts produced by all centers. Unsuccessful centers divert their activities away from productive uses and toward meeting the performance targets but reap no budgetary rewards. Successful centers produce more net impacts in the next period because they have more resources, but these additional impacts may not suffice to make up for the reductions in impacts in the current period from the centers that failed to reach the performance targets despite diverting resources away from present value maximization. If the increases in the present value of net impacts from the successful centers do not exceed the decreases from the unsuccessful centers, then aggregate output falls.

PERFORMANCE STANDARDS AND BUDGETARY DYNAMICS: THE REAL WORLD

As described in Chapters 2 and 4 and in more detail for WIA in Heinrich (2007), both JTPA and WIA built budgetary rewards into their performance systems. However, in both programs, the budgetary awards did not simply get added to the budget for the following period, as we have assumed for simplicity in our model. Instead, in JTPA, individuals served using the budgetary reward money did not count against the performance measures in the following period. This allowed centers to focus these funds on, in most cases, the hard to serve. In the context of our model, they spent them to maximize their utility in terms of $\psi(S,B,J)$, $Q(S)$, and $N(S)$ without worrying about $R[M(S)]$. Similarly, under WIA, most states spend their bonus funds on program improvements, either in the form of new initiatives or enhancements to current program infrastructure and services (e.g., trying to develop learning programs that engage dropouts, at-risk youth, and disadvantaged adults, improving outreach activities, and so on). Taking into account the realities of the programs does not change the basic dynamics outlined in the preceding two sections. For certain parameter values, centers might still find it optimal to take a hit in terms of current period utility in order to obtain the reward money, provided the additional utility obtained in the next period more than makes up for the loss when discounted back to the current period.

Moreover, with economies of scale in center operations, the real world budgetary rewards in JTPA and WIA may still generate the sort of incumbency effects described in the preceding section. Centers in JTPA and WIA could spend their reward money in part on administrative costs. If, for example, they would buy productivity-increasing office equipment or hire better managers with this money, this should spill over to the participants served under the regular budget B. In the model, we could capture this by making $c(e)$ declining in $N(S)$ to reflect economies of scale that arise from using physical or human capital more intensively.

STRATEGIC BEHAVIOR IN A DYNAMIC ENVIRONMENT

Another dynamic incentive induced by performance standards arises when centers have some flexibility over the period in which their participants count for the purposes of the performance measures. As documented for JTPA in Chapter 7, centers have some flexibility in the timing of termination decisions for their participants. Thus, around the end of one period (a program year in JTPA or WIA) they have some choice regarding whether to count particular participants in the current period or in the next period. When centers face nonlinear reward functions, like the simple one considered above in which the center receives R for attaining some threshold level of performance τ but has no incentive to do better at the margin either above or below τ, centers above the cutoff in the current period will want to move "good" participants to the following period. In contrast, a center with performance well below τ in the current period will want to move "bad" participants who might otherwise finish participating in the next period back to the current period, where they can do no harm to a "lost cause."

Our formal model does not capture this particular strategic response to performance standards, though we could modify it to do so. The simplest change would add the capacity for centers to count some current period participant realizations against performance in the following period. Doing so would have some per-participant cost that increased with the number of current period participants counted in the next period. The increasing per-participant cost captures the effect of rules, such as those in JTPA and WIA, that govern how long centers can keep participants "on the books" without spending money on them, as well as the fact that some program services (such as occupational training courses) have fixed durations, thus limiting flexibility. A set of more complicated changes to the model would also allow centers to bring forward good outcomes from the following period.

SUMMARY AND CONCLUSIONS

This chapter has laid out a (relatively) simple model of training center behavior in the context of a generic performance standards system similar to those used in active labor market programs around the world. Such performance standards systems have a variety of justifications, including aligning center behavior with the preferences of politicians who fund but do not operate them, solving a principal-agent problem by increasing the effort levels of center staff, and providing "quick and dirty" pseudo-evaluations of the extent to which the program improves the labor market outcomes of participants.

This model clarifies the ways in which performance standards systems affect center behavior, and the conditions under which those changes will increase the earnings or employment gains from participation, as well as the conditions under which they have positive or negative equity effects by changing the set of persons served among the eligible. We clarify the discussion of cream skimming in the literature in the context of our model. We show that the effects of introducing a performance standards system depend in part on center preferences and in part on empirical parameters such as the correlation between the short-term participant outcomes typically utilized as performance measures and the long-term behavioral impacts that represent the real goal of most programs.

We extend our simple model to include strategic behavior by training centers seeking to "game" the performance measures, whether by playing tricks with measurement in a static context or by manipulating the period in which participants count against the performance measures in a dynamic context. We examine two dynamic versions of our model in which centers receive budgetary rewards in each period based on their measured performance in the prior period. In this dynamic context, further distortions of center choices can result, as they may have an incentive to trade off utility (and perhaps discounted net impacts) in one period to achieve high performance and thus a larger budget in the following period.

Overall, this model provides a framework for thinking about the effects of performance standards on organizational behavior in the context of ALMPs and in broader contexts such as schools. In so doing, it motivates and provides a theoretical context for the empirical investigations presented in the later chapters of this book. Finally, in our view, the analysis in this chapter, along with the empirical evidence presented elsewhere in the book, suggests that policymakers who have mandated such systems, as well as the administrators who have determined their details and undertaken their practical implementation, have often failed to appreciate the difficulty of designing a performance system that makes things better (rather than making them worse), as well as the dependence of the effects of performance standards systems on empirical parameters that remain generally unknown and little investigated.

Notes

1. See Hanushek (2002) for a discussion of accountability systems in education based on performance standards at the teacher and school level. See, for example, Barnow (1992) and Barnow and Smith (2004) for additional discussions of performance standards in publicly provided training programs.
2. Wilson (1989) and Dixit (2002) discuss conflicts regarding the objectives of programs as outcomes of a political process.
3. On the issue of the timing of participation, see, for example, Sianesi (2004), Heckman and Navarro (2007), and Fredrikkson and Johansson (2008) and the papers cited therein.
4. It can also be negative in the long run, as indeed it was for male youth in JTPA. Bloom et al. (1993), Bloom et al. (1997), and Orr et al. (1996) provide more detail regarding the experimental impact estimates from the National JTPA Study.
5. Heckman, Lochner, and Taber (1998) present evidence on the importance of general equilibrium effects in evaluating large scale educational programs and Lise, Seitz, and Smith (2004) provide evidence of such effects in an earnings supplement program.
6. Note that r may represent a social discount factor.
7. We assume interior solutions. Sufficient conditions for an interior solution are concavity of Equation (3.2) in e for all $Y^0_{a,i}$, convexity of $c_i(e_i)$ for each i, and Inada conditions on both cost and technology. For some S, the constraint in Equation (3.4) may be slack (that is, $\lambda = 1$ can be obtained).
8. There may be more than one S that qualifies. If so, we assume the training center picks one of them at random.
9. There is an additional stage to the allocation process that we do not consider, namely, the allocation of the overall program budget among centers. From the standpoint of economic efficiency, the budget should be allocated to equate returns at the margin for all centers.
10. We ignore other methods for aligning training center behavior with politicians' preferences, such as developing a professional culture among caseworkers. See, for example, Wilson (1989) for further discussion.
11. See the related discussion in Sosin (1986) regarding the interaction between rules and caseworker discretion in the old Aid to Families with Dependent Children (AFDC) program.
12. In thinking about cream skimming from a policy perspective, two other facts should be kept in mind. First, as shown in Chapter 6, even if cream skimming occurs, the operation of program eligibility rules means that

even the cream consists of relatively disadvantaged individuals. Thus, at least in programs like JTPA or WIA, cream skimming does not generally mean that program resources were spent on, for example, middle-class people. Second, in the United States, many federal, state, local, and voluntary sector employment and training programs coexist at any given point in time. For example, National Commission for Employment Policy (1995) documents that dozens of other programs coexisted with JTPA. When thinking about cream skimming in a particular program, such as WIA, it should be kept in mind that other programs may provide services better suited to the hardest to serve among that program's eligible population. Determining whether cream skimming, should it occur, is good or bad, requires more thought than the literature typically devotes to it.

13. The finding in Heckman, Smith, and Clements (1997) will hold in general for programs with small mean impacts relative to the mean untreated outcome, so long as the impacts are not strongly negatively correlated with the untreated outcome.
14. In models with regressors, this assumption is $\Delta_{a,i}(X) = Y^1_{a,i} - Y^0_{a,i} = \Delta_a$ for all i, yielding equal impacts for all persons with the same X.
15. See JTPA Directive No. D98-15, February 22, 1999.
16. In this heuristic problem, we assume that the second order conditions are satisfied.

References

Anderson, Kathryn, Richard Burkhauser, Jennie Raymond, and Clifford Russell. 1992. "Mixed Signals in the Job Training Partnership Act." *Growth and Change* 22(3): 32–48.

Barnow, Burt. 1992. "The Effects of Performance Standards on State and Local Programs." In *Evaluating Welfare and Training Programs*, Charles Manski and Irwin Garfinkel, eds. Cambridge, MA: Harvard University Press, pp. 277–309.

Barnow, Burt S., and Daniel B. Gubits. 2002. "Review of Recent Pilot, Demonstration, Research, and Evaluation Initatives to Assist in the Implementation of Programs under the Workforce Investment Act." ETA Occasional Paper No. 2003-10. Washington, DC: USDOL.

Barnow, Burt, and Jeffrey Smith. 2004. "Performance Management of U.S. Job Training Programs: Lessons from the Job Training Partnership Act." *Public Finance and Management* 4(3): 247–287.

Bell, Stephen, and Larry Orr. 2002. "Screening (and Creaming?) Applicants to Job Training Programs: The AFDC Homemaker–Home Health Aide Demonstration." *Labour Economics* 9(2): 279–301.

Bloom, Howard, Larry Orr, Stephen Bell, George Cave, Fred Doolittle, Winston Lin, and Johannes Bos. 1997. "The Benefits and Costs of JTPA Title II-A Programs: Key Findings from the National Job Training Partnership Act Study." *Journal of Human Resources* 32(3): 549–576.

Bloom, Howard, Larry Orr, George Cave, Stephen Bell, and Fred Doolittle. 1993. *The National JTPA Study: Title IIA Impacts on Earnings and Employment at 18 Months*. Research and Evaluation Report Series 93-C. Bethesda, MD: Abt Associates.

Carneiro, Pedro, Karsten Hansen, and James Heckman. 2003. "Estimating Distributions of Treatment Effects with an Application to the Returns to Schooling and Measurement of the Effects of Uncertainty on College." *International Economic Review* 44(2): 361–442.

Courty, Pascal, Do Han Kim, and Gerald Marschke. Forthcoming. "Curbing Cream Skimming: Evidence on Enrollment Incentives." *Labour Economics*.

D'Amico, Ron, and Jeffrey Salzman. 2004. *An Evaluation of the Individual Training Account/Eligible Training Provider Demonstration*. Social Policy Research Associates final interim report to the USDOL-ETA. Oakland, CA: Social Policy Research Associates.

Dixit, Avinash. 2002. "Incentives and Organizations in the Public Sector: An Interpretative Review." *Journal of Human Resources* 37(4): 696–727.

Djebbari, Habiba, and Jeffrey Smith. 2008. "Heterogeneous Program Impacts: Experimental Evidence from the PROGRESA Program." *Journal of Econometrics* 145(1–2): 64–80.

Doolittle, Fred, and Linda Traeger. 1990. *Implementing the National JTPA Study*. New York: Manpower Demonstration Research Corporation.

Dyke, Andrew, Carolyn Heinrich, Peter Mueser, and Kenneth Troske. 2006. "The Effects of Welfare-to-Work Program Activities on Labor Market Outcomes." *Journal of Labor Economics* 24(3): 567–608.

Fredrikkson, Peter, and Per Johansson. 2008. "Dynamic Treatment Assignment: The Consequences for Evaluations Using Observational Data." *Journal of Business and Economic Statistics* 26(4): 435–445.

General Accounting Office (GAO). 2002. *Improvements Needed in Performance Measures to Provide a More Accurate Picture of WIA's Effectiveness*. Report to Congressional Requesters. GAO-02-275. Washington, DC: GAO.

Hanushek, Eric. 2002. "Publicly Provided Education." In *Handbook of Public Finance*, Alan Auerbach and Martin Feldstein, eds. Amsterdam: North-Holland, pp. 2045–2141.

Hayek, Frederick. 1945. "The Use of Knowledge in Society." *American Economic Review* 35(4): 519–530.

Heckman, James. 1992. "Randomization and Social Program Evaluation." In *Evaluating Welfare and Training Programs*, Charles Manski and Irwin Garfinkel, eds. Cambridge, MA: Harvard University Press, pp. 201–230.

Heckman, James, Carolyn Heinrich, and Jeffrey Smith. 2002. "The Performance of Performance Standards." *Journal of Human Resources* 37(4): 778–811.

Heckman, James, Robert LaLonde, and Jeffrey Smith. 1999. "The Economics and Econometrics of Active Labor Market Programs." In *Handbook of Labor Economics,* Vol. 3A, Orley Ashenfelter and David Card, eds. Amsterdam: North-Holland, pp. 1865–2097.

Heckman, James, Lance Lochner, and Christopher Taber. 1998. "Explaining Rising Wage Inequality: Explorations with a Dynamic General Equilibrium Model of Labor Earnings with Heterogeneous Agents." *Review of Economic Dynamics* 1(1): 1–58.

Heckman, James, and Salvador Navarro. 2007. "Dynamic Discrete Choice and Dynamic Treatment Effects." *Journal of Econometrics* 136(2): 341–396.

Heckman, James, and Jeffrey Smith. 1999. "The Pre-Programme Dip and the Determinants of Participation in a Social Programme: Implications for Simple Programme Evaluation Strategies." *Economic Journal* 109(457): 313–348.

Heckman, James, Jeffrey Smith, and Nancy Clements. 1997. "Making the Most Out of Programme Evaluations and Social Experiments: Accounting for Heterogeneity in Programme Impacts." *Review of Economic Studies* 64(4): 487–535.

Heckman, James, Jeffrey Smith, and Christopher Taber. 1996. "What Do Bureaucrats Do? The Effects of Performance Standards and Bureaucratic Preferences on Acceptance into the JTPA Program." In *Advances in the Study of Entrepreneurship, Innovation, and Economic Growth,* Vol. 7: *Reinventing Government and the Problem of Bureaucracy*, Gary Libecap, ed. Greenwich, CT: JAI Press, pp. 191–218.

Heinrich, Carolyn. 1999. "Do Governments Make Effective Use of Performance Management Information?" *Journal of Public Administration Research and Theory* 9(3): 363–393.

———. 2007. "False or Fitting Recognition? The Use of High Performance Bonuses in Motivating Organizational Achievements." *Journal of Policy Analysis and Management* 26(2): 281–304.

Hotz, V. Joseph, Guido Imbens, and Jacob Klerman. 2006. "Evaluating the Effects of Alternative Welfare-to-Work Training Components: A Reanalysis of the California GAIN Program." *Journal of Labor Economics* 24(3): 521–566.

Lazear, Edward. 1995. *Personnel Economics*. Cambridge, MA: MIT Press.

Lechner, Michael, Ruth Miquel, and Conny Wunsch. 2004. "Long-Run Effects of Public Sector Sponsored Training in West Germany." IZA Discussion Paper No. 1443. Bonn, Germany: IZA.

Lechner, Michael, and Jeffrey Smith. 2007. "What is the Value Added by Caseworkers?" *Labour Economics* 14(2): 135–151.

Lise, Jeremy, Shannon Seitz, and Jeffrey Smith. 2004. "Equilibrium Policy Experiments and the Evaluation of Social Programs." NBER Working Paper No. 10283. Cambridge, MA: National Bureau of Economic Research.

National Commission for Employment Policy. 1995. *Understanding Federal Training and Employment Programs*. Washington, DC: National Commission for Employment Policy.

Orr, Larry, Howard Bloom, Stephen Bell, Fred Doolittle, Winston Lin, and George Cave. 1996. *Does Training for the Disadvantaged Work? Evidence from the National JTPA Study*. Washington, DC: Urban Institute Press.

Prendergast, Canice. 1999. "The Provision of Incentives in Firms." *Journal of Economic Literature* 37(1): 7–63.

Radin, Beryl. 2006. *Challenging the Performance Movement: Accountability, Complexity, and Democratic Values*. Washington, DC: Georgetown University Press.

Sianesi, Barbara. 2004. "An Evaluation of the Swedish System of Active Labor Market Programs in the 1990s." *Review of Economics and Statistics* 86(1): 133–155.

Smith, Jeffrey. 2004. "Evaluating Local Economic Development Policies: Theory and Practice." In *Evaluating Local Economic and Employment Development: How to Assess What Works among Programmes and Policies*, Alistair Nolan and Ging Wong, eds. Paris: Organisation for Economic Cooperation and Development, pp. 287–332.

Smith, Jeffrey, Alexander Whalley, and Nathaniel Wilcox. 2010a. "Evaluating Participant Self-Evaluation." Book manuscript under preparation.

———. 2010b. "Are Participants Good Evaluators?" Unpublished manuscript. University of Michigan, Ann Arbor, MI.

Social Policy Research Associates. 2004. *The Workforce Investment Act after Five Years: Results from the National Evaluation of the Implementation of WIA*. Report prepared for the USDOL-ETA, Office of Policy Development, Evaluation and Research. Oakland, CA: SPRA.

Sosin, Michael. 1986. "Legal Rights and Welfare Change, 1960–1980." In *Fighting Poverty: What Works and What Doesn't?* Sheldon Danziger and Daniel Weinberg, eds. Cambridge, MA: Harvard University Press, pp. 260–282.

Trutko, John, Burt Barnow, Mary Farrell, and Asaph Glosser. 2005. *Earnings Replacement Outcomes for Dislocated Workers: Extent of Variation and Factors Accounting for Variation in Earnings Replacement Outcomes across State and Local Workforce Investment Boards*. Final report to the U.S. Department of Labor. Washington, DC: USDOL, Employment and Training Administration.

Wilson, James. 1989. *Bureaucracy: What Government Agencies Do and Why They Do It*. New York: Basic Books.

4
The JTPA Incentive System

Implementing Performance Measurement and Funding

Pascal Courty
Gerald Marschke

This chapter outlines the specifics of JTPA's performance incentives, which provide necessary background information for subsequent chapters in this monograph. It also speaks generally to the challenges that must be met in formulating performance measures and incentives anywhere in government.[1] In particular, we argue that the decisions about what should be measured, and how, when, and by whom it should be measured, make a critical difference for the success of incentive-backed performance measurement.

The JTPA organization was conceived in the spirit of New Federalism. Proponents of New Federalism have argued that more decentralized decision making leads to "laboratories of the states" that foster innovation and creativity and hence, in the end, superior policies. In JTPA, states indeed used their discretion to produce a wide variety of performance measurement and incentive structures. The federal government retained control over some important aspects of the incentive system. The discretion left to the states, however, was important for determining the character of performance measurement and the incentives.

By providing an analytical description of performance measurement in JTPA, this chapter complements the institutional literature on the JTPA bureaucracy (Barnow 1992; Svorny 1996). Although this literature provides a good understanding of how JTPA's performance incentives worked at the federal level, it has little to say about its implementation at the state level. By offering a more complete description of JTPA performance incentives, this chapter lays the foundation for understanding how the JTPA incentive system determined bureau-cratic behavior and program outcomes. Previous studies of the impact of JTPA's performance incentive scheme on bureaucratic behavior (Anderson, Burkhauser, and Raymond 1993; Courty and Marschke 2004; Heckman, Smith, and Taber 1996; and Marschke 2002) have used only the federal guidelines, which provide an incomplete and possibly misleading representation of the true incentive systems.[2] Along with others (see, e.g., Wholey 1999, p. 305), we believe that such case studies of operational performance measurement systems are important inputs into developing theories to understand and recommendations to improve performance measurement in the public sector.

We limit our description to the state incentive and performance measurement policies for the years 1987–1989 for a sample of 16 states (identified in Table 4.1).[3] In describing JTPA's performance-based incentive system, we address three questions. First, what was the nature of the training center's incentive? Or, how much was at stake? Second, which dimension of performance did JTPA reward? That is, what mattered? According to the act, Congress intended the performance incentives to measure the training centers' success in developing participants' labor-market specific human capital (U.S. Congress 1982, Section 106[a]). Because direct measures of human-capital value-added are unavailable, the program's federal overseers have resorted to proxies of value-added. At the heart of the JTPA incentive system is a set of performance measures based on the labor market outcomes of enrollees at or shortly after training. We describe these performance measures.

Third, what is the relationship between performance and awards? In JTPA, states determined awards in three steps. First, they standardized the performance outcomes to make them comparable across training centers. States rewarded training centers not for the absolute level of performance but for their performance in excess of a numerical threshold, or performance standard. The performance standard depended on factors that were specific to each training center and outside the centers' control. The performance standards were intended to establish reasonable counterfactual levels of performance that one would expect given the environment in which the training center operated. The second step was to establish the training center's eligibility for an award. Training centers were usually eligible only if they exceeded the standards associated with all or a defined subset of the performance measures.

Finally, the states formulated award functions that translated training centers' excess performances into budgetary awards. The sensitivity of the award to excess performance determined the strength of the incentive and varied across states and over time.

The chapter is organized as follows. The first section investigates the bureaucrats' motivations for seeking awards. The second section explains the JTPA performance measures and also how performance outcomes across the population of training centers were adjusted to level the playing field. The third section describes the incentive award, and the last section concludes and summarizes our main findings.

AWARDS AND BUREAUCRATIC PREFERENCES

The JTPA incentive system takes the form of increases in training centers' training budgets. We start by describing the sizes of these increases. By focusing solely on the absolute award amounts, however, one risks overlooking potentially important influences of performance awards on bureaucratic behavior and program outcomes. These nonfinancial reasons are reviewed next.

Award Size

The act required that states allocate about 7 percent of their total JTPA training budget to their incentive programs.[4] States then decided how to allocate this sum among the three categories of expenditures: 1) awards for successful training centers, 2) administration of the incentive programs, and 3) "technical assistance" for unsuccessful training centers. JTPA mandated that the state set aside funds for technical assistance, but left the amount set aside up to the state. Technical assistance provided resources to improve managerial performance to training centers that failed to meet performance standards.

While the act intended that the training centers use the awards primarily for training, awards could also be used for staff bonuses and payroll increases. A training center was required to spend at least 70 percent of the award on training activities, leaving 30 percent, at most, for staff compensation. By comparison, training centers were permitted

Table 4.1 State Funding of the JTPA Incentive Program States of the National JTPA Study, 1987–1989

	Program year 1987		Program year 1988		Program year 1989	
State	Award fund as percentage of 6 % funds	Percentage of award funds allocated to federal performance standards	Award fund as percentage of 6 % funds	Percentage of award funds allocated to federal performance standards	Award fund as percentage of 6 % funds	Percentage of award funds allocated to federal performance standards
CA	85	100	85	88	85	88
CO	95	100	85	100	85	100
FL	—	—	—	—	—	—
GA	75	100	75	90	75	90
IA	75	99	75	99	75	99
IL	75	100	75	100	75	100
IN	93	40	92	60	78	60
MN	85	50	85	50	85	50
MO[a]	100	100	100	100	100	100
MS	100	70	98	70	98	70
MT[a]	66	100	66	100	66	100
NE	85	60	85	60	85	60
NJ	80	33	80	33	80	33
OH	80	100	80	60	70	60
RI	75	100	75	100	75	100
TX	76	90	77	90	81	80

NOTE: JTPA allowed each state to use up to 6 percent of its JTPA appropriation for direct cash payments to job training centers for performance on federal and state performance measures. The first column for each year lists the fraction of the 6 percent that was set aside for the award fund. This fraction represents the maximum amount that would be rewarded to training centers for performance relative to federal and state standards. The second column for each year represents the fraction of the award fund that is set aside for federal performance standards alone. — = data not available.

[a]The 1987 values for Missouri and Montana in the first column are taken from the NCEP-SRI survey, which interviewed training center personnel in 1986 concerning the program year 1986. They are not calculated from training center policy documents.

to spend no more than 15 percent out of budgetary funds on payroll. The higher cap for payroll expenses alone may have motivated training centers to pursue awards.

Table 4.1 shows the share of the incentive fund set aside for the award for a sample of 16 states in the years 1987–1989. We collected data on these 16 states because they contained the 16 training agencies that participated in the late 1980s USDOL-commissioned National JTPA Study (NJS). The NJS was an important experimental study involving approximately 20,000 enrollees that was designed to measure the impact of job training in JTPA on participants' earnings and employment prospects. The analyses contained in Chapters 5, 6, and 9 are at least in part based on the NJS data. The second, fourth, and sixth columns show the award size as a percentage of the 7 percent incentive fund for 1987, 1988, and 1989, respectively. Although states varied in the portion set aside for awards, as Table 4.1 shows, most states made available a majority of the incentive fund to training centers as potential awards. Montana set aside the smallest share—66 percent of the incentive fund—while Missouri and Mississippi (in 1987) set aside the entire fund to be paid out as an incentive award. While the portion set aside varied significantly across states, it was stable over the 1987–1989 period. For example, between 1987 and 1989, Illinois devoted 75 percent of its 7 percent fund to the award fund. It reserved the other 25 percent for technical assistance. Only in Indiana did a significant change take place. Between 1987 and 1989, Indiana lowered the portion set aside for the award from 93 percent of the incentive allocation to 78 percent. The other states devoted a constant (or nearly constant) share of the incentive funds to awards.

In some states, not all of the funds that the state made available for awards were paid out. Not all funds were awarded because many training centers did not perform well enough to meet the states' award eligibility requirements. Nevertheless, as Table 4.2 shows, the amounts paid out were substantial. Table 4.2 shows the actual award amounts disbursed as a fraction of the training center's budget for a sample of 448 training centers in program year 1987. The average disbursement was equivalent to 7 percent of the training center's budget.[5] The highest disbursements were equivalent to 60 percent of the training center's budget. Rewards this large, however, were not possible in all states.

Table 4.2 Size of Incentive Award

	Allocation ($)	Incentive award ($)	Fraction of training center's budget
Mean	2,326,191.42	119,663.79	0.07
(Std. dev.)	(3,043,936.68)	(145,751.12)	(0.07)
First quartile	1,003,308.50	33,000.00	0.03
Median	1,627,151.50	93,550.00	0.06
Third quartile	2,398,462.00	160,534.00	0.09
Maximum	29,408,455.00	1,407,853.00	0.57
Number of obs.	448	385	385

NOTE: Data are from the National Commission for Employment Policy and SRI, Inc. (see their description in Dickinson et al. [1988]).

We expect that if incentives matter, the intensity of the behavioral responses to the incentives should depend on the size of the award. Tables 4.1 and 4.2 show that the award amounts available varied significantly by state. Everything else equal, we might expect that JTPA incentives produced greater responses among training centers in Missouri than Montana where the award disbursement was the greatest (i.e., 100 percent of the award fund). In addition, the kind of behavioral response we observe would likely have depended upon how states divided award money between state and federal measures of performance. The division matters because state and federal performance measures stressed different aspects of training center output.

Why Should Training Centers Care about Awards?

As a rough approximation, the awards might have increased salaries by as much as 15 percent.[6] This figure corresponds to the purely financial part of the incentive. This by itself represents a substantial increase even compared with private sector bonuses. There is, however, little evidence that training center administrators paid out such a large share of the award as salary bonuses.[7] Why, then, should bureaucrats care about the awards?

There are at least three reasons why a training center may wish to increase its budget. First, Niskanen (1971) and others argue that everything the bureaucratic manager desires (salary, staff, power, professional reputation, and perquisites) derives from the bureau's budget.

Because of their training and the orthodoxy of the social work profession, welfare bureaucrats—like the ones in JTPA—may behave as selfless advocates for their clients (Lipsky 1980). Nevertheless, even as client advocates, JTPA bureaucrats would desire extra award funds to expand their clients' training resources.

Second, performance levels and the awards they represent might have been used by local elected officials for political gain. The act gave local elected officials—often these are city mayors—some authority over the operation of training centers. The administrative headquarters of training centers were frequently situated in these elected officials' offices. These elected officials often touted performance awards as measures of their administration's success in the local fight against poverty.

Third, bureaucrats might have sought performance awards for the professional recognition they convey. Bureaucrats faced no other objectives—and the public and bureaucratic superiors have no other evaluation criteria—as precisely defined, quantifiable, and available as these performance measures. Tirole (1994, p. 7) argues that government bureaucrats might be "concerned by the effect of their current performance not so much on their monetary reward, but rather on their reputation or image in view of future promotions, job prospects in the private and public sectors."[8] Moreover, by performing well compared to the standards, bureaucrats could protect themselves against attack from outside critics and political enemies.

As a final point, note that because awards were based on group performance, individual bureaucrats had an incentive to free-ride on the effort of colleagues. Free-riding may have muted the influence of incentives at the level of caseworkers. Ultimately, the issue of the influence of budget-based awards and the significance of the free-riding problem must be resolved empirically.

PERFORMANCE MEASURES

The act directed the USDOL to formulate measures of performance that captured the gains produced in the employment and earnings of participants and the reductions in their reliance on welfare programs (Chapter 2). Reliable measures of earnings and employment impacts of job training, however, were prohibitively costly to obtain, and instead, the USDOL issued measures that assessed the effectiveness of job training through the labor market outcomes of enrollees at training end.

JTPA required states to use the USDOL's performance measures in constructing their incentive system. Nevertheless, the USDOL permitted states to impose additional performance measures, and many states did. Whereas the federally designed performance measures were concerned with labor market outcomes, state measures (described below) tended to focus on inputs. While many states developed their own measures, they typically devoted a disproportionately small share of the award to them, leaving the bulk of the award for the federally designed measures.

The following section discusses the federal and state-designed measures and how states divided their awards between them. In addition, this section discusses the possible consequences of the construction of these measures for JTPA training practices. Over time, state and federal authorities replaced or redefined those performance measures whose effects were possibly counterproductive. We also discuss these modifications.

Federal Performance Measures

Table 4.3 defines the federal performance measures in place during the period 1987–1989. For the adult portion of the program, the system's performance measures were employment rate at termination, the average wage at termination, the cost per employment, the employment rate at 90 days after termination—i.e., at follow-up, the average weeks worked at follow-up, and the average weekly earnings at follow-up. For the youth portion of the program, the system's performance measures were the employment rate at termination, the cost per employment, the positive termination rate, and the employability enhancement rate. The youth employment rate at termination and youth cost per employment were defined as for adults. Youth positive termination rate and youth employability enhancement rate evaluated the acquisition of certain kinds of general or labor market skills, such as the completion of a major level of education, or completion of a GED certification (see Table 4.3, especially the last part of the note).

Table 4.3 National JTPA Performance Measures in Effect in Years 1987–1989

Performance measure	Definition
Adult performance measures	
Employment rate at termination	Fraction of terminees employed at termination
Welfare employment rate at termination	Fraction of terminees receiving welfare at date of application who were employed at termination
Average wage at termination	Average wage at termination for terminees who were employed at termination
Cost per employment	Training center's year's expenditures on adults divided by the number of adults employed at termination
Employment rate at follow-up	Fraction of terminees who were employed at 13 weeks after termination
Welfare employment rate at follow-up	Fraction of terminees receiving welfare at date of application who were employed at 13 weeks after termination
Average weekly earnings at follow-up	Average weekly wage of terminees who were employed 13 weeks after termination
Average weeks worked by follow-up	Average number of weeks worked by terminees in 13 weeks following termination
Youth performance measures	
Youth employment rate at termination	Fraction of youth terminees employed at termination
Youth employability enhancement rate	Fraction of youth terminees who obtained employment competencies (see note below)
Youth positive termination rate	Fraction of youth terminees who were "positively terminated" (see note below)
Youth cost per employment	Training center's year's expenditures on youths divided by the number of youths positively terminated

NOTE: The date of termination is the date the enrollee officially exits training. A terminee is an enrollee after he has officially exited training. All measures are calculated over the year's *terminee* population. Therefore, the average follow-up weekly earnings for 1987 was calculated using earnings at follow-up for the terminees who terminated in 1987, even if their follow-up period extended into 1988. Likewise, persons who terminated in 1986 were not included in the 1987 measure, even if their follow-up period extended into 1987. A positive termination is entering unsubsidized employment, attaining youth employment "competencies" (through coursework, training and/or tests in work maturity, basic education, or job-specific skills), entering non-JTPA training, returning to school full time, or completing a major level of education.

All federal performance measures for adult participants had three characteristics in common. All performance measures were 1) year-end summaries of yearly cumulated performance, 2) based on aspects of the enrollee's labor market status on the date the enrollee officially terminated the program or at three months after termination, and 3) averages of outcomes over the population of the year's terminees (not participants). Thus, training centers did not face a piece rate in the sense that training centers received compensation per unit of output: e.g., per enrollee employed, or per dollar increase in an enrollee's earnings ability. Instead, training centers received awards for achieving high average labor market outcomes. For example, the employment rate at termination for the fiscal year 1987 was defined as the fraction of persons terminated between July 1, 1987, and June 30, 1988, who were employed on their termination date.[9] Awards were thus independent of the number of persons who obtained high outcomes.

The use of performance measures varied across states. In 1987, the USDOL required states to base incentives on seven termination-based measures: the adult employment rate at termination, adult welfare employment rate at termination, adult cost per employment, average wage at termination, youth employment rate at termination, youth positive termination rate, and youth cost per employment. In 1988–1989, the USDOL extended the list of measures to the 12 described in Table 4.3 and required states to choose any 8 or more of these 12 measures. The years 1988 and 1989 marked the beginning of the phaseout of termination-based performance measures and the cost measure.[10] After 1992, the USDOL prohibited the states from using any cost measures of performance. Moreover, after 1992, all performance measures based on measures of output became follow-up measures.[11]

Performance measures based on labor market outcomes may have influenced training center behavior in several ways. First, because they measure aspects of an enrollee's employment state and not the impact of job training, they may have led training centers to select enrollees most able to achieve high levels of employment at high wages, instead of the enrollees most likely to benefit from the program. This behavior has been called cream skimming (see Chapters 6 and 9).

Second, the performance measures may have encouraged training centers to offer "quick fixes," that is, employment-oriented job search or on-the-job training services. These services, rather than more intensive kinds that result in greater skill development, would more frequently lead to employment on the measurement date, whether or not the employment match was suitable and likely to last beyond the end of training. The reason why quick fixes may have been preferred is because the employment and wage measures focused on labor market success at a point in time rather than over a period of time. Cream skimming is an example of dysfunctional behavior that results when the performance measures are not well-aligned with the goals of the organization. If quick fixes generate smaller welfare gains per dollar spent than more intensive services they also constitute dysfunctional behavior (see Bloom et al. [1997] for evidence on the relative effectiveness of different training types in JTPA). See Blau (1955) for an early discussion of unintended responses to performance measures.

Third, because these measures were based on averages instead of aggregate outcomes, training centers had no incentive to spend their entire budget. Actually, the optimal training strategy from a pure performance point of view was to enroll only the most promising applicant. More generally, enrolling a smaller than efficient population would typically be an optimal strategy in areas where able applicants were scarce. In these areas, rather than enroll less able enrollees who lower per capita scores, training centers would prefer to leave some of their budget unspent.

Fourth, the role of the cost measure was ambiguous. The cost measure was defined as the total expenditure divided by the number of persons employed at training end. Holding spending constant, the cost measure becomes an incentive to produce as many employed terminees as possible. Bureaucrats could produce greater numbers of employed terminees either by increasing their employment rates at termination or by enrolling more applicants (holding the employment rate constant). Viewed in this way the cost measure would have countered the incentive to serve small populations. The elimination of the cost measures in the last years of JTPA would have added an additional incentive to reduce the number of enrollees served. Training centers would enroll less than the efficient number of enrollees because small enrollee populations increased the per capita spending, and greater per capita spending increased the per capita performance outcomes (Barnow [1992] makes this point).

Federal Performance Standards

The impact of the performance measures on bureaucratic behavior depended critically on the threshold the bureaucrat had to meet. For example, a training center did not receive an award for the wage measure if its year-end average wage outcome (the average wage at termination) failed to meet the average wage standard. Thus, the wage measure would produce no effect on behavior if the wage standard was set too high so that no amount of effort would push the wage outcome over the standard. Another reason why the performance standards were crucial was because the performance awards did not depend on absolute performance but on excess performance, that is, on the difference between the performance outcome and the performance standard.

This subsection describes the heights of the standards and how they were tailored to the different environments faced by the training centers. The USDOL adjusted the performance standards to the local conditions faced by training centers in an attempt to level the playing field.

For each performance measure, the numerical standard started with the national "departure point." The USDOL set the departure point for all but the cost and wage measures at the 25th percentile of the distribution of performance in the system in the preceding two years. That is, 75 percent of the training centers would have exceeded the performance standard on average. For the cost measure, good performances were low performances. Successful training centers had to produce an outcome below the standard. The USDOL set the departure point for the cost measure at the 90th percentile. For the wage measure, the department set the departure point at the 50th percentile.[12]

Training centers faced different costs of meeting these departure points. Costs varied because labor markets, training costs, and the characteristics of the eligible populations varied. Imposing uniform standards would have favored low-cost training centers by increasing their resources relative to high-cost training centers. Only in the case that low-cost training centers tended also to be more efficient would such incentives enhance the efficiency of the allocation of training resources. Believing that this probably was not the case, the USDOL established an adjustment model that took into account features of the training center's environment that may be correlated with costs. For example, by taking into account local unemployment measures and other measures of the labor market, the adjustment methodology lowered the employment rate standard for training centers in depressed job markets, compared to training centers in robust job markets.

Although the USDOL allowed states some flexibility in developing standards, most states used the department's adjustment methodology.[13] All states participating in the NJS used the USDOL's adjustment model during the NJS years. We describe this method here.

USDOL adjustment model

Consider an arbitrary performance measure and let S_l be the outcome produced by training center l. The USDOL adjustment scheme posited that the following function generates performance outcome S_l.

$$(4.1)\quad S_l = \alpha + \beta_1(x_{1l} - \overline{x}_1) + \beta_2(x_{2l} - \overline{x}_2) + \ldots + \beta_M(x_{Ml} - \overline{x}_M) + \varepsilon_l,$$

where $x_{1l}, x_{2l}, \ldots, x_{Ml}$ are training center l's realizations for the M factors chosen, $\overline{x}_1, \overline{x}_2, \ldots, \overline{x}_M$, are the average realizations of these factors over all JTPA training centers, and ε_l is a site-specific error term. Biannually the USDOL estimated the coefficients β with the most recent two years of training center–level data using ordinary least squares. β_m expresses the impact of an increase in the factor x_{Ml}, on the outcome S_l, holding other factors constant. The USDOL chose a different set of factors for each performance measure. It chose those economic factors and demographic variables based upon their availability and whether the factors were statistically correlated with the performance outcomes. In addition, political considerations may have played a role.[14]

Table 4.4 presents an example of a JTPA worksheet for adjusting the adult employment rate at termination in 1987. The first six adjustment factors in the table are enrollment population characteristics (the percentage of the participant population that is female, black, Hispanic, Asian, handicapped, and welfare recipients). The last two adjustment factors are measures of the local economy (unemployment rate and population density). Column B presents factor values for a hypothetical training center. Columns C and E present the actual national factor averages and the weights from the USDOL adjustment model for 1987. These weights are the estimated effects of each characteristic on the performance outcome adult employment rate at termination (estimated

Table 4.4 U.S. Department of Labor's Performance Standard Adjustment Model Performance Standard: Adult Employment Rate at Termination

A. Local factors	B. Training center factor values	C. National averages	D. Difference (B – C)	E. Weights	F. Effect of local factors
% Female	49.9	52.8	−2.9	−0.020	0.058
% Black	41.2	23.8	17.4	−0.081	−1.41
% Hispanic	30.1	7.9	22.2	−0.009	−0.20
% Asian	2.1	2.4	−0.3	−0.022	0.01
% Handicapped	9.5	9.1	0.4	−0.093	−0.04
% Welfare recipient	35.0	29.8	5.2	−0.276	−1.44
Unemployment rate	8.8	8.0	0.8	−0.623	−0.50
Population density	0.21	0.6	−0.39	0.771	−0.3
	G. Total effect of local factors on performance expectations				−5.77
	H. National departure pcint				62.4
	I. Model-adjusted performance level (G + H)				56.6

NOTE: Local factors listed in column A are determined by the USDOL. Percentages are of year's participant population. Values for columns C, E, and H are given by the USDOL. Values for column B are for a hypothetical training center.

β's from Equation 4.1). The training center's realization of each of the factors is compared to the national average and the difference is multiplied by a weight. For example, suppose the hypothetical training center served 1,000 persons during 1987, of which 499 were female. Thus, its percentage female factor was 49.9 percent. To obtain the adjustment to the standard for the female participation factor, one multiplies the difference between the training center's factor value and the national average (49.9 − 52.8 = −2.9) by the adjustment weight (−0.020). The adjustment weight reflects how the enrollment of women historically affected the employment rate outcome.

For the other factors, weighted differences were calculated similarly. The total effect of local factors on performance expectations (column F)—the sum of the weighted differences—was added to the national departure point. The departure point (the 25th percentile value) for the measure was 62.4. The final performance standard (56.6) is the sum of the departure point (62.4) and adjustment factor (−5.8). The state used the final standard to establish whether the training center had met its adult employment rate target.

The USDOL intended that the bar be set to a height appropriate to the training center's circumstances. Thus it included measures of the local unemployment rate and of local population density to capture aspects of the local labor market in which the training center operated. For example, as one can see from Table 4.4, the weight on the local unemployment rate measure was negative: a one-point increase in the local unemployment rate lowered the standard by about two-thirds of a point. Because training centers were small relative to the local labor market, the unemployment rate is an example of an influence on the performance outcome which was likely to be beyond the training center's control.

As Table 4.4 also makes clear, an important class of characteristics for which the USDOL adjusted standards was the composition of the enrollment pool. While the enrollment pool reflected in part the composition of the local eligible population (an influence beyond the training center's control), it was at least partly a choice variable. Adjusting the performance standard in this way may have encouraged the training center to enroll not only persons who would boost performance outcomes, but also persons who would lower standards.

Table 4.4 also reveals that the USDOL adjustment model did not take into account training services as a relevant control variable, although these data were available to the department. Thus, the nature of the adjustment procedure meant that the incentive system held training centers accountable for the kinds of training provided but not the kinds of enrollees enrolled; both choices have consequences for the effectiveness and efficiency of training. Neither did the adjustment model directly control for the training services available in the training centers' local area. This is more surprising; by not controlling for the availability and costs of training facing training centers, the incentive system implicitly favored those training centers located in markets where there was a competitive and efficient training industry.[15]

State Performance Measures and Standards

States were permitted to develop their own performance measures. While state measures played a smaller role than federal measures in the determination of the awards, the number of NJS states using their own measures increased from 10 to 13 between 1987 and 1989. The increase in importance of state-formulated measures was apparently a nationwide trend.

In Table 4.1, the second column under each year shows the percentage of the total award set aside allocated to federal measures, as opposed to state measures. Although state-defined measures were common among the NJS states, they comprised a relatively small fraction of the award. Excluding New Jersey, the average split between federal—or performance-based—measures and state measures was 82/18. The split ranged from a low of 50/50 to a full allocation of the money to the federal award.

We broke down the state measures into four categories. The most important category of state measures comprised input or enrollment measures. In the mid-1980s, states became increasingly concerned that federal performance incentives were driving training center bureaucrats to enroll from the eligible population only those enrollees who were likely to get jobs at the end of training—i.e., who were "job ready." Many states implemented a set of enrollment-based performance measures designed to encourage training centers to enroll the more difficult cases. In 1988, for example, 9 out of 16 states set up standards that compensated training centers for the number of or the rate at which persons in target groups were enrolled.[16] These target groups varied by state but were typically the least successful in the labor market among the eligible and included high school dropouts, minority youths, Women/ Infant Nutrition program participants, and older workers. For example, in addition to compensating performance based on federal performance measures, Minnesota rewarded training centers for the fraction of enrollees who were receiving public aid. In these cases, compensation was contingent upon meeting a numerical standard, frequently based on the fraction of eligible persons in the local population who belonged to the target group. Studies of the effect of incentives on the enrollment decision can be further refined by allowing for these enrollment quotas to influence the enrollment decision.

The other categories of state measures were more idiosyncratic. Some states compensated training centers for the fraction of their budgetary allotment spent. For example, in 1987 and 1988, Mississippi paid a portion of its award money to training centers that spent at least 85 percent or more of their budgets. Training centers might have left portions of their budgets unspent because, as we noted above, the kinds of applicants who would produce high-performance outcomes may have been scarce. Rather than enrolling less able enrollees who lower per capita scores, training centers might have enrolled fewer enrollees than the maximum their budgets would have allowed.

Three of the 16 states sought to encourage JTPA training centers to coordinate their activities with other state agencies that helped the poor.[17] In promoting these goals, states typically evaluated performance subjectively, without well-defined performance standards. Finally, although state performance measures usually were not based on participant labor market outcomes, some states used their own measures to encourage training centers to seek longer-term employment matches before the USDOL began offering the follow-up measures in 1988. In 1987, New Jersey used a separate measure for employment retention, similar to the federal employment rate at follow-up measure.

THE JTPA AWARD

This section describes how states used performance outcomes and standards to reward training centers. In particular, we discuss the states' eligibility rules that determine which training centers received awards and the award functions themselves. The award functions translate the performance of eligible training centers to award amounts.

The states were entirely free to design the eligibility rules and the performance awards as they saw fit, which led to great variation in both across states. In fact, no two award functions (or eligibility rules, for that matter) were identical. Because of space constraints, we do not report the exact computation rules for the awards. Instead, we define some broad dimensions that are important from a behavioral point of view, to categorize the different types of award functions, illustrating where appropriate with specific details from the state incentive systems.

Qualifying for Awards

Here we discuss the qualifying criteria for the 16 NJS states in years 1987–1989. Some states (such as Indiana) required training centers to meet all standards as a prerequisite for earning any award money. Other states required training centers to exceed a subset of standards to qualify. For example, in 1987 Minnesota required training centers to exceed five of seven performance standards to qualify for awards. Other states had no qualification criteria. These states (such as Iowa) simply rewarded training centers for each performance standard exceeded.

Some qualification criteria were quite complicated. For example, in 1987, Illinois divided the seven federal measures in place at the time into three groups. To qualify for an incentive grant, a training center had to meet both standards in the first group, one of two standards in the second group, and one of three standards in the third group.[18] In addition, the training center had to meet a slightly higher version of the standards for at least one measure.

The number and kind of standards a training center had to meet to win an award may have been an important determinant of the influence of incentives upon behavior. States that required the training center to meet all standards discouraged training centers from specializing in the production of certain performance outcomes at the expense of others. Moreover, the greater the number of performance standards that training centers were required to meet, the lower their likelihood of obtaining an award. By lowering the chances to qualify for an award, such qualification criteria may have discouraged training centers from attempting to win awards.

Award Function

The award functions varied along several important dimensions. The three most important dimensions, discussed below, address three broad questions: Which performance measures mattered? How competitive was the incentive system? Did excess performance cease to matter after some point?

Performance measure weighting. By exercising their discretion over which measures they included in their awards (see Table 4.2) and in their construction of the eligibility criteria, states could emphasize some performance measures and de-emphasize others. In addition, states used explicit weighting schemes in the award function for the same purpose. Although many states weighted each measure used equally, some states weighted performance measures differently to emphasize some measures over others.

Consider, for example, New Jersey in 1987 and 1988. While a training center there had to meet its cost standards to qualify for an award, its cost outcomes did not figure into the award's calculation. Moreover, the award calculation up-weighted the follow-up-based measures compared to the termination-based measures. In de-emphasizing the cost- and termination-based measures, New Jersey intended to encourage training centers to provide more intensive training and enroll more difficult-to-train enrollees (see Note 12).

Competition among training centers. In many states (such as Texas), a training center's award depended only on its own performance. In Illinois's scheme, the size of a successful training center's award depended on the number of training centers that qualified: the lower the number of training centers that qualified, the greater the allocation to the successful ones.

Other examples of interdependence more closely resemble the relative performance evaluation schemes found in the incentive literature in economics. New Jersey is an example of a state that pitted training centers against one another in a form of head-to-head competition. In New Jersey's tournament system, a training center received an award based not on an absolute level of performance but on its position in a ranking of its fellow training centers.

Evaluating a training center on its relative performance may have stimulated competition between training centers by accentuating social comparisons. Another reason for relative performance evaluation is that it holds training centers harmless for influences that are beyond the training center's control and that affect all training centers uniformly. Thus, relative performance evaluation should be most effective in states where training centers are homogeneous (e.g., operate in similar environments) and if the performance standards do a poor job of controlling for factors that are outside the training centers' control.[19]

Marginal incentive. The marginal incentive measures the change in incentive award for a small change in performance. Marginal incentives are constant when the award function is linear, as in a piece rate compensation system. However, they may depend on the level of performance. When the marginal incentives vary with the level of performance, incentives are said to be nonlinear. In JTPA, the main source of nonlinearity was the performance standard: in many states, training centers were paid only contingent upon achieving standards. Many states (such as Georgia) paid out the entire award merely for meeting the standards. Such states provided no pecuniary incentive to exceed the standards. Other states, however, compensated training centers for performance in excess of the standard, at least over some range of performance. For example, in Illinois in 1987, a training center's award increased with its performance, until its performance exceeded the standard by 40 percent. For performance in excess of 40 percent of the standard, the training center received no additional compensation. The marginal incentives for performances above 40 percent of the standard were zero.

As with many incentive systems based upon attaining standards, training centers may have been able to manipulate the award intertemporally by selectively choosing when to report good and bad performances. In this way, training centers would have been able to increase their performance outcomes without actually increasing the effectiveness of their training. Deadline effects have been described in the behavior of military recruiters whose bonuses depend on recruitment quotas (Asch 1990), salespersons whose commissions depend on achieving sales targets (Oyer 1995), and CEOs whose bonuses depend on performance targets linked to measures of corporate earnings (Healy 1985). See Courty and Marschke (1996, 1997) for evidence of deadline effects in JTPA, and Courty and Marschke (2004) for an attempted estimation of the efficiency costs of these effects.

CONCLUSION

This chapter details a description of the incentives in place under JTPA. The incentive awards amount to budgetary increases that training center bureaucrats valued for professional, personal, and political reasons. The potential size of the bonus award varied by state and program year. In program year 1986, for example, the total bonus was about 7 percent of the training budget. These awards, however, could have been a substantial added source of training funds. Depending on the state and the year, this amounted to as much as 60 percent of a training center's yearly allocation of funds.

The heart of the JTPA incentive system was the set of performance measures and their standards. Job training programs illustrate the difficulty of devising performance measures that are aligned with programmatic goals. In the early years of JTPA, performance measures were based on employment outcomes measured at training end, thus possibly encouraging training centers to pursue high employment rates instead of increased earnings-capacities. Moreover, because they were based on average outcomes, performance measures may have reduced the number of disadvantaged people served, raised the expenditure per enrollee, and produced budget surpluses. In later years, some states adopted expenditure-based performance measures, possibly to counteract the incentives created by federal measures to leave some of their budgets unspent.

Training centers received awards when the outcomes of performance measures exceeded numerical standards. The USDOL attempted to adjust performance standards to reflect the environment in which the training center operated so that training centers in healthy and in depressed economies had to exert complementary levels of effort to achieve their standards. The USDOL's adjustment scheme offers a real-world example of strategies for adjusting performance measures that have been proposed in the literature (Stiefel, Rubenstein, and Schwartz 1999). Performance standards were also adjusted for the characteristics of persons enrolled, so as to discourage cream skimming, but not adjusted for the kinds of training offered. Excluding training from the adjustment method may have promoted employment-oriented services —such as job clubs and on-the-job training—and these services may not have produced either stable employment relationships or significant improvements in the long-term employability of enrollees. This study has revealed numerous ways in which performance measures might have been misaligned with the agency's goals. With the exception of some cream skimming studies and a study of deadline effects, these distortionary effects have not been investigated. We believe that further research on the behavioral responses to JTPA's incentives would lead to much useful information for developing and refining performance measures for many kinds of public sector organizations.

The federal government left the formulation of many of the details of the award to the states. Consequently, the form of the award varied. States established eligibility criteria that modified the JTPA incentive system by reducing the incentive to specialize in the production of one or two performance measures, lowering the training center's likelihood of obtaining an award, holding effort constant, and emphasizing some performance measures over others.

The strength of the award varied greatly across states, suggesting that the magnitude of responses to performance incentives depended on the state. States also differed in the degree of competition among training centers and in the interdependence of awards. Head-to-head competition among training centers in some states may have heightened the impact of the incentive system on behavior. States also differed in the extent to which they compensated exceptional performance. In some states, training centers received no more award money for meeting standards than exceeding them. In other states, training centers received additional money for higher performance. States also designed and implemented their own performance measures that promoted different goals than the goals implicit in the federal measures. Thus, the objectives transmitted to the training center depended on the state in which it operated.

Notes

This chapter introduces features of the JTPA incentive system that will be used extensively in the remainder of this monograph. Some of these features have been discussed and analyzed in detail elsewhere (Courty and Marschke 1997, 2002, 2003, and 2004), and parts of this chapter borrow from these sources.

1. Discussions of general criteria for choosing performance measures and constructing performance measurement systems, for example, are found in Hatry (1980), Hurst (1980), Usilaner and Soniat (1980), Wholey (1999), and GAO (1996).
2. Cragg (1997) and Marschke (2002) are exceptions.
3. We chose to limit the number of states and years for which we collected incentive policies because of the difficulty and expense of obtaining these records. We collected data on these 16 states because they contained the training agencies that participated in the late 1980s USDOL-commissioned National JTPA Study, described in Chapter 2.
4. The JTPA funds were allocated in three subfunds: 1) 78 percent were set aside for training services, 2) 6 percent were set aside for the incentive system, and 3) the remaining 16 percent were set aside for other special services. The award fund as a fraction of total training budget was 7.1 percent (6/[78+6]) if one assumes that all award funds were eventually distributed as training budget. The actual figure may have been a little lower because some of the incentive set aside fund was spent on the administration of the incentive funds.
5. These figures are based on the data set of SRI, International and Berkeley Planning Associates. See Dickinson et al. (1988) for a description of these data.
6. Salary payroll represented at most 15 percent of training budget that was itself only 78 percent of total JTPA training funds (see Note 7). The award fund was 6 percent of JTPA funds and at most 30 percent could be distributed as salary. The award salary bonus as a fraction of total salary was at most $(0.06 \times 0.3)/(0.15 \times 0.78) = 0.15$.
7. In a survey of 30 training centers conducted by Dickinson et al. (1988), only three administrators indicated that this was their practice. In a 1994 telephone survey administered to 11 of the 16 training centers of the National JTPA Study, all training center administrators that we spoke to denied that they ever distributed a portion of the award for salary bonuses.
8. Thompson (2000) describes the merit pay system at the Social Security Administration, ushered in with the enactment of the Civil Service Reform Act of 1978. Under this system one half of managers' annual pay increases were determined by

their performance relative to a set of output indicators. While originally set up as a basis for rewarding pay increases, these indicators became the basis for promotion decisions as well. According to one former manager, they became "the basis for your career . . . if you do well on those four measures. You can write your own ticket" (p. 270).

9. Note that persons who entered the program already employed, and then terminated employed, holding the same job they began training with, say, were numbered among the successfully trained—i.e., were *employed at termination*—for award accounting purposes.
10. In the first years of JTPA (through 1987), the USDOL required states to use a cost measure. Nevertheless, some policymakers and analysts, alarmed at the short length of training (the average length of training is about five months in JTPA), instigated investigations by the GAO and other interested parties into the link between cost measures and short, low-intensity services. As a consequence of this inquiry, the USDOL encouraged states to phase out the cost measure, "to encourage [training centers] to provide more comprehensive programming and increased services for those individuals who are most in need" (Division of Employment and Training, New Jersey Department of Labor 1990). Moreover, in response to a number of Labor Department investigations, which concluded that training centers were emphasizing "quick fixes" with job-placement-oriented services that had no long-term impact on enrollees' skills, the department formulated a number of follow-up measures: the measures based on outcomes three months after termination, presented in Table 4.3. The USDOL introduced follow-up measures to "[promote] effective service to participants and [assist] them to achieve long-term economic independence" (Division of Employment and Training, New Jersey Department of Labor 1990).
11. That is, the employment rate at termination and average wage at termination gave way to the employment rate, the average weeks worked, and average weekly earnings at follow-up (13 weeks after termination).
12. Actually, the USDOL's JTPA Technical Assistance Guide, PY1988, reports that the cost standard's departure point was set "above the 25th percentile. It more closely resembles an estimate of average performance." We interpret this statement to mean the department set the wage standard at the 50th percentile.
13. State governors had the option to 1) set the performance standard at the national departure point; 2) adjust the national departure point for specific economic, geographic, and demographic factors within the state or local service delivery areas using the regression model established by the USDOL; or 3) propose their own adjustment method to the USDOL. Between the end of the National JTPA Study and the end of JTPA, more states abandoned the USDOL adjustment method for their own (option 3).
14. Barnow (1992) writes that "when estimated coefficients have an unexpected sign, the variables are dropped from the models and regressions are re-estimated" (p. 292). For example, in some regressions, the USDOL dropped an indicator variable for Hispanic enrollees because it apparently showed a positive effect on performance outcomes.

15. For more on the specification of USDOL's regression model, see Barnow (1992) and Trott and Baj (1987). One significant shortcoming they describe is that estimating the Equation with training center–level data, as opposed to enrollee-level data, biased the estimates of the model's coefficients. Using enrollee-level data, Trott and Baj demonstrated that the practice of pooling the data by training center significantly changes some of the estimates of β_m. For a general discussion of the theory of adjusting performance measures, what factors should and should not be used to adjust performance measures, see Stiefel, Rubenstein, and Schwartz (1999).
16. These states were California, Iowa, Indiana, Minnesota, Missouri, Mississippi, Nebraska, New Jersey, and Ohio.
17. These states were Georgia, Iowa, and Ohio.
18. The first group consisted of the adult employment rate at termination and the adult cost per employment. The second group consisted of the youth positive termination rate and the youth employment rate at termination. The third group consisted of the average wage at termination, the welfare employment rate at termination, and the youth cost per positive termination.
19. The USDOL's performance standard adjustment methodology—to the extent that it accounted for external factors that affect performance—produced the same effect.

References

Anderson, Kathryn, Richard Burkhauser, and J. Raymond. 1993. "The Effect of Creaming on Placement Rates under the Job Training Partnership Act." *Industrial and Labor Relations Review* 46(4): 613–624.

Asch, B.J. 1990. "Do Incentives Matter? The Case of Navy Recruiters." *Industrial and Labor Relations Review* 43(3): S89–106.

Barnow, Burt. 1992. "The Effect of Performance Standards on State and Local Programs." In *Evaluating Welfare and Training Programs*, Charles F. Manski and Irwin Garfinkel, eds. Cambridge, MA: Harvard University Press, pp. 277–309.

Blau, P. 1955. *The Dynamics of Bureaucracy: A Study of Interpersonal Relations in Two Government Agencies*. Chicago: University of Chicago Press.

Bloom, Howard S., Larry L. Orr, Stephen H. Bell, George Cave, Fred Doolittle, Winston Lin, and Johannes M. Bos. 1997. "The Benefits and Costs of JTPA Title II-A Programs: Key Findings from the National Job Training Partnership Act Study." *Journal of Human Resources* 32(3): 549–576.

Courty, Pascal, and Gerald Marschke. 1996. "Moral Hazard under Incentive Systems." In *Advances in the Study of Entrepreneurship, Innovation, and Economic Growth*, G. Libecap, ed. New York: JAI Press, pp.157–190.

———. 1997. "Measuring Government Performance: Lessons from a Federal Bureaucracy." *American Economic Review* 87(2): 383–388.

———. 2002. "Performance Incentives with Award Constraints." *Journal of Human Resources* 37(4): 812–845.

———. 2003. "Performance Funding in Federal Agencies: A Case Study of a Federal Job Training Program." *Public Budgeting and Finance* 23(3): 22–48.

———. 2004. "An Empirical Investigation of Gaming Responses to Performance Incentives." *Journal of Labor Economics* 22(1): 23–56.

Cragg, Michael. 1997. "Performance Incentives in the Public Sector: Evidence from the Job Training Partnership Act." *Journal of Law, Economics, and Organization* 13(1): 147–168.

Dickinson, Katherine P., Richard W. West, Deborah J. Kogan, David A. Drury, Marlene S. Franks, Laura Schlichtmann, and Mary Vencill. 1988. *Evaluation of the Effects of JTPA Performance Standards on Clients, Services, and Costs.* Research Report No. 88-16. Washington, DC: National Commission for Employment Policy.

Division of Employment and Training, New Jersey Department of Labor. 1990. *State of New Jersey Performance Standards Manual, PY 1988–89.* Trenton, NJ: Division of Employment and Training, New Jersey Department of Labor.

General Accounting Office (GAO). 1996. *Executive Guide: Effectively Implementing the GPRA.* GAO/GGD-96-118. Washington, DC: GAO.

Hatry, Harry. 1980. "Performance Measurement Principles and Techniques: An Overview for Local Government." *Public Productivity Review* 4(4): 313–315.

Healy, P. 1985. "The Effect of Bonus Schemes on Accounting Decisions." *Journal of Accounting and Economics* 7(1–3): 85–107.

Heckman, James, Carolyn J. Heinrich, and Jeffrey A. Smith. 1997. "Assessing the Performance of Performance Standards in Public Bureaucracies." *American Economic Review* 87(2): 389–395.

Heckman, James J., and Jeffrey A. Smith. 1995. "The Performance of Performance Standards: The Effects of JTPA Performance Standards on Efficiency, Equity, and Participant Outcomes." Unpublished manuscript. University of Chicago.

Heckman, James J., Jeffrey A. Smith, and Christopher Taber. 1996. "What Do Bureaucrats Do? The Effects of Performance Standards and Bureaucratic Preferences on Acceptance into the JTPA Program." NBER Working Paper No. 5535. Cambridge, MA: National Bureau of Economic Research.

Hurst, E. 1980. "Attributes of Performance Measures." *Public Productivity Review* 4(1): 43–46.

Lipsky, Michael. 1980. *Street Level Bureaucracy: Dilemmas of the Individual in Public Services.* New York: Russell Sage Foundation.

Marschke, Gerald. 2002. "Performance Incentives and Bureaucratic Behavior: Evidence from a Federal Bureaucracy." Unpublished manuscript. University at Albany, State University of New York.

Niskanen, William A. 1971. *Bureaucracy and Representative Government.* Chicago: Aldine-Atherton.

Oyer, P. 1995. "The Effect of Sales Incentives on Business Seasonality." Unpublished manuscript. Princeton University, Princeton, NJ.

Stiefel, Leanna, Ross Rubenstein, and Amy Ellen Schwartz. 1999. "Using Adjusted Performance Measures for Evaluating Resource Use." *Public Budgeting and Finance* 19(3): 67–87.

Svorny, Shirley. 1996. "Congressional Allocation of Federal Funds: The Job Training Partnership Act of 1982." *Public Choice* 87(3–4): 229–242.

Thompson, James R. 2000. "The Dual Potentialities of Performance Measurement." *Public Productivity and Management Review* 23(3): 267–281.

Tirole, Jean. 1994. "The Internal Organization of Government." *Oxford Economic Papers* 46(1): 1–29.

Trott, Charles E., and John Baj. 1987. *Development of JTPA Title II-A Performance Standards Models for the States of Region V.* DeKalb, IL: Center for Governmental Studies, Northern Illinois University.

U.S. Congress. 1982. *Job Training and Partnership Act.* Public Law 97-300, 29 U.S.C. §1501. Washington, DC: U.S. Government Printing Office.

Usilaner, B., and E. Soniat. 1980. "Productivity Measurement." In *Productivity Improvement Handbook for State and Local Government*, G. Washnis, ed. New York: Wiley.

Wholey, Joseph S. 1999. "Performance-Based Management: Responding to the Challenges." *Public Productivity and Management Review* 22(3): 288–307.

5
Setting the Standards

Performance Targets and Benchmarks

Pascal Courty
Carolyn J. Heinrich
Gerald Marschke

A key element in the design of performance measurement and accountability systems is the establishment of appropriate benchmark levels (or standards) of performance to guide the evaluation of program outcomes. Performance benchmarks shape system incentives and influence the responses of public managers and staff operating programs. In systems with rewards and sanctions linked to results, performing above or below the standards can have important short-term consequences (e.g., budgetary rewards or revisions, positive or negative recognition), as well as long-term ones (e.g., promotion, structural reorganization).

In this chapter, we review the literature in information economics, contract theory (see, for example, Dixit [2002] and Prendergast [1999]), and public administration to draw out theoretical implications for the construction of performance standards in public organizations.[1] We then assess alternative methods that are commonly used to construct performance standards and consider the relevance of these lessons for the design of performance measurement systems in public programs. An important premise of our work is that the method used to construct performance standards can change the way employees behave and influence the internal efficiency of organizations. Focusing in particular on performance benchmarking in U.S. workforce training programs (i.e., JTPA and WIA programs), we assess whether the design of performance standards in these programs is efficient and consistent with basic principles derived from theory.

The exercise of performance assessment clearly serves important functions in public organizations other than promoting efficiency.

Marshall et al. (2000) describes three primary functions: 1) accountability for public expenditures, 2) the production of comparative information to inform customer choices in public services, and 3) improvement of professional practice and program management. For example, public managers may use performance information to identify best practices and to communicate to outside constituencies legitimate information about organizational achievements. We acknowledge the possibility that the introduction of performance measurement may transform organizations through channels other than those we discuss in our literature review. We likewise recognize that political and ethical concerns also influence the construction of performance standards and the use of performance data. We discuss these issues to a greater extent in our case study analysis of performance benchmarking in public training programs.

THEORY-BASED FRAMEWORK FOR PERFORMANCE BENCHMARKING

We frame our discussion in terms of the principal-agent model, a theoretical framework commonly applied in the economics and public administration literatures. There are critics of this model who argue that it overemphasizes the self-seeking behavior of agents and neglects social interactions and motivators. In his classic study of organizations, Thompson (1967), for example, describes the importance of cliques, social controls based on informal norms and status that influence the performance of organizations. Similarly, stewardship theory emphasizes collective goals and public managers "whose motives are aligned with the objectives of their principals," or who highly value cooperative behavior even when their interests and those of the principal diverge (Davis, Donaldson, and Schoorman 1997, p. 21). Although we acknowledge the roles of social and cultural norms and the influence of political and personal power relationships as described in these alternative theoretical frameworks, we rely primarily on principal-agent theory in modeling behavior and relationships in this study.

In our application of principal-agent theory to the study of performance standards systems, we call the party who designs the measurement system the principal and the party whose performance is measured the agent. We denote the measured performance *P*, and the benchmark level of performance, or the performance standard, P_0. The difference between the performance outcome (*P*) and the performance standard (P_0) is denoted ΔP, that is, $\Delta P = P - P_0$.

We are interested in the methods that are used to construct the performance benchmark P_0 and in the kind of information that these methods incorporate in the benchmark. Although we recognize that there may not exist a single method of construction that could be effectively applied in all situations, we still believe that some methods are largely more effective than others. We say that a standard is poorly constructed or "ineffective" if it is missing key pieces of information and/or if it is likely to send the wrong signals and to stimulate behavioral responses with negative implications. In addition, we recognize that, in practice, organizations will often use multidimensional measurement systems with multiple measures and performance benchmarks. Although we explicitly discuss these issues, for the sake of conciseness, we focus in our literature review on the simplest case with a single performance measure, as this is sufficient to highlight the main lessons from the literature without loss of generality.

We assume that the agent has some control over the performance outcome, and following the economics literature, effort constitutes the agent's choices and exertions that influence the performance outcome. We denote the effort choice *e* and assume that higher effort levels increase the performance outcome, that is, $P(e)$ increases with *e*. We model effort as a one-dimensional choice by the agent. It is useful, however, to think of *e* as a vector of activities; the agent chooses not only how hard to work, but also how to allocate her time and effort across different activities. For example, in job training centers, caseworkers allocate their efforts toward recruiting participants, assessing their training "needs," networking with other social service organizations and managing contracts with external vendors, and bookkeeping, to name a few of their activities. The lessons we draw from our model based on a simple formulation—assuming that *e* is a scalar—are robust to this more realistic assumption.

In the simplest formulation, performance is equal to effort $P = e$, and value added is equal to $\Delta P = e - P_0$. We think of value added here as the agent's contribution to the principal's welfare, net of costs. In the case of a job training program, assuming its objective is to raise the earnings and employability of the poor, value added is the value of the labor market skills enrollees acquire due to the exertions of training center workers, net of training costs.

As discussed above, setting the absolute level of the performance standard is a critical task in performance measurement systems. In the federal programs we study—JTPA and WIA—and others since the U.S. Government Performance and Results Act (GPRA) of 1993, government officials are required to undertake this task annually. We assume (consistent with practice in these programs) that the performance standard determines the level of acceptable performance below which sanctions are imposed and above which rewards are given. By increasing the standard, the principal boosts incentives to improve performance, because the agent has to supply more effort to meet the standard and avoid sanctions.

Large or incessant increases in the standard, however, also diminish the credibility of the measurement system, with the consequence that the agent may simply give up or search for alternative, possibly unproductive ways to increase measured performance. In our model, we assume that the agent receives a level of compensation that is independent of performance, and we define the level of effort that one would expect for that base compensation as e_0. In an efficiently functioning system, prevailing competitive forces determine this level of effort. In other words, it is the amount of effort a representative agent would expect to exert for the base level of compensation. In this case, the performance standard is set at the level of performance that occurs when the agent provides the competitive level of effort, $P_0 = P(e_0)$.

The rationale behind setting the performance standard at this level is that if the performance standard were set above $P(e_0)$, then the principal would be unable to attract and retain the agent. Agents would not apply or compete for the job or contract. On the other hand, if the performance standard were set below $P(e_0)$, the principal would be overcompensating the agent.

To illustrate this definition of the performance standard, consider a simple manufacturing production example. We use this example because manual work constitutes the occupational class where performance benchmarking was first used in a systematic way (and is still common practice). Taylor (1911) was perhaps its most famous early proponent. His ideas arose from his experience as a machinist in a steel plant. Miller (1992, p. 102) also used a piece-rate production setting to analyze "managerial dilemmas" and to consider how an incentive system could "harness individual self-interest in pursuit of organizational goals," "transforming an organizational social dilemma into an organizational 'invisible hand.'" This choice of example is without loss of generality, as we will argue that the problems that arise with the construction of performance standards in public organizations do not fundamentally differ from those arising in production manufacturing.

Suppose a manual worker in a factory is paid a wage (w) per hour. The wage is paid independently of the level of worker performance. In addition to the fixed wage, the principal may wish to reward the worker for superior performance and impose sanctions for inferior performance. The number of pieces the worker produces per hour is by itself insufficient to assess whether to reward or sanction the agent. One way to address this question is to conduct time-and-motion studies to establish a benchmark level of performance, or an hourly rate, $P_0 = e_0(w)$, which a representative worker earning w would achieve, and then use this benchmark to evaluate actual performance. In other words, the principal actually assesses the level of performance that occurs under competitive effort and uses this information to set the performance standard. The difference between the worker's performance and the performance standard is used as a measure of value added. Under that interpretation, value added corresponds to what the agent adds, because of superior effort, to what we would expect to prevail in the market.

This method of establishing the performance standard requires estimating the production technology available to the agent, that is, the relation between effort and outcomes. Once this relationship is understood, it is possible to infer the agent's excess effort relative to the competitive level of effort. Counterfactual experiments such as time-and-motion studies, however, are practical only in a few occupations that typically involve manual work. Many public and private sector work situations involve nonmanual work, complex group interactions, and nonstandardized outputs, making experimental studies to construct counterfactual performance benchmarks very costly.

These complications mean that the methods typically used to construct performance standards are imperfect. Real world methods necessarily balance the cost of establishing fair and appropriate standards and the expected return to the organization from assessing value added more precisely; and of course, in the "real world," non-economic factors—e.g., political goals, legislative requirements, etc.—may also influence standard setting processes. These challenges and trade-offs will become evident in the case study analysis of the JTPA and WIA performance standards that follow. First, however, we review a set of generic problems that any method of setting performance targets must address.

Leveling the Playing Field

Thus far, we have considered the case of a principal who manages a single agent working in a single environment. It often happens, however, that the agent works in multiple environments or that the principal manages multiple agents who face different work conditions. To illustrate, we return to the time-and-motion study example presented above and assume that there are multiple workers assigned to different machines. We also assume that the machines vary in their productivity in the sense that the amount of effort required to produce a unit of output varies by machine. (One might model this idea formally by defining the performance outcome from machine k when effort is e as $P(e) = ke$, where $k > 0$ and k is different from machine to machine.) Assume that each machine's productivity is known to both the principal and the agent.

If the agent is allowed to refuse to work on a machine, the principal must factor the difference in marginal products of effort across agents into the determination of the performance standard. In fact, if the principal sets the same performance standard for all machines, say, $P_0 = e_0$, then the agent will only agree to work with machines that exhibit high marginal productivities. An important point is that time-and-motion studies would have to be conducted in each work environment to control for the special circumstances of the environment that are commonly observed by the principal and the agent.

Consider, for example, the job-training caseworker with the responsibility to assess clients and place them into jobs at a rate required by the performance standard. The caseworker will prefer to work with the most motivated and capable clients and direct them into the most effective employment preparation activities. Consequently, in the absence of adjustments to the standard, the caseworker would respond by discriminating against low-ability enrollees and directing only the higher-ability trainees into services with the highest measured performance outcomes (e.g., job-placement activities).

Insurance and Uncontrollable Risk

The time-and-motion study example assumed no uncertainty about the worker's performance outcome. Consider a more realistic example where the worker produces a number of pieces that depend on his or her effort and also on some external shock or influence, for example, a power outage that slows production (or in the job-training example, an economic recession that dampens job placement success). The performance outcome is now equal to $P + \Delta$ and the worker's value added is $\Delta P = (P + \varepsilon) - P_0$, where ε is a mean zero random variable that is realized only after the agent has chosen his or her level of effort. Setting the standard at a level that does *not* take into account these circumstances or context implies that a worker who supplies the effort level that is required to achieve the performance standard will sometimes overperform and other times underperform relative to the standard. In this situation, value added is equal to $\Delta P = \Delta$ when $e = e_0$. Outside shocks do not influence the worker's choice of effort because additional effort still increases expected performance. They do, however, change the realized level of performance and value added, and therefore, the worker's compensation.

Although a risk-neutral worker will not suffer any disutility from this variation in compensation, a risk-averse worker will, and this establishes a first rationale to construct as fair a performance standard as possible. The merit of performance standards will depend in part on their ability to control for outside risk (i.e., circumstances beyond the control of public managers or staff). The logic of agency theory is that standards that properly account for external influences reduce compensation risk, thereby increasing the agents' welfare. Lowering the risk faced by the agent is also desirable for the principal, as it means that he does not have to offer the agent a higher wage to compensate for risk bearing.

The key challenge for performance standards system designers is to identify the sources of controllable versus uncontrollable factors that influence the performance outcome. In other words, it is important to hold the worker responsible for effort, *e*, but not for external influences, ε. At the same time, the principal does not want to discount factors that are within the agent's control. For example, the principal does not want to lower the performance standard in the event that the worker's machine breaks down if the agent might have anticipated and prevented the breakdown. In the context of the job-training example, the principal *does* want to hold the caseworker responsible for (and reward) efforts made to appropriately assess clients and facilitate better worker-employer matches. But it would be unfair and inefficient to penalize the caseworker (or job-training center) for a lower rate of worker-employer matches if it is due to a declining number of labor market (job) opportunities.

As suggested above, though, risk aversion is not the only reason the agent may experience disutility from performance standards that fail to control for outside risks. Another closely related concern is fairness. The issue of income variability drives the concern under risk aversion, while other considerations, such as interpersonal comparisons, may foster concerns about fairness. For example, the agent may experience more disutility from an idiosyncratic shock that lowers only her performance and not the performance of her coworkers, compared to a group shock that lowers all workers' performance. The former shock generates different treatments amongst individuals who have essentially behaved identically. As under risk aversion, if workers value fairness, the principal benefits from discounting factors that are outside the worker's control.

Hidden Information, Adverse Selection, and Distortions

We show in the previous section that in setting performance standards, the principal may want to take into account information about shocks that influence the performance outcome and that are outside the agent's control. These shocks are observed only after the agent has chosen a level of effort, implying that they do not influence this choice. We now consider a different kind of information that plays an important role in the construction of performance standards. This information is observed only by the agent, and not by the principal, and it is observed before the agent chooses his/her level of effort. For example, assume that when the agent is assigned to a new machine, she alone knows the productivity of that machine and can use this information to make her effort choice. We say that the information is privately known by the agent, and consistent with the literature, we characterize such situations as hidden information (Holmstrom 1982; Miller 1992).

Hidden information further complicates the problem of setting standards. To illustrate, we return to the job training program example and again assume that the training efforts of caseworkers in this program are evaluated in part according to the rate at which their clients secure jobs. Caseworkers observe relevant information about applicants on the likely success of training investments, (e.g., personal motivation and employment barriers). Based on this information, the caseworkers can predict how likely the applicant is to obtain employment by the end of training. Assume furthermore that those applicants who are more likely to perform well on the performance measure are not necessarily those who benefit most from training. Indeed, some applicants to the job-training program may be highly likely to obtain employment on their own. As a result the caseworkers may overinvest in easy-to-serve applicants and underinvest in hard-to-serve ones, and it may be impossible for the principal to correct these investment distortions.

For example, a given effort level e could produce performance outcome $P = e + h$, where $h < 0$ if a hard-to-serve participant is enrolled, and $h > 0$ if an easy-to-serve participant is enrolled. We denote hidden information by h to distinguish this kind of information from information that is publicly known, such as the information about varying productivities of machines. If the caseworker observes the applicants' type, he has an incentive to enroll only easy-to-serve applicants because they produce better outcomes.

In fact, the only way the principal could try to correct these distortions would be by controlling for the type of applicants who have been served, adjusting upward the performance of those agents who have enrolled a larger fraction of hard-to-serve applicants. By assumption, however, only the agent knows this information. If the principal were to ask the agent what type of participants he has enrolled, the agent would have an incentive to report enrolling only hard-to-serve enrollees, and the principal would have no way to verify that the agent is telling the truth.

Practically speaking, the principal could correct these distortions by developing a specific measure to target the hard-to-serve groups, for example, using observable variables such as welfare recipient or limited English proficiency as proxies for "hard-to-serve." This would assume that welfare recipients or nonnative English speakers are harder to serve because they require higher investments for equal outcomes. The principal could set a lower performance standard for these individuals, for example, $P_0' = e_0 - h$, where $P_0' < P_0$ by construction. Of course, we know that not all welfare recipients (or nonnative English speakers) are identical; some are easier to serve than others, and the agent observes this information. Again, the agent will be inclined to select a nonrepresentative sample of these groups. This implies that the principal has corrected some distortions because the agent's attention is now focused on a needier target population, but the agent will still select those applicants who are the easiest to serve within these subpopulations of applicants.

Note that a slightly different problem from hidden information, known as adverse selection in the literature, occurs when there are multiple agents who are privately informed. In our example, it could be the case that different agents face different costs, observed privately, of meeting the standard. In the job training case, this happens when there are multiple caseworkers who face different eligible populations, and when the caseworkers privately observe this information. The distinction between adverse selection and hidden information has to do with the point in time when the agent becomes privately informed. Under hidden information, the agent becomes privately informed after agreeing to the contract, while under adverse selection, the agent is informed before agreeing to the contract. As a consequence, adverse selection introduces the possibility that the agent's private information will influence the agent's decision to accept the contract or not.

To illustrate, assume that the principal offers all agents the option to run special programs that are only for hard-to-serve populations. The principal lowers the standards for these special programs, and using our terminology, this would constitute a new optional contract. The agent agrees or declines to participate. The agents will choose to run such programs on the basis of their private information about the population they face. Presumably, the agents who face the best chances to meet the lower performance standards will decide to run such programs. However, these agents may not be those who generate the highest returns from the principal's perspective. The agent's selection rule poses a problem when it does not correspond to the rule that the principal would use, had the principal had the same information as the agent.

Multiple Principals

Another distinctive feature of performance standards systems in the public sector is the greater likelihood that agents will work for more than one principal. In the context of public organizations, one should think of principals as a widely defined category that includes all constituencies or interest groups that may influence the actions of the agent, either directly through explicit rewards or indirectly through more subtle channels. For example, in the context of our application to the JTPA and WIA programs, Congress, the USDOL, and state governments would be the main principals, since these are the actors who directly define the goals and activities of the organization, both through the design of the incentive system, performance standards, and also through other organizational features. But local politicians, private industry council representatives, and other interest groups should also be viewed as secondary principals, since these parties likewise have roles in influencing training program priorities and agency actions.

The key implication of the presence of multiple principals is increased complexity in the incentive system, particularly if the interests of the different principals are not aligned, e.g., emphasizing different priorities or outcomes. The agent has to choose how to allocate his/her effort level e across the various goals or objectives of the principals, which might be represented in a performance standards system by multiple standards, P_1, P_2, P_3, etc.

Dixit (2002) proposes an analysis of multiple principals competing noncooperatively for the agent's effort. As expected, the agent will allocate more effort toward the objectives of principals who compensate at a higher rate (or provide greater rewards for achievement in some form or another). In other words, if $w_1 > w_2$, then $e_1 > e_2$ and $P_1 = e_1(w_1) > P_2 = e_2(w_2)$; performance is higher on the outcome set by the principal who calls for P_1 and provides greater rewards for its achievement. Dixit demonstrates that the marginal level of effort applied by the agent (e_1, e_2, e_3, etc.) toward the achievement of the various outcomes will be decreasing in the number of principals. The reason is simply that each principal will reward the agent for success on the particular dimension(s) of effort that concern him or her, but he will also insure the agent against failure on dimensions of effort that concern the other principals. If principals choose the level of incentive noncooperatively, the desire to insure the agent will conflict with the desire to provide incentives.

In investigating how the principals compete for the agent's effort, Dixit also shows that the declines in agents' marginal level of effort (as the number of principals increases) will be exacerbated if the efforts across principals' objectives are substitutes. In other words, the principals undermine one another, and the impact of the incentives is diminished. In equilibrium, all principals call for effort, but since efforts are substitutable, the incentive effects on total effort are reduced.

Dixit's analysis calls for two recommendations for organizational design. First, one should allocate and organize tasks across agents based on whether they are complements or substitutes. Complementary activities can be grouped together, but the grouping of substitute activities should be avoided. In the context of the JTPA program, if there are some principals who are more concerned about equity of allocation (local government) and others more concerned about efficiency (the federal government), then it may be optimal to divide up the functions of enrollment and training and to assign each of these activities to two separate agencies.

In addition, the model has implications for how the principals should be allowed to compete. In particular, the principal *i* should not be permitted to excuse or cover for the agent's poor performance toward meeting principal *j*'s objective. This "compartmentalization principle" has implications in a public organization. Consider, for example, the conflict between enrollment and training in the JTPA program described above, and assume that the proposed solution of breaking up these tasks is not feasible for administrative or practical reasons. In this situation, the principals who are concerned primarily with reaching hard-to-serve populations will try to set the performance standard in such a way that training agencies are not penalized for achieving low performance outcomes. Similarly, principals who care mainly about efficiency will try to minimize the emphasis placed on enrollment choices. A possible result would be that agencies would face low performance standards and no constraints on enrollment. To avoid this outcome, one would want to minimize principals' interference with one another in the setting of performance standards.

Although there is considerable discussion of "multidimensionality" or multiple principals in the literature, there is little mention of situations in which there may be a hierarchy among the principals. The political science literature discusses "political multidimensionality" and the difficulty of identifying an "ultimate principal," e.g., the competing interests of House and Senate chambers, committees, and other political actors that have implications for the stability of agents' behavior (Maltzman and Smith 1994). However, it is also possible that in a political hierarchy such as that established in the JTPA system, with service providers taking signals from local job-training authorities and state and federal policy directives at the same time, agents might allocate their efforts toward alternative objectives of these principals according to the principals' position in this hierarchy.

Dynamic Issues

Measurement systems are often changed from time to time. There are many reasons why the principal may update performance standards. First, the principal may want to set low standards when a new performance measure is introduced to give the agent time to adjust to the change. Second, the principal may correct performance measurement systems as she acquires new information about the effectiveness of different measurement schemes or about the influence of external factors on performance. Third, the principal may revise the standard to account for changes in the environment or in the production technology.

The agent will take into account the possibility of future changes, and most importantly, the fact that current performance outcomes may be used in setting future standards. In both the JTPA and WIA programs, this has been a central component of the performance standard setting process. The WIA legislation explicitly identifies "continuous performance improvement," in which performance targets increase each year, as a central tenet of the performance standards system. Such a rule also implicitly exists in any organization that uses past agent performance to estimate the production function and set standards for the present. Assume the agent systematically outperforms the standard, and the principal consequently increases it. It could be that the agent was outperforming the standard because the agent was exerting exceptional effort. The agent will then anticipate that current performance influences future standards. The natural response to such a rule is to stop supplying high effort because it increases the standard (and the level of effort required to obtain the same reward in the future). Thus, a simple static view of incentive systems may fail to capture such behavioral responses that arise only when one considers the dynamic nature of performance measurement.

In the economics and management literature, this phenomenon is known as the ratchet effect (Holmstrom and Milgrom 1987; Miller 1992). The agent's belief about the principal's policies regarding future standards will significantly influence his behavior and the success of the incentive system. To eliminate the ratchet effect, the agent must trust that the principal will not change the standard. Trust is more likely to develop under repeated interactions when the principal can create a reputation for not reneging on the contract. Miller (1992, p. 157) likewise recognizes the importance of trust in these situations, noting that "'trustworthiness' on the part of managers seems to be a necessary element of an effective incentive system." Another way the principal can eliminate the ratchet effect is by committing to never change a standard, or more realistically, by committing to strict rules for changing the standard. Such commitment is likely to eliminate fear of the ratchet effect and reinforce incentives for effort.

OVERVIEW OF PERFORMANCE STANDARD–SETTING APPROACHES

We now present a brief overview of alternative methods for constructing performance standards (informed by the theoretical discussion above) and consider the environments where these methods are likely to work well.

Estimating the Production Function

Most basically, the principal (or public agency) can attempt to estimate the production function (i.e., the level of productivity expected from a given level of effort) to set the standard. It is sometimes possible to establish a standard through experimentation or through statistical methods. Such an approach will only be valid, however, for production processes that are stable over time and across environments. This is relatively rare, for example, in public social service provision. The use of data on past performance outcomes to construct estimates of the production function is a more common application of this method. A potential problem with this method, as discussed earlier, is the introduction of a ratchet effect if higher performance outcomes increase future standards. This method is also unlikely to work well in nonstationary environments where the production technology is subject to transient shocks.

Relative Performance Evaluation

Relative performance evaluation (RPE) is possible when the principal manages multiple agents. RPE can take many forms. In one form, the principal ranks the agent's performance as in a tournament (e.g., akin to the Job Corps Center annual performance rankings). Alternatively, the principal could compare the agent's performance to the average performance among all agents who perform the same work. RPE works well for "insurance purposes" because it controls for shocks that are common to all agents. In this way, the model provides a rationale for benchmarking by comparing performance across similar workers/agencies, as called for by some public administration scholars (Hatry 1999). Of course, this method has its limitations, too, in that it may exacerbate competition and may also result in wasteful behaviors (e.g., sabotage, monitoring others, etc.).

Negotiating the Standard

With this method, the principal and agent negotiate (agree on) the performance standard. If objective information on the production function is absent and relative performance evaluation is not a viable alternative, this may be the only solution available. This approach requires an environment of mutual trust between the agent and principal(s), i.e., one in which the agent does not withhold important information about her effort and capabilities, and where the principal can be trusted to use performance information fairly, e.g., not to increase the standard in the event of performance outcomes above the standard. The resulting performance standard (and the corresponding distribution of risk between the principal and agent) may be more a function of the relative bargaining ability of the parties, however, rather than reflecting principles of effective performance standard setting processes.

PERFORMANCE-STANDARD SETTING IN FEDERAL JOB-TRAINING PROGRAMS

In the U.S. government's largest job-training program, individual providers of government training have been evaluated by their performance relative to specific, numerical standards. Congress has also legislated important changes in the formulation of these numerical standards, as described in Chapter 4. A major redesign of the program five years ago introduced an entirely different approach to setting performance standards, and we will devote considerable attention to the implications of these changes for the system's incentives and functioning.

Under JTPA, Congress, the USDOL, and state authorities shared in designing and implementing the program's incentive policies. The Labor Department established expected performance levels using a regression-based model with national departure points. States could use the optional department adjustment model or develop their own adjustment procedures, although the state-developed procedures and any adjustments made by the governor had to conform to the USDOL's parameters (see Chapter 4 and Social Policy Research Associates [1999]). A majority of states adopted these models and used the USDOL-provided performance standards worksheets to determine performance targets (some with modifications).

The WIA program that replaced JTPA in 2000 introduced a new approach to setting performance standards that involves the negotiation of performance targets. States negotiate with the USDOL and local workforce investment areas to establish performance standards, using estimates based on historical data (or past performance) that are intended to take into account differences in economic conditions, participant characteristics, and services delivered. The pretext for making this change to a system of negotiated standards was to promote "shared accountability," described as one of the "guiding principles" of WIA (USDOL 2001, p. 8).

In our case analysis of the JTPA and WIA performance measurement systems, the USDOL, Congress, and the states constitute multiple principals in the organizational structure, while local implementing authorities (in government entities or training centers) function as the agents, undertaking the business of enrolling, training, and finding employment for the program clients. Table 2.1 in Chapter 2 (p. 22) shows the performance measures currently in effect in the WIA program and also indicates which of these are new to WIA (i.e., that were not used in the JTPA program).

Determining the Base Level of Performance

The first challenge in setting performance standards is to establish the "counterfactual" level of performance, i.e., the level of performance that would occur under a competitive level of effort. Consider for example the entered employment rate measure. What employment rate outcome would an agent who supplies a competitive level of effort achieve?

In general, the USDOL has attempted to address this question through the use of data on past performance. For example, prior to the start of JTPA, the Labor Department collected performance data on outcomes during the final years of the training program that preceded JTPA and used these data to determine the performance standards in the first year of JTPA. Now assume that past performance in a representative training environment gives a distribution of performance, and that differences in performance outcomes are due only to differences in effort. Then if the department believes that only 50 percent of the training centers have supplied at least the competitive level of effort, the performance standard should be set at the 50th percentile of the distribution of past performance.

In the JTPA measurement system, the performance standard was set at the outcome produced by the training center at the 25th percentile of performance among all training centers nationwide. Thus, the USDOL evaluated a training center's effort, *e*, against an effort level *e'*, that corresponded to the effort level of the training center at the 25th percentile of systemwide performance. An interpretation of this choice is that 25 percent of the training centers in the previous program were not supplying a competitive level of effort.

Under WIA, the more systematic approach for setting standards described above was abandoned. With discretion for setting performance standards transferred to the negotiation process between states and localities, the use of past performance information varied widely. The USDOL did provide some guidance for negotiated targets under WIA using data on the performance of seven early implementing states. However, among the majority of states that used baseline performance measures in determining appropriate levels for the standards, the sources of these data differed considerably. The various types of data used included the projected national averages for the negotiated standards provided by the Labor Department; federal baseline numbers (available in the federal performance tracking system, i.e., Standardized Program Information Reporting [SPIR] data); unemployment insurance (UI) data; and states' own performance baselines from previous program years. Georgia, for example, used program year (PY) 1998 state performance records combined with the projected national averages in negotiations with regional office representatives and local-level officials to determine the performance targets for the first three years of WIA. Some states, such as New Hampshire and Ohio, used UI data from earlier periods (PY 1994–1997) combined with USDOL performance data available in the SPIR to set performance levels. These considerable differences across states in the performance standard setting process have important implications for the ability of the principal to create a level playing field for all agents.

Is the Playing Field Level?

Although our discussion thus far has centered on a representative training center, there are important differences across centers in the populations from which they draw their enrollees and in their labor markets. For example, training centers located in relatively depressed labor markets should reasonably expect lower performance outcomes than those located in relatively tight labor markets. The USDOL recognized this problem and provided states with a method to adjust standards that took into account features of the training center's population and environment that may have been correlated with the performance outcome.

Under JTPA, this method established the 25th percentile only as a starting or departure point. For each training center, the departure point was adjusted using a regression model, taking into account the extent that the training center's characteristics differed from the average training center's characteristics. Thus, continuing the above example, the adjustment approach would lower the entered employment rate standard for training centers in depressed job markets relative to those in robust ones.

In the WIA program, the formal performance standards adjustment models were discarded by nearly all of the states (the exceptions being Texas, Maryland, and the District of Columbia). At the same time, the USDOL instructed states to take into account differences in economic conditions, participant characteristics, and services provided. For a majority, these adjustments to standards were made informally during the review of past performance data and in negotiations. For example, Wisconsin reported using PY 1997 data and the projected averages in negotiations with local officials to set the standards. A comparison of these data shows that when Wisconsin's PY 1997 baseline was above the projected national averages, the projected averages were established as the targets. When Wisconsin's baseline numbers were below the projected national averages, the baseline values were typically set as the targets. Other states (e.g., Washington, Nebraska, South Carolina, and others) followed a similar process.

Adjusting for Uncontrollable Risks

In addition to accounting for factors (demographic, economic, or others) known at the time that performance standards are established, it is important to allow for adjustments to standards that will offset future or unknown risks of poor performance due to conditions or circumstances beyond the control of agents. In other words, the adjustment methodology should also correct for the risk generated by a random shock (ε) in the model. While exceptional performance is still an unbiased estimator of excess effort even in the presence of a random shock, such a shock introduces noise in the measure of value added, and therefore in the training center's award. Because of risk-averse training staff and uncertain budgets, it is in the principal's interest to formulate performance standards that control both for persistent differences across training centers and transitory or idiosyncratic shocks.

As described above, many states used past performance data to set performance standards for the first year of the WIA program. In addition, most states also built in anticipated performance improvements for the two subsequent years. However, economic conditions changed significantly between the pre-WIA period and first three years of the program's implementation. Between 1998 and 1999, unemployment rates were declining on average, with 75 percent of all states experiencing a decline. Then between 2000 and 2001, this trend reversed. More than 75 percent of the states experienced an increase in unemployment rates, and the increases were even greater between 2001 and 2002, following the September 2001 World Trade Center terrorist attacks.[2] As unemployment rates were increasing in the first three years of WIA (from 3.94 percent to 5.35 percent, on average) and creating adverse labor market conditions for trainees, the standards for performance achievement in the program were also increasing (from 66.44 percent to 70.94 percent, on average).

Year-to-year variations in job availability typically cannot be anticipated by training centers, much less an economic shock of the magnitude precipitated by the September 11 terrorist attacks. However, by adjusting a training center's standards for the local unemployment rate each year, the variance in performance due to unpredictable changes in the environment is reduced. And although these types of adjustments were made in the JTPA system, they were not standard practice under WIA. A 2002 GAO report confirmed that WIA program administrators were seriously concerned about their ability to meet performance targets. All state program administrators reported that some of the performance targets were set too high for them and that the performance standards negotiation processes did not allow for adequate adjustments to varying economic conditions and participant demographics. In fact, the proportion of states meeting or exceeding their performance standards dropped between PY 2001 and PY 2002 for nearly all measures, some dramati-

Table 5.1 Percent of States Meeting or Exceeding Their Negotiated Performance Standards in PYs 2000–2002

Performance measure/standard	PY 2000	PY 2001	PY 2002
Adult entered employment rate	56.7	66.5	61.5
Adult employment retention rate	54.0	60.7	57.7
Adult earnings change	49.3	64.6	48.1
Adult credential rate	36.7	45.6	46.2
Dislocated worker entered employment rate	52.7	65.5	55.8
Dislocated worker employment retention rate	42.0	58.7	51.9
Dislocated worker earning replacement rate	54.7	74.8	61.5
Dislocated worker credential rate	36.7	58.7	55.8
Older youth entered employment rate	58.7	63.6	42.3
Older youth employment retention rate	52.0	61.2	48.1
Older youth earnings change	52.7	64.6	59.6
Older youth credential rate	29.3	31.6	23.1
Younger youth retention rate	38.0	59.2	57.7
Younger youth skill attainment rate	72.0	69.4	53.9
Younger youth diploma rate	25.3	45.6	50.0
Employer satisfaction	45.3	75.7	69.2
Participant satisfaction	51.3	78.6	76.9

SOURCE: Heinrich (2004).

cally, such as the 21 percent decrease in the proportion of states meeting their older youth entered employment rates (see Table 5.1).

Cream Skimming and Quick Fixes

The pressures generated by a high-stakes performance measurement system can lead to undesirable behavioral responses on the part of agents. The performance standards under both JTPA and WIA were not only "noisy," but they were also vulnerable to manipulation by agents. One way to increase $P - P_0$ (and the corresponding performance award) was to increase effort. Another way to increase $P - P_0$ that required no additional effort, however, was to select among the eligible applicants only the high-*h* types. That is, training centers might enroll persons who would produce high employment rates and earnings, even in the absence of training. This behavior has been called cream skimming (in addition to Chapter 6, see, e.g., Anderson, Burkhauser, and Raymond [1993];

Cragg [1997]; Heckman and Smith [2003]; and Heckman, Smith, and Taber [1996]).

To prevent cream skimming, the USDOL adjusted the JTPA standards for the effects of the characteristics of enrollees on *P*. As illustrated in Chapter 4, the adjustment method compensated training centers for enrolling persons such as the handicapped who tended to lower posttraining employment rates and earnings outcomes. Training centers that enrolled lower than average numbers of welfare recipients and handicapped were required to achieve higher standards. That is, the USDOL adjusted performance standards for the effect of the training center's enrollment policies on *P*.

These adjustments under JTPA, which apparently did not fully account for all low-*h* characteristics, may have reduced cream-skimming behavior, but they did not eliminate it (Heckman, Heinrich, and Smith [2002]). In addition, the adjustment method did not account for training centers' choices about the training services made available. Thus, the performance measures generated incentives to emphasize short-run, "quick fix"–type job placement activities in lieu of longer-term activities with more training content (Courty and Marschke 2003). Courty and Marschke (1997, 2004a) also showed how program managers strategically managed their "trainee inventories" and timed participant program exits to maximize end of the year performance levels. For a more detailed overview of the findings described in this subsection, see Chapters 6 and 7.

Implications of Multiple Principals

The federal government's efforts to encourage service delivery to the hard-to-serve and the provision of more intensive training activities were also frustrated by the presence of multiple principals with differing priorities. Although state authorities followed suit in placing more emphasis on these same goals, some local job-training authorities continued to demand low-cost placements from their service providers (Heinrich 1999). Heinrich found that service providers were aware of the new federal and state policy directives but focused primarily on job placement rates and costs per placement in their efforts, largely because these were the outcomes directly rewarded with contract renewals and other forms of recognition at the local level.

The change under WIA to a system in which regional USDOL representatives, state authorities, and local representatives engage in negotiations to determine performance standards might have presented an opportunity for greater coordination in aligning these principals' interests and reducing problems associated with divided agent efforts. In practice, however, the lack of formal adjustment mechanisms for standards under the new system only exacerbated these problems. After interviewing WIA program administrators in 50 states and visiting five sites, the GAO (2002) concluded that "the need to meet performance levels may be the driving factor in deciding who receives WIA-funded services at the local level" (p. 14). The GAO report and a subsequent study (Heinrich 2004) describe how some local areas have limited access to services for individuals who they perceive are less likely to get and retain a job. For example, some have responded to these pressures by augmenting the screening process for determining registrations or by limiting registrations of harder-to-serve job seekers, including dislocated workers whose preprogram earnings were more difficult to replace. A Texas official indicated that even with Texas's relatively sophisticated statistical model for setting and adjusting performance standards, adequate adjustments had not been made for economic conditions.

In her empirical analysis of WIA program performance across the states, Heinrich (2004) estimates OLS regressions using as dependent variables states' actual performance levels, and in separate regressions, the differentials between their actual performance and the negotiated standards. The objective of these analyses is to assess the relationship of local participant characteristics and economic conditions to measured performance and to determine if "adjustments" made in the negotiation process (i.e., to establish fair standards) were effective in accounting for these factors. For example, states with a comparatively high number of high school dropouts participating in their programs could have negotiated a lower employment retention rate or earnings change standard in anticipation that their less educated populations would have fewer or less attractive employment opportunities. If the states' initial processes for adjusting performance standards through such negotiations had worked as intended, one would expect to see fewer or weaker relationships between the performance *differentials* and these baseline characteristics (compared to their relationships with actual performance levels). In other words, only state and local program efforts—not characteristics of their populations or economic conditions that were beyond program managers' control—should explain why they met, exceeded, or fell below their negotiated performance standards.

Heinrich estimates separate regressions for each of the 17 performance standards for these two dependent variables. In *both* sets of models, characteristics such as race, education, and work history were statistically significant predictors of performance relative to some standards, suggesting that adjustments for participant characteristics were inadequate. In fact, the most consistent, negative predictors of performance levels and differentials were unemployment rates. These findings confirm that states were not prepared to adjust for what turned out to be significant risks of failure to meet performance standards due to the economic downturn and aftermath of the September 11 terrorist attacks.

Dynamics

Under JTPA, the practice of pegging the performance standard to the performance of the training center at the 25th percentile in the prior period likely contributed to unsustainable changes in the level of effort exerted by training centers over time. If training centers responded to incentives and strived to exceed the performance standard, the distribution of training centers' performances would shift to the right, implying that the new 25th percentile (which would become the basis of the standard in the next year) would exceed the old 25th percentile. As long as training centers can keep up with effort, the standard grows ever higher, and the amount of effort necessary to meet the standard also increases, leading to higher outcomes and future increases in the standard. More realistically, at least if performance improvement or inflation goes on for long enough, such a system implies that some training centers will eventually fall behind and fail to meet the standard. If such a system would be used for long enough, performance inflation should eventually stop and about 25 percent of training centers would perform below the standard: an unsatisfactory outcome.

Table 5.2 reports the departure points for a number of the original JTPA performance measures (i.e., the adult employment rate at termination, the adult welfare employment rate at termination, and the youth employment rate at termination). These departure points were consistently set at the 25th percentile of a previous year's distribution of

Table 5.2 Departure Points for First-Generation JTPA Standards

Program year	Adult employment rate at termination (%)	Adult welfare employment rate at termination (%)	Youth employment rate at termination (%)
1984	47.0	—	21.4
1985	57.1	—	36.4
1986, 1987	62.4	51.3	43.3
1988, 1989	68.0	56.0	45.0

NOTE: — = data not available.
SOURCE: Courty and Marschke (2004b).

outcomes. As predicted, Table 5.2 shows a general increase in departure points over this period of the early JTPA years. The departure points in 1986–1987 were much higher than those in 1984–1985, which is not unexpected given that they were based on performance under JTPA's predecessor program and the initial nine months of JTPA (during which training centers were not subject to incentive policies).

Under WIA, the USDOL strongly encouraged states and localities to set standards that would motivate improved performance from year to year. In fact, in the effort to promote "continuous performance improvement," the states set standards that not only required that they improve over time, but also that the magnitude of the improvements increase from year to year. This approach gave states an implicit incentive to negotiate lower standards in the early years, and some of the states, in fact, attempted to do this. North Carolina, for example, was asked by the USDOL to increase the level of its negotiated standards before the start of the WIA program, as they were judged to be too low relative to other states and North Carolina's past performance (Heinrich 2004). For the most part, though, states and localities complied with WIA requirements by building yearly increases into the standards.

As the analysis by Heinrich shows, however, this approach failed due to the lack of adjustments for changing economic conditions in the early years of WIA. Two years into the program's operation, 38 states were identified as having failed to achieve at least 80 percent of their performance goals for two consecutive years and were at risk for sanctions. More generally, these findings suggest that the types of formal performance standards adjustments made in the JTPA system to control for factors outside program managers' control are critical to the success of a system intended to promote continuous performance improvements. The presence of conditions that drive ratchet effects in WIA also suggests that the design of performance incentives may not always follow a strictly economic logic.

CONCLUSIONS

In this chapter, we have drawn from the information economics, contract theory, and public administration literatures to discern basic lessons for the construction of performance standards. We demonstrate the relevance of these lessons in the context of two public programs, the U.S. JTPA and WIA federal job training programs. We find evidence that performance measurement system designers have attempted to "level the playing field" over time to provide equivalent performance incentives across states and localities. Performance standard adjustment methods were established to account for "shocks" that are outside an agent's control and to reduce the risk faced by the agent. Policymakers have also tried to reduce the potential negative distortions due to hidden information.

At the same time, it is not surprising that in a public sector program with multiple principals and political relationships influencing administration, the evidence suggests that these problems were not fully resolved. We identified some negative dynamic properties of the performance measurement system that threaten its sustainability. In both JTPA and WIA, the dynamics of performance benchmarking and the challenges of effectively adjusting performance expectations for external influences beyond program managers' control likely contributed to inefficiencies and generated incentives to influence performance in ways other than increasing effort. Selecting trainees according to observed characteristics associated with their labor market success, limiting the availability of more intensive training services, and demonstrating lower performance early on to allow for performance improvements over time are some examples of strategic behaviors that were unintended by system designers and potentially harmful to the system and program outcomes. In the WIA system, where rewards (up to $3 million in grants) and sanctions (up to a 5 percent reduction in grants) had potentially important implications for program functioning, the performance standards should have provided appropriate incentives and feedback to operators about the effectiveness of their activities in improving service quality and participant outcomes.

Politicians, along with economists and private sector representatives, have been calling for a more businesslike administration of government for more than a century, most recently in the "reinventing government" and New Public Management reform initiatives. The use of performance measurement systems and bonuses in public sector programs has been a key component of these recent initiatives, although both policymakers and scholars have begun to uncover evidence of their "dark side," including some of the negative or unintended consequences described in this study (Radin 2000). Our research confirms both the potential of these systems to be effectively managed to promote performance improvements, and the limitations of these systems' design, which are guided not only by economic theory, but also by political demands and the complexities of representative governance. Although our research doesn't point to cogent solutions for all of the problems that public sector performance measurement system designers face, we do suggest some specific actions public managers can take to improve these systems, such as the proper incorporation of different types of information into the standard, coordination among multiple principals with conflicting interests, and more careful attention to the dynamic implications of performance measurement. More generally, we also hope that the framework for analysis of these issues that we present might better guide policymakers' or other scholars' understanding and consideration of how these systems and public program performance might be improved.

Notes

1. Both Dixit and Burgess and Ratto (2003) evaluate this literature in the context of incentive provision inside government organizations.
2. In New York City alone, it is estimated that about 430,000 job-months and $2.8 billion in wages were lost in the three months following the September 11 attacks (Makinen 2002).

References

Anderson, Kathryn, Richard Burkhauser, and J. Raymond. 1993. "The Effect of Creaming on Placement Rates under the Job Training Partnership Act." *Industrial and Labor Relations Review* 46(1): 613–624.

Burgess, Simon, and Marisa Ratto. 2003. "The Role of Incentives in the Public Sector: Issues and Evidence." *Oxford Review of Economic Policy* 19(2): 285–300.

Courty, Pascal, and Gerald Marschke. 1997. "Measuring Government Performance: Lessons from a Federal Bureaucracy." *American Economic Review* 87(2): 383–388.

———. 2003. "Performance Funding in Federal Agencies: A Case Study of a Federal Job Training Program." *Public Budgeting and Finance* 23(3): 22–48.

———. 2004a. "An Empirical Investigation of Gaming Responses to Performance Incentives" (with P. Courty). *Journal of Labor Economics* 22(1): 23–56.

———. 2004b. "Benchmarking Performance." *Public Finance and Management* 4(3): 288–316.

Cragg, Michael. 1997. "Performance Incentives in the Public Sector: Evidence from the Job Training Partnership Act." *Journal of Law, Economics, and Organization* 13(1): 147–168.

Davis, J. H., L. Donaldson, and F. D. Schoorman. 1997. "Toward a Stewardship Theory of Management." *Academy of Management Review* 22(1): 20–47.

Dixit, Avinash. 2002. "Incentives and Organizations in the Public Sector." *Journal of Human Resources* 37(4): 696–727.

General Accounting Office (GAO). 2002. *Improvements Needed in Performance Measures to Provide a More Accurate Picture of WIA's Effectiveness*. Report to Congressional Requesters. GAO-02-275. Washington, DC: GAO.

Hatry, Harry. 1999. "Mini-Symposium on Intergovernmental Comparative Performance Data." *Public Administration Review* 59(2): 101–104.

Heckman, James J., Carolyn Heinrich, and Jeffrey A. Smith. 2002. "The Performance of Performance Standards." *Journal of Human Resources* 37(4): 778–811.

Heckman, James J., and Jeffrey A. Smith. 2003. "The Determinants of Participation in a Social Program: Evidence from the Job Training Partnership Act." IZA Discussion Paper No. 798. Bonn, Germany: IZA.

Heckman, James J., Jeffrey A. Smith, and Christopher Taber. 1996. "What Do Bureaucrats Do? The Effects of Performance Standards and Bureaucratic Preferences on Acceptance in the JTPA Program." In *Advances in the Study of Entrepreneurship, Innovation, and Economic Growth*, Vol. 7: *Reinventing*

Government and the Problem of Bureaucracy, Gary Libecap, ed. Greenwich, CT: JAI Press, pp. 191–217.

Heinrich, Carolyn J. 1999. "Do Government Bureaucrats Make Effective Use of Performance Management Information?" *Journal of Public Administration Research and Theory* 9(3): 363–393.

———. 2004. "Improving Public-Sector Performance Management: One Step Forward, Two Steps Back?" *Public Finance and Management* 4(3): 317–351.

Holmstrom, Bengt. 1982. "Moral Hazard in Teams." *Bell Journal of Economics* 13(2): 324–340.

Holmstrom, Bengt, and Paul Milgrom. 1987. "Aggregation and Linearity in the Provision of Intertemporal Incentives." *Econometrica* 55(2): 303–328.

Makinen, Gail. 2002. *The Economic Effects of 9/11: A Retrospective Assessment*. Congressional Research Service report, September 27. Washington, DC: Library of Congress. http://www.fas.org/irp/crs/RL31617.pdf (accessed May 28, 2010).

Maltzman, Forrest, and Steven S. Smith. 1994. "Principals, Goals, Dimensionality, and Congressional Committees." *Legislative Studies Quarterly* 19(4): 457–476.

Marshall, Martin, P. Shekelle, R. Brook, and S. Leatherman. 2000. *Dying to Know: Public Release of Information about Quality of Health Care*. London: Nuffield Trust.

Miller, Gary J. 1992. *Managerial Dilemmas: The Political Economy of Hierarchy*. New York: Cambridge University Press.

Prendergast, Canice. 1999. "The Provision of Incentives in Firms." *Journal of Economic Literature* 37(1): 7–63.

Radin, Beryl A. 2000. "The Government Performance and Results Act and the Tradition of Federal Management Reform: Square Pegs in Round Holes?" *Journal of Public Administration Research and Theory* 10(1): 11–35.

Social Policy Research Associates. 1999. *Guide to Performance Standards for the Job Training Partnership Act for Program Years 1998 and 1999*. Oakland, CA: SPRA.

Taylor, Frederick Winslow. 1911. "Principles and Methods of Scientific Management." *Journal of Accountancy* 12(2): 117–124.

Thompson, James D. 1967. *Organizations in Action: Social Science Bases of Administrative Theory*. New York: McGraw-Hill Book Company.

U.S. Department of Labor (USDOL). 2001. *2002 Annual Performance Plan for Committee on Appropriations*. Washington, DC: USDOL, Employment and Training Administration.

6
Do the Determinants of Program Participation Data Provide Evidence of Cream Skimming?

James J. Heckman
Jeffrey Smith

This chapter considers the extent to which detailed data on the process of participation in a social program can provide researchers and policymakers with meaningful evidence on the nature and extent of cream skimming caused by a performance-management system. We illustrate our discussion with an empirical analysis of data collected as part of the National JTPA Study (NJS). These data allow us to empirically decompose the process of participation in the JTPA program into a series of stages: eligibility for the program, awareness of the program, application to the program, acceptance into the program, and enrollment into the program. This chapter reframes and reinterprets the analysis in Heckman and Smith (2004) for this volume.[1]

Conceptually, this chapter contributes to the literature by clarifying how and when data on multiple stages of the program participation process provide credible evidence on the effect of performance standards on program participation. Decomposing the process into stages allows researchers to compare the determinants of participation across stages. Dividing the stages into those on which program staff (and thus performance standards) have an important influence and those on which they do not provides suggestive evidence on the importance of performance standards for program participation.

Empirically, we make two major contributions. First, we document the importance of factors other than cream skimming induced by performance standards in accounting for differences in JTPA participation among subgroups. In particular, the eligibility rules for JTPA play a major role in driving subgroup differences. Conditional on eligibility, further subgroup differences emerge at the stage of program awareness, something over which program staff have at most limited control. These findings suggest caution regarding the conclusions from existing analyses that presume strong effects of cream skimming based solely on comparisons of the characteristics of program eligibles and program participants.

Second, our analysis of the determinants of program enrollment conditional on application and acceptance into the program (the stage where we expect program staff to have the most control over the process) yields some suggestive evidence consistent with cream skimming.

The remainder of the chapter proceeds as follows. First we put this chapter into the context of the broader literature. We then present a framework for analyzing data on multiple stages of the program participation process and discuss what such data can reveal regarding the empirical importance of cream skimming induced by performance standards in determining who gets served. The next section documents aspects of the JTPA program relevant for our analysis but not covered in Chapter 2. We then describe the data we use and the four training centers from the National JTPA Study at which much of the data were collected, followed by a detailed examination of four stages in the JTPA participation process: eligibility, program awareness, application and acceptance into the program, and formal enrollment. We decompose the program participation process in order to focus on how overall differences in participation probabilities across subgroups break down into effects at each stage of the participation process. The last section reviews our conclusions and places them in the context of the volume as a whole.

CONTEXT

Our analysis fits into two broader literatures, one on the determinants of participation in social programs and the other on the effects of performance management systems in social programs in general and in active labor market programs in particular. Currie (1996) surveys the literature on the determinants of participation in social programs; see also the long list of references in Heckman and Smith (2004).[2]

The majority of this literature focuses on participation in U.S. entitlement programs such as Temporary Aid to Needy Families (TANF), Food Stamps, and Unemployment Insurance. Persons eligible for such programs are legally entitled to their benefits. In addition to the decisions of potential participants, bureaucratic discretion plays a role even in entitlement programs as program staff can affect eligibility decisions—see, e.g., Parsons (1991) for the case of disability insurance—and can affect the information available to potential participants as well as the hassle costs of participation in other program contexts. Empirical analyses of participation in entitlement programs typically focus on the demand side and analyze the effects of variation in the costs and benefits of participation among eligibles.

A smaller literature considers U.S. nonentitlement programs, such as many employment and training programs, where participation conditional on eligibility depends explicitly on both decisions by potential participants and decisions by program gatekeepers; we call such programs mutually voluntary programs. The JTPA program that we study represents such a program, as do National Science Foundation grants and admission to (selective) state colleges and universities (and many other programs). As noted in Chapter 2, under WIA (JTPA's successor), so-called core services, such as job search assistance, represent an entitlement while more expensive services, such as classroom training, require participant interest, program staff approval, and meeting eligibility requirements. Analyses of the determinants of participation in mutually voluntary programs have many purposes, including informing, developing, and implementing econometric evaluation estimators; documenting or explaining differences in participation rates across groups; and examining the role of performance standards (and, in our case, the cream skimming they encourage) on participation patterns. Recent analyses in the context of active labor market programs include Mitnik (2009), Skedinger and Widerstedt (2007), and Weber (2008); see also the earlier references in Heckman and Smith (2004).[3]

A vast general literature on the effects of performance management systems in government has arisen in the past two decades. Osborne and Gaebler (1992) and Osborne and Plastrik (1997) provide important popular treatments, while Heinrich and Lynn (2000), Forsythe (2001), and Radin (2006), among others, offer more scholarly overviews. In the narrower context of active labor market programs, the chapters in this volume touch on many of the major strands of the literature, including analyses of participation and service assignment patterns (as in this chapter), analyses of the effects of cross-sectional and time-series variation in the nature or presence of performance incentives on outcomes (as in Chapter 7), studies of performance-based contracting (as in Chapter 8), and the correlation of performance measures with experimental or econometric estimates of the causal effects of programs (as in Chapter 9). Chapters 7, 8, and 9 review the corresponding literatures in depth.

Our analysis in this chapter takes its inspiration from both of these literatures. The literature on participation in employment and training programs influences our choice of variables, including our examination of recent labor force status patterns. It also influences our interpretation of the results. The broader literature on program participation motivates our emphasis on variation across individuals in the expected costs and benefits of participation and our concern with program awareness. As discussed in more detail in the next section, the literature on the effects of performance management systems influences our thoughts on the evidentiary value of our analysis.

A FRAMEWORK FOR ANALYZING PARTICIPATION IN SOCIAL PROGRAMS

This section outlines a descriptive framework for analyzing the determinants of participation in a social program using data on the characteristics of random samples of individuals observed at each stage of the process and considers its analytic value. The framework follows individuals through multiple stages of a linear participation process, in which participation requires passing through a sequence of stages in a specific order. The particular stages in our framework spring from the data available to us and the (not unrelated) institutional details of the JTPA program examined in our empirical application. Generalizing our framework to allow for a nonlinear participation process (say, by explicitly accounting for the small fraction of JTPA participants sentenced to participate in the program by a judge or for individuals who reach JTPA via a referral from a service provider) or for a larger number or smaller number of stages is straightforward. Moreover, our framework, and our discussion of the evidence it provides, both generalize well beyond JTPA and well beyond the context of active labor market policies.

In order for a person to participate in JTPA, he or she must be eligible for it, must be aware of it, must apply for it, must be accepted into it, and must be formally enrolled in it. Figure 6.1 depicts the process of selection into the program. Different factors govern each stage of the process. Legislators define the eligibility criteria that program staff members apply to each applicant. Program awareness depends on outreach efforts by program operators, on other aspects of the informational environment surrounding potential participants, such as friends who have participated or interaction with staff from other programs, and on potential participants' prior beliefs about the costs and benefits of learning about employment and training programs.

Potential participants make application decisions based on the expected benefits and perceived costs of participation. Acceptance into a program depends on bureaucratic preferences over applicant types, which in many programs are determined in part by formal performance standards systems. Acceptance also depends on the willingness of the applicant to pursue the application process to its conclusion and on further changes in opportunity costs, such as sudden illnesses or the arrival of job offers, during the application process.

Formal enrollment depends on both bureaucratic and personal preferences. For example, as noted in Chapter 4, the JTPA performance

Figure 6.1 The JTPA Selection Process

Eligibility for JTPA

↓

Awareness of JTPA

↓

Application to JTPA

↓

Acceptance into JTPA

↓

Enrollment into JTPA

standards system counted only the employment and wages of enrollees in a specified period following termination from the program. As a result, local JTPA offices had an incentive to gain additional information about the potential employability of persons accepted into the program and to use it to guide their enrollment decisions. At the same time, the passage of time between acceptance and enrollment (as when waiting for a particular course to begin or looking for an employer willing to offer an OJT position) leads to changes in opportunity costs that may cause accepted applicants to decline enrollment when offered.

To more formally describe the participation process, consider the following conditional probabilities for a person with characteristics x: 1) the probability of eligibility, 2) the probability of program awareness given eligibility, 3) the probability of application given eligibility and awareness, 4) the probability of acceptance given application, and 5) the probability of formal enrollment conditional on acceptance into a program. In formal terms, we have

(6.1) $\Pr(el = 1 \mid x)$,

(6.2) $\Pr(aw = 1 \mid el = 1, x)$,

(6.3) $\Pr(ap - 1 \mid aw = 1, el = 1, x)$

(6.4) $\Pr(ac = 1 \mid ap = 1, aw = 1, el = 1, x)$,

(6.5) $\Pr(en = 1 \mid ac = 1, ap = 1, aw = 1, el = 1, x)$,

where $el = 1$ if a person is eligible for a program and zero otherwise, $aw = 1$ if a person is aware of a program and zero otherwise, $ap = 1$ if a person applies to a program and zero otherwise, $ac = 1$ if a person applies to and is accepted into a program and zero otherwise, and $en = 1$ if a person is formally enrolled in a program and zero otherwise.

As persons only participate in the program if they are eligible $el = 1$, are aware $aw = 1$, apply $ap = 1$, are accepted $ac = 1$, and formally enroll $en = 1$, we can decompose the probability of participation given $X = x$, $\Pr(par = 1 \mid x)$, into the five components on the right-hand side of Equation (6.2):

(6.6) $\Pr(par = 1 \mid x) =$

$$\Pr(en = 1 \mid ac = 1, ap = 1, aw = 1, el = 1, x) \Pr(ac = 1 \mid ap = 1, aw = 1, el = 1, x)$$

$$\Pr(ap = 1 \mid aw = 1, el = 1, x) \Pr(aw = 1 \mid el = 1, x) \Pr(el = 1 \mid x),$$

where *par* = 1 if a person participates in a program and zero otherwise. By estimating each of the five component probabilities, we can determine the effect of each variable in x on the overall probability of participation and where and how it influences program participation. A variable that has no effect on the overall probability of participation may have strong, but offsetting, effects on the component probabilities.

In the sections that follow, we apply this framework to analyze participation in the JTPA program. Data limitations force us to combine application and acceptance into a single step, which we call "application/acceptance." We equate acceptance into the program with reaching the stage of random assignment during the experimental evaluation of JTPA. Only eligible applicants who completed the aptitude and achievement tests required at most JTPA training sites and who received a written JTPA service plan were subject to random assignment. These conditions required a substantial commitment by JTPA training centers to continued interaction with the applicant, but fall short of formal enrollment into JTPA. The section titled "The Determinants of Enrollment in JTPA" presents two sets of decompositions based on Equation (6.6). The first set includes four stages: eligibility, awareness, application/acceptance, and enrollment. In the second set, we decompose $\Pr(ac = 1 \mid el = 1, x)$, the probability of application and acceptance conditional on eligibility, into separate stages of awareness given eligibility and acceptance given awareness. Focusing solely on these two stages allows us to examine the effects of explanatory variables not included in the full decomposition due to data limitations or because they are perfect predictors of eligibility.

What can we learn from the analyses undertaken in the remainder of the chapter regarding the empirical importance of cream skimming induced by the JTPA performance standards system for the overall patterns of participation in JTPA among various groups? To begin with, we can use institutional knowledge to divide the stages of the participation process into those affected and not affected by program staff. Subgroup differences in the determinants of passing through stages not affected by program staff, such as eligibility and (in the main) awareness clearly cannot result from cream skimming. The full decompositions presented in the section "The Determinants of Application/Acceptance into JTPA" reveal the relative importance of these stages for overall group differences.

For stages of the participation process potentially affected by both the decisions of potential participants and the decisions of caseworkers, our framework yields at best suggestive evidence. Consider a particular characteristic *Z* that positively affects employment and earnings outcomes in the absence of participation and that both the caseworker and the researcher observe. Now consider a stage of the participation process over which caseworkers have some control. A positive effect of *Z* on the probability of passing through this stage is consistent with cream skimming by caseworkers and so provides some suggestive evidence in that regard. At the same time, high-*Z* individuals might participate at higher rates even without cream skimming, perhaps because of a correlation between observed *Z* and unobserved motivation or because high-*Z* individuals expect to benefit more from program participation. By contrast, a negative effect of *Z* indicates that cream skimming is not the dominant influence on whether or not high-Z individuals transit this stage of the participation process. It does not, however, demonstrate the absence of cream skimming, because a negative estimated effect might simply result from other factors working in the opposite direction overpowering caseworker efforts.

Our empirical analysis is deliberately descriptive. We seek to establish empirical regularities about the participation process in the JTPA program as it existed at the time our data were generated. These regularities suggest interesting behavioral relationships governing the process of program participation. They are not causal (or "structural" in the sense that economists use that term). For example, we would expect substantive changes in the eligibility rules to change not only the determinants of eligibility, but the conditional determinants at the other stages as well. We do not require causal effects to make the inferences we do. The analyses in this chapter complement, rather than substitute for, related analyses in the literature that aim to estimate the causal effects of performance standards on program behavior by making use of plausibly exogenous variation in the presence or details of such standards. Examples of such analyses include Chapters 7 and 8 in this volume, as well as Cragg (1997), Courty and Marschke (2008), and Courty, Kim, and Marschke (forthcoming).

THE JTPA PROGRAM

JTPA was the primary U.S. federal employment and training program for the disadvantaged until replaced by the programs financed under WIA in 1998. JTPA provided classroom training in occupational skills, remedial education, job search assistance, work experience, and subsidized on-the-job training (essentially a temporary wage subsidy) at private firms for approximately one million persons each year. Chapter 2 gives an overall picture of the program, compares it to its predecessors and to WIA and, along with Chapter 4, details its performance management system. This discussion focuses on the details of JTPA eligibility determination, which have special relevance to the analysis in this chapter.

There were two primary avenues to eligibility for JTPA. The first and most important avenue was economic disadvantage, which occurred if one of two criteria were met: 1) low *family* income in the six months prior to application to the program, or 2) being in a family receiving cash public assistance such as Aid to Families with Dependent Children (AFDC), general assistance, or Food Stamps.[4] The short window for income eligibility allowed highly skilled and normally highly paid workers to become eligible for JTPA after being out of work only a few months. According to the USDOL (1993), in program year 1991 around 93 percent of JTPA participants qualified because they were economically disadvantaged. A second avenue to eligibility was an "audit window" that allowed up to 10 percent of participants at each JTPA training center to be noneconomically disadvantaged persons with other barriers to employment such as limited ability in English.[5] Due to the subjective nature of these barriers, and the resulting difficulty in determining who is affected by them, at some stages in the participation process (described in more detail below) we consider only persons eligible by virtue of being economically disadvantaged. Devine and Heckman (1996) discuss the eligibility rules for JTPA and their implications for the composition of the eligible population.[6]

There are some differences between the eligibility criteria and services offered in JTPA compared to its predecessors, the Comprehensive Employment and Training Act (CETA) and the Manpower Development and Training Act (MDTA), and its successor, the WIA program.

Barnow (1993) suggests that these differences are modest in regard to CETA and MDTA. USDOL (1998), O'Shea and King (2001), and Social Policy Research Associates (2004; see especially Exhibit 1) document the details of the WIA program. Universal eligibility for low-intensity core services under WIA represents the largest difference between WIA and JTPA. By law, local programs must give priority to transfer program participants and other low income individuals when allocating intensive and training services. For these more expensive services, but not for the core job finding services, the WIA participation process remains broadly similar to that under JTPA.

DATA

The primary source of our data is the NJS, an experimental evaluation of the JTPA program conducted from 1987 to 1989.[7] We use data on JTPA, even though the program no longer exists, because similar data do not exist for the WIA program. As argued in Chapter 3, the programs have enough in common in terms of the populations they serve, the services they provide, and the institutions that provide them that, at a general level, the inferences we make regarding the relative importance of cream skimming and other factors in determining participation patterns likely carry over to WIA.

In the NJS, persons accepted into JTPA at a nonrandom sample of 16 JTPA training centers were randomly assigned into either a control group excluded from JTPA (for 18 months) or a treatment group given access to JTPA services. In order to learn more about the JTPA-eligible population, and to facilitate the development of better nonexperimental evaluation methods, data were collected on JTPA-eligible nonparticipants (ENPs) at 4 of the 16 centers. We describe these 4 centers in detail in the next section. The ENP sample includes only individuals eligible via the economic disadvantage criterion as determined by a short household screening instrument.

Detailed information on demographic characteristics, labor market histories, transfer program participation, and family composition and income was collected on the ENPs and on experimental control group members at the same four sites. We use this information for our analyses of awareness of JTPA and of application/acceptance into JTPA. For the experimental treatment group, we have only the limited information on characteristics collected shortly before random assignment. We use these data to study enrollment into JTPA at the four sites.

The NJS did not collect data on persons ineligible for JTPA. In order to analyze the determinants of eligibility we use a national sample drawn from the 1986 Panel of the Survey of Income and Program Participation (SIPP). Devine and Heckman (1996) use the SIPP for their detailed study of JTPA eligibility; our dataset is a close cousin of theirs. The SIPP data are well suited to this purpose because they contain sufficient information to precisely determine JTPA eligibility via economic disadvantage. We treat the SIPP panel as a series of repeated cross-sections, and create a dataset consisting of person-months.[8]

The data we use have, not surprisingly, both advantages and disadvantages. In terms of advantages, both the SIPP and ENP data measure eligibility via economic disadvantage relatively precisely. All of the surveys from the NJS obtained relatively high response rates; the SIPP does less well on this dimension. Measurement of both acceptance and enrollment in JTPA relies on administrative data, and so avoids the problems of systematic measurement error in survey measures of program participation documented by Smith and Whalley (2009) for JTPA and by Meyer, Mok, and Sullivan (2009) for a wide variety of other programs. The key disadvantages associated with our data include the lack of separate information on program application and our reliance on only four nonrandomly selected sites for the ENP and JTPA participant data. The latter becomes problematic when combined with national-level data from the SIPP and when attempting to generalize to the overall JTPA eligible and participant populations.

THE FOUR SITES FROM THE NATIONAL JTPA STUDY

Detailed data on ENPs were collected from the geographic areas served by four training centers: Corpus Christi, Texas; Fort Wayne, Indiana; Jersey City, New Jersey; and Providence, Rhode Island. Table 6.1 provides descriptive information about these centers in order to provide some context for our analysis. The table notes provide details on the sources and definitions of the variables.

The first three columns of Table 6.1 present the race/ethnicity of the eligible adult population at each site, constructed using the data on the ENPs and the experimental control group. The sites vary widely on this dimension, with a strong Hispanic majority in Corpus Christi, a strong African American majority in Jersey City, almost exclusively whites in Fort Wayne, and a broad mix in Providence. The fourth column presents mean years of schooling among adult eligibles at each site. Here we find less variation, though Providence stands out as an outlier on the low side, with a mean below 11 years.

The fifth and sixth columns provide economic context in the form of the unemployment and the poverty rates, respectively. Corpus Christi and Jersey City have relatively weak economic situations at this time, while Providence and (especially) Fort Wayne were experiencing relatively low unemployment and poverty rates.

The final three columns summarize the service recommendations that the JTPA participants in the experimental samples at these training centers received prior to random assignment. In the jargon of the National JTPA Study, the "CT-OS treatment stream" denotes individuals recommended for classroom training in occupation skills (and possibly other services, but not on-the-job training), the "OJT treatment stream" denotes individuals recommended for on-the-job training (and possibly other services, but not classroom training in occupational skills), and the "other treatment stream" is a residual category. Most of those recommended for CT-OS either receive it or do not enroll at all (and thus receive at most very minimal services), but many of those recommended for OJT end up enrolling but receiving only job search assistance because no employer can be found who will offer them an on-the-job training slot. The sites differ in their service mix for a number of reasons, including the availability of local training providers of sufficient size and quality, the state of the local economy, and whether the center leadership has a "work first" or "learn first" orientation. Among the four sites in our study, Jersey City emphasizes classroom training, Fort Wayne and Corpus Christi emphasize on-the-job training, and Providence emphasizes other services.

Table 6.1 Characteristics of the Four Sites from the National JTPA Study

	Eligibles								
Name	Fraction white	Fraction black	Fraction Hispanic	Average years of schooling	Unemploy-ment rate	Poverty rate	Fraction CT-OS treatment stream	Fraction OJT treatment stream	Fraction other treatment stream
Corpus Christi	0.25	0.08	0.66	11.33	10.2	13.4	34.3	51.5	14.1
Fort Wayne	0.74	0.23	0.02	11.28	4.7	5.9	6.4	66.2	27.3
Jersey City	0.05	0.68	0.24	11.51	7.3	18.9	46.0	35.7	18.3
Providence	0.32	0.28	0.31	10.72	3.8	12.1	32.3	13.0	54.7

SOURCE: Characteristics of the adult eligible population at each site come from the authors' calculations using the National JTPA Study data on the ENPs and the experimental control group. Following Heckman and Smith (1999), we assign the ENPs a weight of 0.97 and the controls a weight of 0.03 in calculating these averages. The numbers for race/ethnicity do not add up to 1.00 because other race/ethnicity individuals are omitted. The unemployment rates (unweighted annual averages for 1987–1989) are from Exhibit 3.3 of Orr et al. (1996). Poverty rates (for 1979) are from Exhibit 3.2 of Orr et al. (1996). The treatment stream recommendation fractions come from Kemple, Doolittle, and Wallace (1993, Table 7.1). As noted in the text, these refer to the services for which individuals in the National JTPA Study were recommended prior to random assignment. The CT-OS treatment stream corresponds to individuals recommended for classroom training in occupational skills and possibly other services not including on-the-job training. The OJT treatment stream refers to individuals recommended for subsidized on-the-job training at private firms plus possibly other services not including CT-OS. The other treatment stream is a residual category.

Overall, these four sites vary on geographic (two in the Northeast, one in the Southwest, and one in the Midwest), demographic, economic, and programmatic dimensions. Although neither the 4 sites nor the 16 sites represent random samples of all JTPA training centers, the sites examined in this chapter nonetheless do a good job of capturing the diversity present in the population of sites. In addition, the site characteristics presented here provide a context for, and aid in the interpretation of, the results that follow.[9]

THE DETERMINANTS OF ELIGIBILITY FOR THE JTPA PROGRAM

This section examines the determinants of eligibility for JTPA. Table 6.2 defines the explanatory variables used in this chapter. Tables 6.3 and 6.4 present the results of logit analyses of the determinants of eligibility. Table 6.3 presents results for adult (aged 22 and above) men and women, and Table 6.4 presents the results for male and female out-of-school youth (aged 16–21). We focus on these four demographic groups throughout our empirical analysis for three reasons. First, they are the groups employed in the experimental impact reports, in our other work utilizing these data, and in some of the other chapters in this volume. Second, because of differences around family responsibilities and education, we would expect men and women, and youth and adults, to behave differently. Third, we have no NJS data on in-school youth, as this group was excluded from the experimental analysis.

The first column for each demographic group in Tables 6.3 and 6.4 displays estimated coefficients and associated standard errors (in parentheses) from logit models of the probability of eligibility derived from the SIPP data. The second column displays estimates of the mean derivative of the probability of eligibility with respect to each characteristic (in square brackets) along with p-values from tests of the null hypotheses that each population coefficient equals zero.[10]

A number of interesting findings emerge from this analysis. First, even after controlling for family income and productivity characteristics, race and ethnicity are very important determinants of the probability of eligibility. For example, for adult females, the difference

Table 6.2 Definitions of Variables

Site indicators
Fort Wayne, Jersey City, and Providence indicate the site of residence. Corpus Christi is the omitted site.

Race and ethnicity
Black, Hispanic, and other race/ethnicity indicate race or ethnicity. Whites are the omitted group.

Age
Age categories indicate age at the time of eligibility determination or of the participation decision. The omitted category is 16–18 years for youth and 22–29 years for adults.

Highest grade completed
Schooling categories indicate the highest grade of formal schooling completed. The omitted category is exactly 12 years.

Low English ability
This variable indicates low ability in English. For the ENPs, this means that the person completed the baseline interview in a language other than English. For the controls, it means that the person indicated a language other than English in response to a survey question on language preference.

Marital histories
These categories indicate the respondent's marital status history. The omitted category is single, never married. In Tables 6.16 and 6.17, the divorced, widowed, and separated category is broken up into two categories, one for persons who were last married from 1–24 months ago and one for persons who were last married more than 24 months ago.

Presence of young children
Children younger than six years old indicates an own child less than six years old in the household.

Current AFDC receipt
This variable indicates that the respondent was receiving benefits under the Aid to Families with Dependent Children program, either as a case head or as part of someone else's case.

Table 6.2 (continued)

Current Food Stamp receipt
This variable indicates that the respondent was in a household receiving Food Stamps.

Current labor force status
These variables indicate whether the respondent was employed, unemployed (not working but looking for work), or out of the labor force (not employed and not looking for work). The omitted category is currently employed.

Labor force status transitions
These categories in Tables 6.8 and 6.9 and Tables 6.16–6.19 indicate the two most recent labor force statuses in the seven months up to and including the month of the participation decision. The second status in each pattern indicates the labor force status at the time of the participation decision. The first status indicates the status of the most recent prior spell during the preceding six months. Thus, the pattern "employed → unemployed" indicates someone who was unemployed at the time of the participation decision but whose most recent prior labor force status within the preceding six months was employed. Persons in the same labor force status for all seven months have repeated patterns of the form "OLF → OLF." The omitted pattern is "employed → employed," indicating persistent employment. In some cases, the "employed → OLF" and "unemployed → OLF" categories are collapsed due to small sample sizes.

Time since most recent employment
These categories indicate the number of months since the person was last employed. The omitted category is currently employed.

Family income in the last year
These categories indicate total family earnings in the past year. The omitted category is less than $3,000. For some tables, the original six categories are combined into four due to small sample sizes.

Table 6.3 Logit Estimates of the Determinants of JTPA Eligibility: Adults

	Adult males		Adult females	
Black	1.315	[0.060]	2.172	[0.129]
	(0.034)	0.000	(0.032)	0.000
Hispanic	1.070	[0.048]	2.270	[0.136]
	(0.036)	0.000	(0.030)	0.000
Other race/ethnicity	1.352	[0.062]	1.551	[0.090]
	(0.087)	0.000	(0.051)	0.000
Aged 30–39	−0.860	[−0.038]	0.018	[0.001]
	(0.030)	0.000	(0.026)	0.489
Aged 40–49	−0.939	[−0.042]	0.144	[0.007]
	(0.040)	0.000	(0.030)	0.000
Aged 50–54	−1.586	[−0.064]	0.047	[0.002]
	(0.049)	0.000	(0.035)	0.176
Highest grade < 10	0.737	[0.033]	0.974	[0.060]
	(0.034)	0.000	(0.029)	0.000
Highest grade 10–11	0.292	[0.012]	0.514	[0.031]
	(0.033)	0.000	(0.028)	0.000
Highest grade 13–15	−0.231	[−0.009]	−0.408	[−0.022]
	(0.031)	0.000	(0.025)	0.000
Highest grade > 15	−0.064	[−0.003]	−1.652	[−0.075]
	(0.036)	0.074	(0.032)	0.000
Currently married	0.157	[0.006]	1.366	[−0.074]
	(0.035)	0.000	(0.029)	0.000
Div.-wid.-sep.	0.177	[0.007]	0.043	[0.003]
	(0.042)	0.000	(0.031)	0.162
Child age < 6 years	−0.205	[−0.008]	0.646	[0.035]
	(0.036)	0.000	(0.027)	0.000
Family income $3,000–$6,000	0.113	[0.019]	−0.367	[−0.039]
	(0.050)	0.024	(0.044)	0.000
Family income $6,000–$9,000	−1.814	[−0.206]	−1.737	[−0.154]
	(0.048)	0.000	(0.043)	0.000
Family income $9,000–$12,000	−3.103	[−0.268]	−2.671	[−0.214]
	(0.056)	0.000	(0.043)	0.000
Family income $12,000–$15,000	−3.857	[−0.295]	−3.318	[−0.249]
	(0.056)	0.000	(0.044)	0.000

Table 6.3 (continued)

	Adult males		Adult females	
Family income > $15,000	−4.966	[−0.331]	−4.461	[−0.301]
	(0.048)	0.000	(0.037)	0.000
Constant	−0.474	[0.000]	4.714	[0.000]
	(0.033)	0.000	(0.043)	0.000
Number of observations	80,598		89,196	

NOTE: Standard errors are in parentheses, mean derivatives are in square brackets, and p-values are below the mean derivatives. Person-month data from the 1986 SIPP full panel. Omitted categories in the logit are white, aged 22–29, highest grade equals 12, never married, no young children, and family income less then $3,000. Using the sample proportion eligible as the cutoff value, the within-sample prediction rates for adult males are 72.48 percent for eligibles and 91.10 percent for noneligibles. The corresponding rates for adult females are 79.82 percent for eligibles and 88.32 percent for noneligibles.

SOURCE: Heckman and Smith (2004).

in the average probability of eligibility for blacks and Hispanics relative to whites exceeds 0.12 holding the resource variables constant.

Being married has a large negative estimated effect on the eligibility probabilities for all groups except adult males. The eligibility status of adult males is driven primarily by their own income, while for adult females and for youth, eligibility status depends in large part on the earnings of other family members. For all demographic groups except adult males, the presence of an own child under the age of six living in the home substantially increases the probability of eligibility for JTPA. Children raise the income cutoff for eligibility by increasing household size but do not add to the family income. In addition, years of schooling have an important impact on eligibility for all groups.

Not surprisingly, the probability of eligibility decreases monotonically with family income for all four demographic groups. The magnitude of the estimated average derivatives is very large for family income categories corresponding to incomes above $6,000. For adult males, raising family income from less than $3,000 to between $9,000 and $12,000 produces a decrease in the average probability of JTPA eligibility of 0.268. For male and female youth, the estimated average derivatives are larger still, reflecting the differential importance of family resources in determining eligibility for these groups.

Table 6.4 Logit Estimates of the Determinants of JTPA Eligibility: Youth

	Male youth		Female youth	
Black	1.111	[0.056]	2.446	[0.155]
	(0.164)	0.000	(0.092)	0.000
Hispanic	2.255	[0.121]	1.114	[0.068]
	(0.103)	0.000	(0.076)	0.000
Other race/ethnicity	1.514	[0.078]	2.065	[0.129]
	(0.195)	0.000	(0.408)	0.000
Aged 19–21	−0.434	[−0.021]	0.124	[0.007]
	(0.082)	0.000	(0.070)	0.079
Highest grade < 10	1.959	[0.100]	0.915	[0.057]
	(0.105)	0.000	(0.107)	0.000
Highest grade 10–11	1.469	[0.074]	0.134	[0.008]
	(0.109)	0.000	(0.086)	0.118
Highest grade > 12	−0.150	[−0.007]	−0.617	[−0.036]
	(0.107)	0.160	(0.072)	0.000
Currently married	−1.657	[−0.068]	0.609	[0.036]
	(0.168)	0.000	(0.082)	0.000
Div.-wid.-sep.	−3.041	[−0.106]	1.511	[0.094]
	(0.380)	0.000	(0.242)	0.000
Child age < 6 years	1.161	[0.061]	1.468	[0.090]
	(0.168)	0.000	(0.081)	0.000
Family income $3,000–$6,000	−2.582	[−0.387]	−1.306	[−0.201]
	(0.153)	0.000	(0.102)	0.000
Family income $6,000–$9,000	−4.370	[−0.547]	−3.008	[−0.436]
	(0.165)	0.000	(0.126)	0.000
Family income $9,000–$12,000	−4.595	[−0.561]	−4.237	[−0.552]
	(0.157)	0.000	(0.144)	0.000
Family income $12,000–$15,000	−5.935	[−0.631]	−5.057	[−0.610]
	(0.204)	0.000	(0.142)	0.000
Family income > $15,000	−6.628	[−0.660]	−6.585	[−0.695]
	(0.153)	0.000	(0.103)	0.000
Constant	6.246	[0.000]	6.164	[0.000]
	(0.170)	0.000	(0.117)	0.000
Number of observations	10,280		11,165	

NOTE: Standard errors are in parentheses, mean derivatives are in square brackets, and p-values are below the mean derivatives. Person-month data from 1986 SIPP full panel. Omitted categories in the logit are white, aged 16–18, highest grade equals 12, never married, no young children, and family income less than $3,000. Using the sample proportion eligible as the cutoff value, the within-sample prediction rates for male youth are 71.95 percent for eligibles and 90.67 percent for noneligibles. The corresponding rates for female youth are 72.72 percent for eligibles and 91.32 percent for noneligibles.
SOURCE: Heckman and Smith (2004).

As we detail in the table notes, the small set of characteristics included in the specifications reported in Tables 6.3 and 6.4 do well at predicting within-sample eligibility status. For all four groups, over 70 percent of the eligibles and almost 90 percent of the noneligibles are correctly predicted when we use the overall eligibility rate within each group to define the cutoff for predicting eligibility. Taken together, our results demonstrate that the eligibility rules for JTPA produced substantial group differences in access to subsidized government training. These differences have no link to the presence of a performance management system within JTPA.

THE DETERMINANTS OF AWARENESS OF THE JTPA PROGRAM

This section investigates the determinants of awareness of the JTPA program using data on the controls and ENPs at the four JTPA sites described earlier. The concept of program awareness is an elusive but important one. Differential access to information about the program can affect awareness and thereby influence participation. Language barriers are an obvious case in point. However, awareness also depends on the incentives a person has to participate in the program. In some cases the desire to participate may influence awareness rather than awareness independently influencing participation.

As we lack evidence on individuals' information-gathering activities, we cannot determine the extent to which information costs, and therefore program awareness, play a causal role in determining program participation choices. However, the evidence presented in this section indicates that awareness of JTPA among those eligible for it is by no means universal, and that program awareness appears to be related to the likelihood of participation in the program, to education, and to language skills. We also present evidence that a sizeable fraction of persons who are eligible for the program do not believe that they are eligible for it. Taken together, this evidence suggests that barriers to information represent an important determinant of program participation.

Each member of the ENP sample was asked whether or not he or she had heard of the JTPA program. In keeping with the decentralized nature of the program, local training sites often selected operating names other than JTPA. To overcome this problem, ENPs were asked about their awareness of JTPA using the program's primary name in their locality. This measure does not capture general awareness of the existence of programs like JTPA among individuals not aware of JTPA by its local name. Persons who indicated that they were aware of the program were then asked whether or not they believed themselves to be presently eligible for it. Control group members are assumed to be aware of JTPA and of their own eligibility for it.

Table 6.5 presents rates of awareness and self-reported eligibility for ENPs in each major demographic group. The first column presents the fraction of the ENPs who have heard of JTPA. These fractions are surprisingly low. For all four groups, the awareness rate is below 50 percent. The rate is higher for youth than for adults, which may indirectly reflect requirements that sites expend 40 percent of their training resources on youth, who constitute much less than 40 percent of the eligible population. The second column gives the fraction of those persons aware of the program who think that they are eligible for it. Note that all

Table 6.5 Awareness of and Self-Reported Eligibility for the JTPA Program: JTPA-Eligible Nonparticipants

	Self-reported awareness of JTPA	Self-reported eligibility for JTPA conditional on awareness	Self-reported eligibility for JTPA unconditional on awareness
Adult males	0.3539	0.3598	0.1274
	(0.0167)	(0.0311)	(0.0116)
Adult females	0.4165	0.4594	0.1913
	(0.0124)	(0.0214)	(0.0099)
Male youth	0.4722	0.5672	0.2678
	(0.0373)	(0.0610)	(0.0330)
Female youth	0.4667	0.5410	0.2525
	(0.0289)	(0.0453)	(0.0251)

NOTE: Standard errors are in parentheses. National JTPA Study data. Respondents are coded as aware of JTPA if they report having heard of JTPA by its most common local name. Respondents are coded as self-reported eligibles if they are aware of JTPA and report that they believe themselves to be presently eligible for it.

SOURCE: Heckman and Smith (2004).

of the ENPs are determined to be eligible at the time of their screening interviews and that nearly all are still eligible at the time the awareness question was asked in the baseline interview. Conditional on awareness, only 36 percent of adult males, 46 percent of adult females, and around 55 percent of youth realize that they qualify for JTPA services. Taking the product of these two probabilities yields the unconditional probability of awareness and self-reported eligibility appearing in the third column. Barely 12 percent of adult male eligibles can identify both the program and their own eligibility for it. Even among youth, only about 25 percent of eligibles are both aware of the program and of their own eligibility for it. These figures suggest that there are substantial costs associated with finding out about social programs such as JTPA and about the rules governing access to their services, and that information costs play an important role in producing demographic differentials in program participation.

The results from a logit analysis of the determinants of awareness of the JTPA program appear in Tables 6.6 and 6.7. These tables have the same basic structure as Tables 6.3 and 6.4. These estimates result from the pooled sample of ENPs and experimental controls at the four sites in the NJS that collected ENP data. Following Heckman and Smith (1999), we weight the data such that the ENPs and controls represent 0.97 and 0.03 of the overall eligible population, respectively.

For all four demographic groups, black eligibles are relatively more likely than white eligibles to know about JTPA. Adult Hispanic eligibles are relatively less likely than whites to know about JTPA, with the difference being statistically significant in both cases. The negative and statistically significant coefficient estimates for Hispanic adult eligibles arise even after controlling for facility with the English language and for level of education.[11] Language skills and educational deficits play a role in explaining this phenomenon but more than just language deficits are involved. Tienda and Jensen (1988) find that Hispanics participate less in government programs compared to non-Hispanics with the same basic economic characteristics; this suggests that they may obtain less information about programs such as JTPA from their social environment.

Consistent with the standard human capital model (see, e.g., Becker [1964]), older adults have statistically significantly lower probabilities of awareness of the program than persons age 22 to 29. This may reflect the reduced demand for skill enhancement programs with age documented in, e.g., Leigh (1995). The pattern with respect to education is hump-shaped. Persons with the lowest levels of schooling have lower conditional probabilities of awareness than those who have completed high school. This evidence supports the notion of substantial information processing costs among those with very low levels of schooling. A lower likelihood of participating in JTPA, and hence a lower value to information about the program, accounts for the evidence that the most educated persons are less aware of the program. More specifically, individuals with high levels of education have low incentives to know about poverty reduction programs, as they are not typically eligible for them.

Among adults, divorced, widowed, or separated eligibles have a higher probability of awareness than do those who are single. The difference is both statistically and substantively significant for adult males. For three of the four groups, living in a family that receives Food Stamps has a positive effect on the probability of being aware of JTPA, while living in a family that receives AFDC has a positive effect only for adult males and for female youth. The estimated effect of living in a family receiving Food Stamps is large, with mean derivatives of 0.164 and 0.133, and it is statistically significant for both adult males and females. As nearly all of the adult female AFDC recipients also receive Food Stamps, the negative (essentially zero) coefficient on the AFDC variable indicates the additional effect of receiving *both* AFDC and Food Stamps, rather than just Food Stamps. Interpreted in this way, the absence of any AFDC effect becomes less surprising. The strong effects observed for Food Stamp receipt are consistent with the practice in that program of providing recipients with information about training opportunities.

Unemployed (i.e., out of work but actively looking for work) eligibles have a higher probability of program awareness for all four demographic groups. This difference between the unemployed and the employed is statistically significant for both male and female adults. In contrast, eligible individuals who are out of the labor force (i.e., not working and not actively looking for work) have lower probabilities of awareness than employed eligibles for all four demographic groups. These results are consistent with the relative value of information about JTPA for the two groups.

Table 6.6 Logit Estimates of the Determinants of JTPA Awareness among JTPA-Eligible Nonparticipants: Adults

	Adult males		Adult females	
Fort Wayne	0.261	[0.055]	−0.187	[−0.039]
	(0.233)	0.264	(0.203)	0.356
Jersey City	0.071	[0.015]	−0.174	[−0.036]
	(0.210)	0.736	(0.191)	0.364
Providence	−0.268	[−0.054]	−0.683	[−0.142]
	(0.231)	0.245	(0.197)	0.001
Black	0.414	[0.094]	0.288	[0.063]
	(0.272)	0.128	(0.194)	0.138
Hispanic	−0.486	[−0.102]	−0.360	[−0.077]
	(0.210)	0.021	(0.185)	0.051
Other race/ethnicity	−0.290	[−0.063]	−0.348	[−0.074]
	(0.279)	0.298	(0.255)	0.174
Low English ability	−0.763	[−0.147]	−1.334	[−0.254]
	(0.180)	0.000	(0.144)	0.000
Aged 30–39	−0.345	[−0.073]	−0.114	[−0.024]
	(0.165)	0.037	(0.137)	0.405
Aged 40–49	−0.372	[−0.078]	−0.235	[−0.050]
	(0.201)	0.064	(0.174)	0.177
Aged 50–54	0.010	[0.002]	−0.126	[−0.027]
	(0.349)	0.977	(0.253)	0.619
Highest grade < 10	−0.476	[−0.100]	−0.836	[−0.180]
	(0.179)	0.008	(0.135)	0.000
Highest grade 10–11	−0.144	[−0.031]	−0.126	[−0.028]
	(0.210)	0.494	(0.173)	0.468
Highest grade 13–15	0.102	[0.022]	−0.263	[−0.058]
	(0.239)	0.671	(0.201)	0.190
Highest grade > 15	−0.387	[−0.082]	−0.646	[−0.141]
	(0.279)	0.166	(0.292)	0.027
Currently married	0.019	[0.004]	−0.239	[−0.051]
	(0.181)	0.918	(0.162)	0.142
Div.-wid.-sep.	0.718	[0.156]	0.112	[0.024]
	(0.273)	0.009	(0.164)	0.494
Child age < 6 years	−0.079	[−0.016]	−0.062	[−0.013]
	(0.161)	0.623	(0.130)	0.635

Table 6.6 (continued)

	Adult males		Adult females	
Current AFDC receipt	0.088	[0.019]	−0.086	[−0.018]
	(0.499)	0.859	(0.218)	0.694
Current Food Stamp receipt	0.756	[0.164]	0.625	[0.133]
	(0.251)	0.003	(0.187)	0.001
Currently unemployed	0.805	[0.176]	0.628	[0.136]
	(0.289)	0.005	(0.250)	0.012
Currently out of the labor	−0.182	[−0.037]	−0.221	[−0.047]
force	(0.258)	0.481	(0.140)	0.115
Family income $3,000–	−0.152	[−0.030]	0.604	[0.129]
$9,000	(0.347)	0.662	(0.239)	0.012
Family income $9,000–	−0.070	[−0.014]	0.389	[0.083]
$15,000	(0.343)	0.838	(0.239)	0.104
Family income > $15,000	0.377	[0.080]	0.156	[0.033]
	(0.340)	0.267	(0.215)	0.469
Constant	−0.359	[0.000]	0.238	[0.000]
	(0.393)	0.361	(0.287)	0.407
Number of observations	1,551		2,436	

NOTE: Standard errors are in parentheses, mean derivatives are in square brackets, and p-values are below the mean derivatives. National JTPA Study data. Omitted categories in the logit are Corpus Christi, white, aged 22–29, highest grade equals 12, never married, no young children, not currently receiving AFDC, not currently receiving Food Stamps, currently employed, and family income less than $3,000. Using the sample proportion aware of JTPA as the cutoff, the within-sample prediction rates for adult males are 63.29 percent for aware eligibles and 62.95 percent for unaware eligibles. The corresponding rates for adult females are 69.44 percent for aware eligibles and 61.82 percent for unaware eligibles.

SOURCE: Heckman and Smith (2004).

Table 6.7 Logit Estimates of the Determinants of JTPA Awareness among JTPA-Eligible Nonparticipants: Youth

	Male youth		Female youth	
Fort Wayne	0.054	[0.011]	0.150	[0.033]
	(0.661)	0.935	(0.490)	0.759
Jersey City	−0.147	[−0.031]	−0.509	[−0.111]
	(0.727)	0.839	(0.461)	0.270
Providence	−0.412	[−0.087]	−0.686	[−0.153]
	(0.666)	0.536	(0.438)	0.117
Black	1.183	[0.242]	0.902	[0.204]
	(0.739)	0.109	(0.464)	0.052
Hispanic	0.189	[0.040]	0.298	[0.068]
	(0.652)	0.772	(0.416)	0.475
Other race/ethnicity	1.348	[0.277]	−0.813	[−0.167]
	(1.370)	0.325	(0.610)	0.183
Low English ability	−2.972	[−0.439]	−2.373	[−0.393]
	(0.751)	0.000	(0.664)	0.000
Aged 19–21	−0.891	[−0.187]	−0.212	[−0.048]
	(0.528)	0.091	(0.300)	0.478
Highest grade < 10	−0.025	[−0.005]	−0.672	[−0.153]
	(0.630)	0.968	(0.368)	0.068
Highest grade 10–11	0.280	[0.059]	−0.077	[−0.018]
	(0.592)	0.636	(0.405)	0.849
Highest grade > 12	−0.254	[−0.053]	0.063	[0.014]
	(0.729)	0.728	(0.496)	0.898
Currently married	1.323	[0.266]	0.136	[0.031]
	(0.819)	0.106	(0.370)	0.713
Div.-wid.-sep.	−0.584	[−0.119]	−0.951	[−0.203]
	(0.830)	0.482	(0.444)	0.032
Child age < 6 years	−0.242	[−0.050]	−0.164	[−0.037]
	(0.758)	0.750	(0.323)	0.613
Current AFDC receipt	−0.838	[−0.170]	0.329	[0.073]
	(1.087)	0.441	(0.420)	0.433
Current Food Stamp receipt	0.494	[0.103]	−0.026	[−0.006]
	(0.813)	0.543	(0.410)	0.950
Currently unemployed	0.522	[0.110]	0.362	[0.081]
	(0.575)	0.363	(0.471)	0.442

Table 6.7 (continued)

	Male youth		Female youth	
Currently out of the labor force	−0.990	[−0.203]	0.000	[0.000]
	(0.594)	0.095	(0.342)	1.000
Family income \$3,000–\$9,000	−0.907	[−0.188]	0.040	[0.009]
	(0.915)	0.321	(0.441)	0.928
Family income \$9,000–\$15,000	−0.395	[−0.082]	−0.321	[−0.072]
	(0.938)	0.673	(0.555)	0.563
Family income > \$15,000	−0.703	[−0.146]	−0.410	[−0.092]
	(1.031)	0.495	(0.534)	0.442
Constant	0.613	[0.000]	0.272	[0.000]
	(1.019)	0.547	(0.633)	0.668
Number of observations	530		700	

NOTE: Standard errors are in parentheses, mean derivatives are in square brackets, and p-values are below the mean derivatives. National JTPA Study data. Omitted categories in the logit are Corpus Christi, white, aged 16–18, highest grade equals 12, never married, no young children, not currently receiving AFDC, not currently receiving Food Stamps, currently employed, and family income less than \$3,000. Using the sample proportion aware of JTPA as the cutoff, the within-sample prediction rates for male youth are 72.31 percent for aware eligibles and 64.86 percent for unaware eligibles. The corresponding rates for female youth are 67.43 percent for aware eligibles and 53.64 percent for unaware eligibles.

SOURCE: Heckman and Smith (2004).

While the concept of program awareness is a conceptually problematic one, the evidence presented here indicates that learning about the JTPA program and its eligibility requirements is not costless, and that the likelihood of becoming aware of the program varies in predictable ways. In particular, we find that differences in information costs, information processing and language skills, and the expected value of information about the JTPA program (which is itself a function of the probability of participation in the program and its expected benefit) can account for the patterns we observe in the data. Both the institutional structure of JTPA and our empirical findings suggest little if any link between awareness and JTPA's performance standards system. While local JTPA offices could in principle influence awareness by targeting specific groups or locations in their (quite limited) marketing efforts or by choosing contractors with links to specific subgroups among the eligible population, the indirect nature of these strategies suggests that even a program that wanted to cream-skim would likely devote its efforts primarily to other margins. Moreover, findings such as the positive effect of Food Stamp receipt on awareness argue against a major role for attempts to cream-skim at this stage in the participation process. Our analysis also suggests, however, that one way to boost program participation is to increase awareness among those eligible.

THE DETERMINANTS OF APPLICATION/ ACCEPTANCE INTO JTPA

This section presents a logit analysis of the determinants of application/acceptance (defined as reaching random assignment) conditional on program awareness using data on controls and ENPs from the NJS. We combine the application and acceptance stages here because we lack the data to examine them separately. Combining these two stages in the program participation process means that the patterns we observe reflect the influence of individual decisions to apply and to persist through the (sometimes lengthy) application process, as well as JTPA staff decisions regarding referrals to other programs, the number of required visits to the JTPA office and other hassle costs, what services to offer, and so on.

Tables 6.8 and 6.9 report estimates of logit models of application/acceptance into the JTPA program as a function of observed characteristics for the four demographic groups. Coefficient estimates and estimated standard errors take account of the choice-based nature of the sample. The training site indicators included in the model have no behavioral interpretation, as the relative numbers of ENPs and controls at each site is an artifact of the study design. The notes to Tables 6.8 and 6.9 summarize the within-sample predictive success of the models.[12]

The most dramatic result in Tables 6.8 and 6.9 is the powerful effect of recent labor force status dynamics on application/acceptance into JTPA.[13] For both adult males and adult females, all of the labor force status pattern indicators have coefficients statistically different from zero, though many of the coefficients cannot be statistically distinguished from one another. In general, unemployed persons are the most likely to apply and be accepted into the JTPA program. For adult men, individuals who recently became unemployed, either by leaving employment or by reentering the labor force, have higher application/acceptance probabilities than the long term (over six months) unemployed. This difference does not appear for adult women.

Older adults have a lower conditional probability of application/acceptance, consistent with conventional arguments that the return to training declines with age. The effect of years of completed schooling on acceptance into the program shows a hill-shaped pattern for adults, with individuals with fewer than 10 or more than 15 years of schooling having differentially low estimated application/acceptance probabilities. This pattern reveals that it is more than just low rates of awareness that cause those with less than a high school education to have low rates of participation in JTPA conditional on eligibility. For youth, the probability of application/acceptance increases monotonically with years of schooling.

Relative to single, never married persons, currently married persons have a statistically significantly lower probability of application/acceptance for three of the four demographic groups. Among adult men, but not the other three demographic groups, divorced, widowed, and separated persons also have lower probabilities of application/acceptance into JTPA.

The effect of living in a family receiving AFDC is negative for all four groups, and statistically significant for three. In contrast, family

Table 6.8 Logit Estimates of the Determinants of Acceptance into JTPA-Aware ENP and Control Samples: Adults

	Adult males		Adult females	
Fort Wayne	2.334	[0.117]	1.878	[0.118]
	(0.450)	0.000	(0.256)	0.000
Jersey City	1.120	[0.040]	1.228	[0.060]
	(0.482)	0.020	(0.238)	0.000
Providence	1.547	[0.054]	1.720	[0.084]
	(0.507)	0.002	(0.280)	0.000
Black	0.159	[0.008]	−0.060	[−0.003]
	(0.304)	0.600	(0.199)	0.763
Hispanic	−0.170	[−0.007]	0.964	[0.067]
	(0.442)	0.701	(0.240)	0.000
Other race/ethnicity	1.228	[0.079]	−0.169	[−0.008]
	(0.455)	0.007	(0.494)	0.732
Aged 30–39	−0.564	[−0.028]	−0.291	[−0.016]
	(0.263)	0.032	(0.160)	0.069
Aged 40–49	−0.836	[−0.038]	−0.226	[−0.013]
	(0.396)	0.035	(0.224)	0.313
Aged 50–54	−0.766	[−0.036]	−0.276	[−0.016]
	(0.518)	0.139	(0.334)	0.408
Highest grade < 10	−0.950	[−0.040]	−0.194	[−0.010]
	(0.341)	0.005	(0.172)	0.258
Highest grade 10–11	−0.103	[−0.006]	−0.112	[−0.006]
	(0.331)	0.755	(0.184)	0.543
Highest grade 13–15	0.327	[0.020]	0.413	[0.027]
	(0.332)	0.325	(0.208)	0.047
Highest grade > 15	−1.420	[−0.053]	−0.500	[−0.024]
	(0.550)	0.010	(0.767)	0.515
Currently married	−0.875	[−0.043]	−0.909	[−0.042]
	(0.314)	0.005	(0.214)	0.000
Div.-wid.-sep.	−0.571	[−0.031]	0.142	[0.010]
	(0.316)	0.071	(0.167)	0.398
Child age < 6 years	−0.166	[−0.007]	−0.185	[−0.010]
	(0.349)	0.634	(0.159)	0.245
Current AFDC receipt	−1.545	[−0.047]	−0.975	[−0.050]
	(0.691)	0.025	(0.232)	0.000
Current Food Stamp receipt	0.189	[0.009]	0.205	[0.012]
	(0.323)	0.558	(0.191)	0.282

Table 6.8 (continued)

	Adult males		Adult females	
Unemployed → employed	1.752	[0.068]	1.722	[0.080]
	(0.390)	0.000	(0.325)	0.000
OLF → employed	2.372	[0.120]	1.122	[0.039]
	(0.447)	0.000	(0.370)	0.002
Employed → unemployed	3.861	[0.328]	2.782	[0.210]
	(0.430)	0.000	(0.277)	0.000
Unemployed → unemployed	2.615	[0.146]	2.862	[0.223]
	(0.536)	0.000	(0.320)	0.000
OLF → unemployed	4.048	[0.360]	2.326	[0.144]
	(0.566)	0.000	(0.324)	0.000
Employed or unemployed →	5.421	[0.610]		
OLF	(0.937)	0.000		
Employed → OLF			1.400	[0.055]
			(0.314)	0.000
Unemployed → OLF			2.242	[0.134]
			(0.452)	0.000
OLF → OLF	1.550	[0.055]	1.093	[0.037]
	(0.556)	0.005	(0.260)	0.000
Family income $3,000–	−1.196	[−0.075]	0.269	[0.016]
$9,000	(0.531)	0.024	(0.232)	0.246
Family income $9,000–	−0.448	[−0.034]	−0.023	[−0.001]
$15,000	(0.480)	0.351	(0.339)	0.946
Family income > $15,000	−1.895	[−0.098]	0.034	[0.002]
	(0.507)	0.000	(0.313)	0.914
Constant	−3.385	[0.000]	−4.857	[0.000]
	(0.564)	0.000	(0.385)	0.000
Number of observations	1,024		1,520	

NOTE: Standard errors are in parentheses, mean derivatives are in square brackets, and p-values are below the mean derivatives. National JTPA Study data. Estimates reflect weighting to account for choice-based sampling. Omitted categories in the logit are Corpus Christi, white, aged 22–29, highest grade equals 12, never married, no young children, not currently receiving AFDC, not currently receiving Food Stamps, "Employed → employed," and family income less than $3,000. The categories "Employed → OLF" and "Unemployed → OLF" are combined due to small sample sizes. Using the population proportion of persons accepted into JTPA (assumed to be 3 percent overall) to determine the cutoff, the within sample prediction rates for adult males are 81.06 for controls (applied and accepted into JTPA) and 81.38 for ENPs (did not apply or not accepted into JTPA). The corresponding rates for adult females are 65.94 for controls and 71.43 for ENPs.

SOURCE: Heckman and Smith (2004).

Table 6.9 Logit Estimates of the Determinants of Acceptance into JTPA-Aware ENP and Control Samples: Youth

	Male youth		Female youth	
Fort Wayne	2.268	[0.127]	0.750	[0.040]
	(0.647)	0.000	(0.506)	0.139
Jersey City	1.445	[0.060]	0.462	[0.022]
	(0.649)	0.026	(0.545)	0.396
Providence	3.627	[0.246]	1.218	[0.067]
	(0.632)	0.000	(0.471)	0.010
Black	−0.793	[−0.030]	0.227	[0.011]
	(0.515)	0.124	(0.434)	0.601
Hispanic	0.717	[0.046]	0.097	[0.005]
	(0.628)	0.254	(0.439)	0.825
Other race/ethnicity	−4.207	[−0.080]	0.971	[0.064]
	(1.252)	0.001	(0.798)	0.223
Aged 19–21	0.285	[0.013]	−0.451	[−0.024]
	(0.460)	0.536	(0.328)	0.169
Highest grade < 10	−0.104	[−0.005]	−0.028	[−0.001]
	(0.508)	0.838	(0.421)	0.947
Highest grade 10–11	−0.187	[−0.009]	−0.392	[−0.018]
	(0.475)	0.693	(0.440)	0.373
Highest grade > 12	0.472	[0.028]	0.236	[0.014]
	(0.845)	0.576	(0.441)	0.592
Currently married	−1.225	[−0.042]	−0.527	[−0.022]
	(0.637)	0.055	(0.436)	0.227
Div.-wid.-sep.	0.155	[0.009]	0.316	[0.018]
	(1.226)	0.899	(0.662)	0.633
Current AFDC receipt	−1.455	[−0.043]	−0.934	[−0.007]
	(0.980)	0.137	(0.399)	0.019
Current Food Stamp	0.555	[−0.043]	1.311	[−0.042]
receipt	(0.580)	0.339	(0.370)	0.000
Child age < 6 years	−1.294	[0.030]	−0.139	[0.083]
	(0.676)	0.056	(0.339)	0.681
Unemployed →	2.110	[0.120]	1.776	[0.059]
employed	(0.629)	0.001	(0.564)	0.002
OLF → employed	−1.331	[−0.021]	2.243	[0.095]
	(0.890)	0.135	(0.597)	0.000

Table 6.9 (continued)

	Male youth		Female youth	
Employed → unemployed	2.087	[0.118]	3.648	[0.293]
	(0.537)	0.000	(0.664)	0.000
Unemployed → unemployed	2.211	[0.130]	2.638	[0.137]
	(0.706)	0.002	(0.591)	0.000
OLF → unemployed	1.285	[0.054]	3.292	[0.229]
	(0.764)	0.093	(0.614)	0.000
Employed or unemployed → OLF	1.959	[0.106]		
	(0.806)	0.015		
Employed → OLF			1.462	[0.041]
			(0.498)	0.003
Unemployed → OLF			0.845	[0.017]
			(0.886)	0.340
OLF → OLF	2.387	[0.150]	1.201	[0.030]
	(0.699)	0.001	(0.549)	0.029
Family income \$3,000–\$9,000	3.867	[0.309]	−0.386	[−0.015]
	(0.748)	0.000	(0.536)	0.472
Family income \$9,000–\$15,000	1.552	[0.055]	0.261	[0.013]
	(0.746)	0.038	(0.691)	0.706
Family income > \$15,000	1.011	[0.028]	1.765	[0.149]
	(0.764)	0.186	(0.535)	0.001
Constant	−6.787	[0.000]	−4.732	[0.000]
	(0.976)	0.000	(0.753)	0.000
Number of observations	436		540	

NOTE: Standard errors are in parentheses, mean derivatives are in square brackets, and p-values are below the mean derivatives. National JTPA Study data. Estimates reflect weighting to account for choice-based sampling. Omitted categories in the logit are Corpus Christi, white, aged 16–18, highest grade equals 12, never married, no young children, not currently receiving AFDC, not currently receiving Food Stamps, "Employed → employed," and family income less than \$3,000. The categories "Employed → OLF" and "Unemployed → OLF" are combined due to small sample sizes. Using the population proportion of persons accepted into JTPA (assumed to be three percent overall) as the cutoff, the within sample prediction rates for male youth are 68.66 for controls (applied and accepted into JTPA) and 76.47 for ENPs (did not apply or not accepted into JTPA). The corresponding rates for female youth are 67.91 for controls and 69.57 for ENPs.

SOURCE: Heckman and Smith (2004).

Food Stamp receipt has a positive influence in all cases. Interpreting the AFDC coefficient as the marginal effect of family AFDC receipt in addition to Food Stamps, it appears that among aware eligibles, AFDC recipients have much lower probabilities of application/acceptance into JTPA than do those receiving only Food Stamps. As the effect of young children in the home is being controlled for, this difference does not result from young children acting as a barrier to work or training outside the home.

The effects of family income differ across groups. High levels of family income reduce the probability of application/acceptance among adult males, have little effect for adult females, and raise the probability of participation for both youth groups. The availability of income from other family members to provide support during training appears to encourage youth to apply to JTPA.

We do not include measures of the state of the local economy at the four sites during the time that the ENP and control samples were collected in the specifications reported here. In other work, we estimate models including both county-level monthly unemployment rates averaged over the counties constituting each of the sites, and interactions between these unemployment rates and the site indicators. Surprisingly, given the strong effects of individual unemployment found here, these variables never attain statistical significance and never have a noticeable impact on the proportion of correct predictions. One reason for this is that the number of ENPs whose month of measured (via the screening interview) eligibility occurs in a given calendar month depends not only on the size of the eligible population in that month, but also on the administrative schedule of the consulting firm doing the screening. A second reason is that the flow into the program, as measured by the number of persons randomly assigned in each calendar month, depends strongly on factors besides the local economy, including the academic schedule of the community colleges that provide much of the JTPA classroom training at these sites.

Our analysis of application/acceptance into JTPA conditional on eligibility reveals the fundamental importance of labor force status dynamics in determining who applies and is accepted into the program conditional on program awareness. A number of other factors including age, schooling, marital status, and family income play important supporting roles. In terms of cream skimming, the institutions appear to drive some measurable effects here, as caseworkers can affect the process once a potential participant applies to JTPA. For example, caseworkers sometimes required extra visits as a way of weeding out potential participants not seriously interested in services and/or employment. The overrepresentation of unemployed individuals who recently lost a job or reentered the labor market is consistent with a cream-skimming story, though it is also consistent with the use of JTPA as a form of job search by such persons. The age, education, marital status, welfare, and family income patterns we estimate do not suggest a dominant role for cream skimming, but they do not rule out a modest one, either.

THE DETERMINANTS OF ENROLLMENT IN JTPA

Formal enrollment constitutes the final stage in the JTPA participation process. In this section we examine the determinants of the transition from acceptance into the program (defined as reaching random assignment) to formal enrollment.[14] A key difference between acceptance and enrollment is that, as noted in Chapters 3 and 4, only the outcomes of persons formally enrolled in JTPA influenced the rewards (or punishments) that a site received under the JTPA performance standards system. Training centers in JTPA had considerable (but not unlimited) discretion regarding whether (and when) to enroll persons accepted into the program. The performance standards system provided an incentive for training centers to delay enrollment until accepted applicants provided evidence that they were likely to obtain a job or to otherwise count favorably toward center performance. In practice, this sometimes meant that individuals receiving job search assistance were not enrolled until they found a job and that persons assigned to receive subsidized on-the-job training at private firms were not enrolled until a firm willing to provide them with such training had been located. For persons assigned to receive classroom training, training centers would often wait until trainees successfully attended class before enrolling them in the program.

Another factor influencing enrollment decisions for persons recommended for classroom training is their ability to maintain themselves during the time they are enrolled in training. Classroom training typically lasts longer than employment-related services such as job search assistance. At the same time, unlike earlier programs such as CETA, JTPA provided no stipends to trainees except in unusual circumstances. Thus, the willingness of a person to pursue classroom training could depend on the availability of a stable income from outside sources. Two important sources of such income are transfer programs such as AFDC and family income. Thus, we would expect AFDC receipt and family income to have positive effects on the probability of enrollment.

At the same time, the lag between acceptance into the program and enrollment may lead to changes in the opportunity costs of participation. Accepted applicants may receive job offers that dominate the training offered by JTPA, or they may experience illness or family problems that make it impossible for them to enroll. Alternatively, they may not care for the particular services offered by their caseworkers, or may not expect them to provide sufficient benefits to justify their time, hassle, and opportunity costs. Thus, even though enrollment represents the stage in the participation process where JTPA staff members have both the greatest incentive to cream-skim and the most leverage to do so, the patterns we observe still represent the combined influence of their efforts and of individual decisions to continue in or drop out of the program.

Tables 6.10 and 6.11 present the results of logit analyses of enrollment for the four demographic groups using data on the experimental treatment group. The notes to the tables discuss the within-sample predictive performance of the model, which is quite good. We find that the four training centers have very different overall enrollment rates, even controlling for the observable characteristics of their accepted applicants. For all four demographic groups, accepted applicants at the Fort Wayne and Jersey City centers have enrollment probabilities substantially lower than similar persons at Corpus Christi, which is the omitted training center in our analysis. These differences reflect in part the differing mix of services offered at the various sites. As documented in Table 6.1, Corpus Christi offered mainly classroom training. This form of service leads to a higher enrollment rate than other JTPA services; see Kemple, Doolittle, and Wallace (1993). In contrast, Fort Wayne and, to a lesser extent, Jersey City, primarily offered on-the-job training and job search assistance. Centers offering these services will have lower enrollment rates among accepted applicants because those who fail to locate a job or for whom no firm is willing to provide on-the-job training often do not ever get enrolled in the program.

Conditional on acceptance into JTPA, older adults are less likely to enroll than younger adults. This finding is consistent with the lower expected returns to training for older persons, which would make them relatively more likely to drop out of the program in response to a given outside opportunity. Family participation in the Food Stamp Program has a negative effect for three of the four demographic groups, with the effect both large and statistically significant for adult females. To the extent that Food Stamp recipients are less likely to find employment than other accepted applicants, this is consistent with creaming induced by the operation of JTPA performance standards. Also consistent with these incentives is our finding that for women and male youth, having no employment experience strongly reduces the probability of enrollment.

Finally, we estimate a large positive effect of family income on the enrollment probability for adults. Family income may allow an accepted applicant to undertake training even in the absence of a stipend. Thus, even though higher family income lowers eligibility, it raises the probability of enrollment among accepted applicants.

Taken together, our findings on the determinants of enrollment provide some suggestive, but not definitive, evidence of cream skimming. The strongest evidence comes from the systematic relationship between enrollment probabilities and service types across sites. Sites emphasizing subsidized on-the-job training, which provides greater enrollment flexibility than classroom training, appear to make strategic use of that flexibility. In terms of the covariates, explanations other than cream skimming can account for the age and family income effects. The rest lack any consistent pattern of precisely estimated coefficients across demographic groups. As such, we conclude only that, based primarily on site effects, our analysis of enrollment offers suggestive evidence in favor of cream skimming.

Table 6.10 Logit Estimates of the Determinants of Enrollment into JTPA Experimental Treatment Group: Adults

	Adult males		Adult females	
Fort Wayne	−0.692	[−0.163]	−1.030	[−0.232]
	(0.177)	0.000	(0.177)	0.000
Jersey City	−1.157	[−0.274]	−1.280	[−0.292]
	(0.204)	0.000	(0.195)	0.000
Providence	0.447	[0.090]	−0.563	[−0.121]
	(0.198)	0.024	(0.199)	0.005
Black	−0.180	[−0.041]	−0.240	[−0.056]
	(0.129)	0.165	(0.132)	0.069
Hispanic	0.271	[0.060]	0.196	[0.045]
	(0.181)	0.135	(0.176)	0.265
Other race/ethnicity	−0.024	[−0.005]	0.637	[0.141]
	(0.283)	0.933	(0.350)	0.068
Low English ability	0.288	[0.065]	−0.082	[−0.019]
	(0.241)	0.231	(0.210)	0.697
Aged 30–39	−0.105	[−0.023]	0.056	[0.013]
	(0.114)	0.358	(0.115)	0.629
Aged 40–49	−0.483	[−0.109]	−0.324	[−0.075]
	(0.165)	0.003	(0.160)	0.042
Aged 50–54	−0.370	[−0.083]	0.055	[0.013]
	(0.285)	0.195	(0.305)	0.856
Highest grade < 10	−0.129	[−0.029]	−0.168	[−0.038]
	(0.140)	0.357	(0.132)	0.203
Highest grade 10–11	−0.210	[−0.047]	−0.041	[−0.009]
	(0.130)	0.105	(0.124)	0.738
Highest grade 13–15	0.001	[0.000]	−0.035	[−0.008]
	(0.156)	0.993	(0.151)	0.817
Highest grade > 15	−0.204	[−0.046]	−0.216	[−0.049]
	(0.260)	0.432	(0.302)	0.475
Currently married	0.325	[0.073]	0.106	[0.024]
	(0.154)	0.034	(0.167)	0.525
Div.-wid.-sep.	0.273	[0.061]	0.203	[0.046]
	(0.135)	0.044	(0.121)	0.093
Child age < 6 years	0.109	[0.024]	0.336	[0.077]
	(0.154)	0.480	(0.115)	0.004

Table 6.10 (continued)

	Adult males		Adult females	
Current AFDC receipt	0.132	[0.029]	0.158	[0.036]
	(0.353)	0.709	(0.138)	0.253
Current Food Stamp receipt	−0.070	[−0.016]	−0.237	[−0.054]
	(0.132)	0.595	(0.117)	0.044
Employed 1–6 months ago	−0.060	[−0.013]	0.308	[0.071]
	(0.164)	0.715	(0.150)	0.040
Employed 7–12 months ago	−0.058	[−0.013]	0.216	[0.050]
	(0.210)	0.781	(0.198)	0.276
Employed > 12 months ago	0.032	[0.007]	0.287	[0.066]
	(0.211)	0.880	(0.177)	0.106
Never employed	−0.085	[−0.019]	0.061	[0.014]
	(0.227)	0.709	(0.192)	0.750
Family income $3,000–	−0.108	[−0.024]	0.211	[0.049]
$9,000	(0.122)	0.378	(0.118)	0.073
Family income $9,000–	0.057	[0.013]	0.441	[0.100]
$15,000	(0.165)	0.728	(0.166)	0.008
Family income	0.483	[0.105]	0.599	[0.135]
> $15,000	(0.204)	0.018	(0.256)	0.019
Constant	0.498	[0.000]	0.596	[0.000]
	(0.365)	0.172	(0.350)	0.088
Number of observations	1,886		2,012	

NOTE: Standard errors are in parentheses, mean derivatives are in square brackets, and p-values are below the mean derivatives. National JTPA Study data. Estimation includes observations with imputed covariates due to relative high levels of item non-response. Omitted categories in the logit are Corpus Christi, white, normal English ability, aged 22–29, highest grade equals 12, never married, no young children, not currently receiving AFDC, not currently receiving Food Stamps, currently employed, and family income less than $3,000. Using the sample proportion of accepted applicants enrolled into JTPA as the cutoff, the within-sample prediction rates for adult males are 62.48 percent for enrollees and 67.94 percent for nonenrollees. The corresponding rates for adult females are 57.64 percent for enrollees and 66.41 percent for nonenrollees.

SOURCE: Heckman and Smith (2004).

Table 6.11 Logit Estimates of the Determinants of Enrollment into JTPA Experimental Treatment Group: Youth

	Male youth		Female youth	
Fort Wayne	−1.213	[−0.241]	−1.266	[−0.253]
	(0.273)	0.000	(0.271)	0.000
Jersey City	−1.350	[−0.274]	−1.557	[−0.324]
	(0.297)	0.000	(0.266)	0.000
Providence	−0.554	[−0.096]	−0.597	[−0.103]
	(0.276)	0.045	(0.276)	0.031
Black	−0.291	[−0.061]	−0.223	[−0.048]
	(0.191)	0.127	(0.210)	0.287
Hispanic	−0.044	[−0.009]	0.212	[0.043]
	(0.241)	0.854	(0.250)	0.396
Other race/ethnicity			0.531	[0.102]
			(0.533)	0.319
Low English ability	−0.360	[−0.070]	0.113	[0.023]
	(0.392)	0.358	(0.391)	0.773
Aged 19–21	−0.429	[−0.087]	0.036	[0.007]
	(0.175)	0.014	(0.167)	0.830
Highest grade < 10	0.060	[0.012]	0.084	[0.017]
	(0.213)	0.779	(0.204)	0.680
Highest grade 10–11	0.000	[0.000]	0.131	[0.027]
	(0.192)	0.999	(0.183)	0.476
Highest grade > 12	0.064	[0.013]	−0.111	[−0.023]
	(0.405)	0.874	(0.355)	0.755
Currently married	0.138	[0.028]	−0.052	[−0.011]
	(0.335)	0.680	(0.302)	0.864
Div.-wid.-sep.	0.338	[0.066]	0.424	[0.083]
	(0.729)	0.643	(0.381)	0.267
Child age < 6 years	0.279	[0.055]	0.092	[0.019]
	(0.313)	0.373	(0.193)	0.632
Current AFDC receipt	−0.699	[−0.151]	0.135	[0.028]
	(0.336)	0.038	(0.241)	0.576
Current Food Stamp receipt	0.157	[0.032]	−0.060	[−0.012]
	(0.219)	0.474	(0.195)	0.757
Employed 1–6 months ago	−0.228	[−0.044]	−0.220	[−0.044]
	(0.254)	0.370	(0.239)	0.357

Table 6.11 (continued)

	Male youth		Female youth	
Employed 7–12 months ago	−0.467	[−0.093]	−0.415	[−0.085]
	(0.341)	0.170	(0.332)	0.211
Employed > 12 months ago	−0.413	[−0.082]	−0.353	[−0.072]
	(0.409)	0.312	(0.328)	0.282
Never employed	−0.657	[−0.134]	−0.276	[−0.055]
	(0.302)	0.030	(0.280)	0.324
Family income $3,000–$9,000	−0.057	[−0.012]	0.086	[0.018]
	(0.185)	0.758	(0.176)	0.627
Family income $9,000–$15,000	−0.463	[−0.099]	0.207	[0.042]
	(0.234)	0.048	(0.272)	0.446
Family income > $15,000	0.301	[0.058]	0.116	[0.024]
	(0.278)	0.279	(0.280)	0.680
Constant	2.505	[0.000]	1.453	[0.000]
	(0.586)	0.000	(0.557)	0.009
Number of observations	923		962	

NOTE: Standard errors are in parentheses, mean derivatives are in square brackets, and p-values are below the mean derivatives. National JTPA Study data. Estimation includes observations with imputed covariates due to relative high levels of item non-response. Omitted categories in the logit are Corpus Christi, white, normal English ability, aged 16–18, highest grade equals 12, never married, no young children, not currently receiving AFDC, not currently receiving Food Stamps, currently employed, and family income less than $3,000. Using the sample proportion of accepted applicants enrolled into JTPA as the cutoff, the within-sample prediction rates for male youth are 60.20 percent for enrollees and 65.08 percent for nonenrollees. The corresponding rates for female youth are 57.51 percent for enrollees and 68.75 percent for nonenrollees.

SOURCE: Heckman and Smith (2004).

DECOMPOSING THE PROCESS OF SELECTION INTO JTPA

In order to determine at what stage—enrollment (*en*), awareness (*aw*), acceptance (*ac*), or eligibility (*el*)—and in which direction particular observed characteristics operate to determine participation in the program, we use the chain rule to decompose the probability of participation in the following way:

$$(6.7)\quad \frac{\partial \Pr(en=1\mid x)}{\partial x} =$$
$$\left[\frac{\partial cond(en)}{\partial x}\right]\cdot cond(ac)\cdot cond(aw)\cdot cond(el)$$
$$+cond(en)\cdot\left[\frac{\partial cond(ac)}{\partial x}\right]\cdot cond(aw)\cdot cond(el)$$
$$+cond(en)\cdot cond(ac)\cdot\left[\frac{\partial cond(aw)}{\partial x}\right]\cdot cond(el)$$
$$+cond(en)\cdot cond(ac)\cdot cond(aw)\cdot\left[\frac{\partial cond(el)}{\partial x}\right]$$

where $cond(en)=\Pr(en=1\mid ac=1, aw=1, el=1, x)$

$cond(ac)=\Pr(ac=1\mid aw=1, el=1, x)$

$cond(aw)=\Pr(aw=1\mid el=1, x)$

$cond(el)=\Pr(el=1\mid x)$.

This equation decomposes the effect of a change in x on the probability of participation in the program into its effect on each constituent probability weighted by the remaining probabilities. In each term, the component in square brackets is the effect of a change in x on one of the conditional probabilities leading to participation in the program. For dichotomous variables, we replace derivatives with finite changes.

Using Equation (6.7), we can assess through which channels, if any, variation in x operates to affect the probability of participation in JTPA. In this section, we present results for two different decompositions. The two decompositions differ in terms of the number of steps included, the set of variables included, and the data used to perform the decomposition. These criteria are interrelated because the probability estimates are derived from different datasets and not all of the datasets contain all of the variables used to estimate the conditional probabilities discussed in the preceding sections. Reducing the number of stages enables us to estimate the effects of more explanatory variables. In addition, for certain variables some of the stages in Equation (6.7) are effectively eliminated. For example, belonging to a family that receives AFDC or Food Stamps makes the probability of eligibility equal to one. It is only informative to examine the effects of AFDC and Food Stamp receipt on the remaining components of the decomposition.

The first decompositions we present appear in Tables 6.12–6.15. The format of each table corresponds directly to Equation (6.7). The estimates of the probability of eligibility are based on the SIPP data. The estimates for the conditional probabilities of awareness, of application/acceptance, and of enrollment all draw on data from the four sites in the National JTPA Study, with the first two constructed using the pooled ENP and control group data and the last obtained from the experimental treatment group. The stark difference in geographic coverage between the samples for the first stage and the later stages of the decomposition weakens our analysis, but this is unavoidable given the lack of comparable data on the ineligible population at the four ENP sites. As in the earlier tables, the reported derivatives consist of sample averages of individual derivatives (or finite differences). They are not the derivatives evaluated at the sample means of the characteristics.[15]

The first column in the table presents the overall effect of a change in the indicated characteristic x on the probability of enrollment; this is the term on the left-hand side of Equation (6.7). These values are expressed in terms of the expected change in the probability of participation resulting from the indicated change in characteristics, multiplied by 100 for ease of presentation. To put the terms in context, note that the unconditional probability of participation is around 0.03, so that an overall effect of −0.867, which is the effect for adult males of switching from a family income of $0–$3,000 to one over $15,000, translates into a change in the probability of −0.00867, or a reduction of nearly one-third relative to the unconditional probability.

The second, fourth, sixth, and eighth columns of the first panel present the four chain rule terms that compose the overall effect. Thus,

Table 6.12 JTPA Participation Simulation Results—Weighted and Unweighted Effects of Changes in Characteristics on the Probability of Participation in JTPA 1986 SIPP Panel Sample of JTPA Eligibles: Adult Males (80,598 observations)

Change from:	Overall effect	Weighted eligibility term	Percent of overall	Weighted awareness term	Percent of overall	Weighted acceptance term	Percent of overall	Weighted enrollment term	Percent of overall
White to									
Black	0.15813	0.17989	113.76	0.06623	41.88	−0.05204	−32.91	−0.03595	−22.74
	(0.00174)	(0.00194)	(0.21)	(0.00068)	(0.20)	(0.00054)	(0.21)	(0.00041)	(0.15)
Hispanic	−0.09954	0.12535	−125.93	−0.08245	82.83	−0.18921	190.08	0.04676	−46.98
	(0.00121)	(0.00137)	(1.30)	(0.00086)	(0.54)	(0.00198)	(1.03)	(0.00053)	(0.30)
Other race/ethnicity	0.19616	0.17773	90.61	−0.07631	−38.90	0.08834	45.03	0.00643	3.28
	(0.00202)	(0.00193)	(0.16)	(0.00081)	(0.19)	(0.00084)	(0.19)	(0.00007)	(0.02)
Aged 22–29 to									
30–39	−0.20738	−0.07229	34.86	−0.04524	21.81	−0.08232	39.69	−0.00752	3.63
	(0.00213)	(0.00078)	(0.05)	(0.00046)	(0.05)	(0.00083)	(0.06)	(0.00009)	(0.01)
40–49	−0.23873	−0.08673	36.33	−0.04657	19.51	−0.05507	23.07	−0.05034	21.09
	(0.00252)	(0.00095)	(0.06)	(0.00048)	(0.04)	(0.00056)	(0.04)	(0.00058)	(0.05)
50–54	−0.31125	−0.12920	41.51	−0.00039	0.012	−0.12280	39.45	−0.05886	18.91
	(0.00330)	(0.00139)	(0.05)	(0.00000)	(0.00)	(0.00127)	(0.05)	(0.00067)	(0.04)
Single, never married to									
Married	−0.05544	0.01257	−22.68	0.01334	−24.07	−0.12037	217.11	0.03899	−70.33
	(0.00052)	(0.00014)	(0.15)	(0.00014)	(0.14)	(0.00117)	(0.69)	(0.00044)	(0.45)
Div.-wid.-sep.	0.09699	0.02779	28.66	0.10393	107.16	−0.06582	−67.86	0.03110	32.06
	(0.00106)	(0.00030)	(0.10)	(0.00106)	(0.18)	(0.00068)	(0.37)	(0.00035)	(0.16)

Highest grade = 12 to									
< 10	−0.07920	0.08490	−107.19	−0.06366	80.37	−0.01038	126.74	−0.00008	0.10
	(0.00091)	(0.00093)	(0.93)	(0.00067)	(0.44)	(0.00105)	(0.53)	(0.00000)	(0.00)
10–11	0.02426	0.03716	153.13	−0.01861	−76.70	0.02108	86.89	−0.01537	−63.33
	(0.00027)	(0.00041)	(0.52)	(0.00019)	(0.46)	(0.00021)	(0.44)	(0.00018)	(0.44)
13–15	0.01822	−0.02288	−125.56	0.00813	44.64	0.01885	103.44	0.01412	77.48
	(0.00019)	(0.00026)	(0.88)	(0.00008)	(0.25)	(0.00019)	(0.41)	(0.00016)	(0.31)
> 15	−0.24466	−0.00939	3.84	−0.05869	23.99	−0.17448	71.32	−0.00210	0.86
	(0.00245)	(0.00010)	(0.01)	(0.00060)	(0.04)	(0.00174)	(0.05)	(0.00002)	(0.00)
No child < 6 years of age to child									
< 6 years of age	−0.09757	−0.02979	30.53	−0.00915	9.38	−0.07291	74.72	0.01429	−14.64
	(0.00097)	(0.00032)	(0.07)	(0.00009)	(0.02)	(0.00072)	(0.10)	(0.00016)	(0.05)
Family income < $3,000 to									
$3,000–$9,000	−0.32777	−0.10544	32.17	−0.02445	7.46	−0.15696	47.89	−0.04095	12.49
	(0.00344)	(0.00116)	(0.04)	(0.00025)	(0.02)	(0.00161)	(0.06)	(0.00047)	(0.03)
$9,000–$15,000	−0.47674	−0.25404	53.29	−0.03367	7.06	−0.15563	32.64	−0.03338	7.00
	(0.00484)	(0.00259)	(0.05)	(0.00035)	(0.02)	(0.00158)	(0.04)	(0.00038)	(0.02)
> $15,000	−0.86666	−0.32102	37.04	0.01048	−1.21	−0.56750	65.48	0.01143	−1.32
	(0.00493)	(0.00250)	(0.09)	(0.00011)	(0.01)	(0.00274)	(0.07)	(0.00013)	(0.01)

(continued)

Table 6.12 (continued)

Change from:	Unweighted eligibility term	Unweighted awareness term	Unweighted acceptance term	Unweighted enrollment term
White to				
Black	0.06693	0.11697	−0.00968	−0.07041
	(0.00018)	(0.00005)	(0.00005)	(0.00005)
Hispanic	0.04687	−0.14448	−0.03352	0.08792
	(0.00013)	(0.00011)	(0.00020)	(0.00000)
Other race/ethnicity	0.06753	−0.13250	0.01774	0.01230
	(0.00020)	(0.00009)	(0.00009)	(0.00000)
Aged 22–29 to				
30–39	−0.02757	−0.08029	−0.01583	−0.01445
	(0.00007)	(0.00004)	(0.00009)	(0.00000)
40–49	−0.03277	−0.08247	−0.01053	−0.09820
	(0.00009)	(0.00004)	(0.00006)	(0.00003)
50–54	−0.04864	−0.00068	−0.02274	−0.11663
	(0.00014)	(0.00000)	(0.00013)	(0.00008)
Single, never married to				
Married	0.00468	0.02359	−0.02424	0.07681
	(0.00001)	(0.00001)	(0.00012)	(0.00006)
Div.-wid.-sep.	0.01056	0.18502	−0.01223	0.05862
	(0.00003)	(0.00006)	(0.00007)	(0.00002)

Highest grade = 12 to				
< 10	0.03184	−0.11108	−0.01834	−0.00016
	(0.00008)	(0.00007)	(0.00010)	(0.00000)
10–11	0.01406	−0.03287	0.00410	−0.02980
	(0.00004)	(0.00001)	(0.00002)	(0.00000)
13–15	−0.00856	0.01443	0.00364	0.02700
	(0.00002)	(0.00000)	(0.00002)	(0.00000)
> 15	−0.00355	−0.10503	−0.03325	−0.00404
	(0.00001)	(0.00003)	(0.00017)	(0.00000)
No child < 6 years of age to child < 6 years of age	−0.01129	−0.01621	−0.01379	0.02742
	(0.00003)	(0.00001)	(0.00007)	(0.00001)
Family income < $3,000 to				
$3,000–$9,000	−0.03797	−0.04304	−0.02817	−0.08075
	(0.00013)	(0.00000)	(0.00017)	(0.00006)
$9,000–$15,000	−0.08709	−0.05927	−0.03101	−0.06552
	(0.00035)	(0.00000)	(0.00019)	(0.00000)
> $15,000	−0.27189	0.01851	−0.22959	0.02226
	(0.00040)	(0.00001)	(0.00043)	(0.00000)

NOTE: Simulations use 1986 SIPP full panel data. Bootstrap standard errors appear in parentheses. The standard errors reflect variation due to the sample used to perform the simulations.
SOURCE: Heckman and Smith (2004).

Table 6.13 JTPA Participation Simulation Results—Weighted and Unweighted Effects of Changes in Characteristics on the Probability of Participation in JTPA 1986 SIPP Panel Sample of JTPA Eligibles: Adult Females (89,196 observations)

Change from:	Overall effect	Weighted eligibility term	Percent of overall	Weighted awareness term	Percent of overall	Weighted acceptance term	Percent of overall	Weighted enrollment term	Percent of overall
White to									
Black	0.18225	0.17694	97.09	0.04858	26.66	−0.01011	−5.55	−0.03316	−18.20
	(0.00074)	(0.00074)	(0.08)	(0.00024)	(0.09)	(0.00005)	(0.01)	(0.00016)	(0.05)
Hispanic	0.05725	0.06722	117.41	−0.03759	−65.65	−0.03785	−66.11	0.06547	114.36
	(0.00027)	(0.00028)	(0.26)	(0.00018)	(0.28)	(0.00018)	(0.25)	(0.00033)	(0.36)
Other race/ethnicity	0.08121	0.06315	77.76	−0.05323	−65.54	0.00495	6.10	0.06633	81.68
	(0.00037)	(0.00026)	(0.15)	(0.00025)	(0.22)	(0.00002)	(0.02)	(0.00033)	(0.18)
Aged 22–29 to									
30–39	−0.06881	0.00439	−6.38	−0.00849	12.34	−0.07057	102.56	0.00587	−8.53
	(0.00031)	(0.00002)	(0.01)	(0.00004)	(0.02)	(0.00032)	(0.00)	(0.00003)	(0.02)
40–49	−0.13415	0.00954	−7.11	−0.02645	19.72	−0.08264	61.60	−0.03461	25.80
	(0.00064)	(0.00004)	(0.02)	(0.00013)	(0.03)	(0.00039)	(0.00)	(0.00017)	(0.03)
50–54	−0.17226	−0.02104	12.21	−0.02611	15.16	−0.13052	75.77	0.00540	−3.13
	(0.00078)	(0.00008)	(0.02)	(0.00013)	(0.02)	(0.00061)	(0.05)	(0.00003)	(0.01)
Single, never married to									
Married	−0.25809	−0.11003	42.63	−0.03753	14.54	−0.13273	51.43	0.02221	−8.61
	(0.00096)	(0.00037)	(0.03)	(0.00018)	(0.02)	(0.00054)	(0.03)	(0.00011)	(0.02)
Div.-wid.-sep.	0.05775	−0.00537	−9.30	0.00975	16.88	0.02610	45.20	0.02727	47.21
	(0.00028)	(0.00002)	(0.02)	(0.00005)	(0.03)	(0.00012)	(0.03)	(0.00014)	(0.04)

Highest grade = 12 to								
< 10	−0.00028	0.12478	−45004.11	−0.09553	34456.05	−0.01200	4329.50	−0.01752	6320.56
	(0.00039)	(0.00050)	(61725.88)	(0.00048)	(47143.37)	(0.00006)	(5926.98)	(0.00009)	(8658.46)
10–11	−0.02252	0.00440	−19.54	−0.00229	10.17	−0.01690	75.04	−0.00773	34.34
	(0.00011)	(0.00002)	(0.05)	(0.00001)	(0.02)	(0.00008)	(0.06)	(0.00004)	(0.03)
13–15	0.00983	−0.02878	−292.81	−0.02655	−270.11	0.06390	650.14	0.00125	12.70
	(0.00010)	(0.00012)	(2.80)	(0.00013)	(2.40)	(0.00030)	(5.07)	(0.00001)	(0.10)
> 15	−0.17329	−0.11342	65.45	−0.08481	48.94	0.04682	−27.02	−0.02190	12.64
	(0.00072)	(0.00045)	(0.07)	(0.00039)	(0.04)	(0.00022)	(0.03)	(0.00011)	(0.02)
No child < 6 years of age to child									
< 6 years	0.00212	0.03731	1763.02	−0.00557	−263.19	−0.06759	−3193.65	0.03797	1794.02
	(0.00012)	(0.00015)	(103.67)	(0.00003)	(15.97)	(0.00033)	(194.88)	(0.00019)	(107.23)
Family income < \$3,000 to									
\$3,000–\$9,000	0.00364	−0.08450	−2322.85	0.06882	1891.74	0.01681	462.23	0.00250	68.81
	(0.00022)	(0.00037)	(139.38)	(0.00034)	(108.34)	(0.00008)	(27.00)	(0.00001)	(4.04)
\$9,000–\$15,000	−0.14105	−0.18756	132.98	0.03819	−27.08	−0.02034	14.42	0.02862	−20.29
	(0.00068)	(0.00084)	(0.13)	(0.00019)	(0.11)	(0.00009)	(0.04)	(0.00014)	(0.08)
> \$15,000	−0.37947	−0.33806	89.09	0.00612	−1.61	−0.08725	22.99	0.03971	−10.46
	(0.00114)	(0.00098)	(0.00)	(0.00003)	(0.01)	(0.00036)	(0.05)	(0.00020)	(0.04)

(continued)

Table 6.13 (continued)

Change from:	Unweighted eligibility term	Unweighted awareness term	Unweighted acceptance term	Unweighted enrollment term
White to				
Black	0.11936	0.10254	−0.00213	−0.07239
	(0.00025)	(0.00000)	(0.00000)	(0.00003)
Hispanic	0.04523	−0.07589	−0.00796	0.13711
	(0.00010)	(0.00003)	(0.00001)	(0.00006)
Other race/ethnicity	0.04237	−0.10664	0.00105	0.13905
	(0.00009)	(0.00004)	(0.00000)	(0.00000)
Aged 22–29 to				
30–39	0.00292	−0.01759	−0.01495	0.01270
	(0.00001)	(0.00000)	(0.00003)	(0.00000)
40–49	0.00633	−0.05442	−0.01792	−0.07575
	(0.00001)	(0.00002)	(0.00004)	(0.00003)
50–54	−0.01395	−0.05343	−0.02759	0.01166
	(0.00004)	(0.00003)	(0.00004)	(0.00000)
Single, never married to				
Married	−0.08046	−0.07888	−0.03365	0.04852
	(0.00017)	(0.00004)	(0.00004)	(0.00002)
Div.-wid.-sep.	−0.00355	0.02033	0.00566	0.05814
	(0.00001)	(0.00001)	(0.00001)	(0.00000)

Highest grade = 12 to				
< 10	0.08384	−0.18277	−0.00254	−0.03823
	(0.00017)	(0.00014)	(0.00001)	(0.00001)
10–11	0.00292	−0.00474	−0.00356	−0.01680
	(0.00001)	(0.00000)	(0.00001)	(0.00000)
13–15	−0.01898	−0.05459	0.01348	0.00270
	(0.00005)	(0.00000)	(0.00002)	(0.00000)
> 15	−0.07569	−0.17394	0.00970	−0.04777
	(0.00020)	(0.00009)	(0.00002)	(0.00002)
No child < 6 years of age to				
child < 6 years	0.02473	−0.01154	−0.01397	0.08169
	(0.00006)	(0.00001)	(0.00003)	(0.00004)
Family income < $3,000 to				
$3,000–$9,000	−0.05266	0.14643	0.00361	0.00541
	(0.00015)	(0.00006)	(0.00001)	(0.00000)
$9,000–$15,000	−0.11255	0.08099	−0.00431	0.06103
	(0.00035)	(0.00000)	(0.00001)	(0.00000)
> $15,000	−0.26155	0.01266	−0.02135	0.08726
	(0.00039)	(0.00001)	(0.00003)	(0.00000)

NOTE: Simulations use 1986 SIPP full panel data. Bootstrap standard errors appear in parentheses. The standard errors reflect variation due to the sample used to perform the simulations.
SOURCE: Heckman and Smith (2004).

Table 6.14 JTPA Participation Simulation Results—Weighted and Unweighted Effects of Changes in Characteristics on the Probability of Participation in JTPA 1986 SIPP Panel Sample of JTPA Eligibles: Male Youth (10,280 observations)

Change from:	Overall effect	Weighted eligibility term	Percent of overall	Weighted awareness term	Percent of overall	Weighted acceptance term	Percent of overall	Weighted enrollment term	Percent of overall
White to									
Black	0.18985	0.13157	69.30	0.19817	104.38	−0.08387	−44.18	−0.05602	−29.51
	(0.00359)	(0.00251)	(0.59)	(0.00360)	(1.21)	(0.00185)	(0.94)	(0.00127)	(0.59)
Hispanic	0.16202	0.27921	172.33	0.00435	2.68	−0.16337	−100.84	0.04183	25.82
	(0.00461)	(0.00559)	(2.31)	(0.00008)	(0.07)	(0.00334)	(3.13)	(0.00098)	(0.80)
Other race/ethnicity	0.11554	0.21151	183.06	0.19799	171.37	−.35420	−306.57	0.06022	52.12
	(0.00528)	(0.00417)	(6.88)	(0.00348)	(7.34)	(0.00742)	(16.67)	(0.00144)	(2.69)
Aged 16–18 to									
19–21	−0.04099	−0.05230	127.60	−0.12499	304.94	0.17496	−426.86	−0.03866	94.32
	(0.00217)	(0.00098)	(5.88)	(0.00224)	(15.65)	(0.00386)	(26.88)	(0.00091)	(5.52)
Single, never married to									
Married	−0.09644	−0.14673	152.14	0.22705	−235.42	−0.20505	212.61	0.02827	−29.31
	(0.00327)	(0.00262)	(3.74)	(0.00400)	(7.59)	(0.00430)	(4.65)	(0.00067)	(0.66)
Div.-wid.-sep.	−0.45773	−0.18594	40.62	−0.16515	36.08	−0.12806	27.98	0.02142	−4.68
	(0.00827)	(0.00319)	(0.18)	(0.00311)	(0.10)	(0.00267)	(0.16)	(0.00051)	(0.04)

Highest grade = 12 to									
< 10	0.27423	0.19428	70.85	0.00450	1.64	0.05394	19.67	0.02152	7.85
	(0.00480)	(0.00358)	(0.36)	(0.00008)	(0.01)	(0.00110)	(0.25)	(0.00051)	(0.10)
10–11	0.31709	0.15118	47.68	0.06286	19.82	0.09853	31.07	0.00451	1.42
	(0.00559)	(0.00287)	(0.35)	(0.00112)	(0.13)	(0.00200)	(0.27)	(0.00011)	(0.02)
> 12	−0.15662	−0.00644	4.11	−0.08392	53.58	−0.06819	43.54	0.00192	−1.23
	(0.00291)	(0.00012)	(0.05)	(0.00152)	(0.17)	(0.00140)	(0.20)	(0.00005)	(0.01)
No child < 6 years of age to child									
< 6 years	−0.06653	0.13831	−207.91	−0.02807	42.20	−0.20069	301.67	0.02392	−35.95
	(0.00296)	(0.00276)	(9.74)	(0.00051)	(1.50)	(0.00411)	(9.40)	(0.00057)	(1.18)
Family income < $3,000 to									
$3,000–$9,000	−0.02934	−0.38646	1317.34	−0.09657	329.20	0.47009	−1602.39	−0.01638	55.82
	(0.00890)	(0.00892)	(577.07)	(0.00178)	(147.80)	(0.00977)	(750.37)	(0.00038)	(25.52)
$9,000–$15,000	−0.62620	−0.36139	57.71	0.00376	−0.60	−0.18625	29.74	−0.08230	13.14
	(0.01208)	(0.00660)	(0.13)	(0.00007)	(0.01)	(0.00378)	(0.08)	(0.00188)	(0.08)
> $15,000	−1.13101	−0.85797	75.86	−0.07077	6.26	−0.22640	20.02	0.02411	−2.13
	(0.00927)	(0.00564)	(0.21)	(0.00126)	(0.07)	(0.00358)	(0.18)	(0.00056)	(0.04)

(continued)

Table 6.14 (continued)

Change from:	Unweighted eligibility term	Unweighted awareness term	Unweighted acceptance term	Unweighted enrollment term
White to				
Black	0.06224	0.23652	−0.01464	−0.10033
	(0.00033)	(0.00027)	(0.00011)	(0.00009)
Hispanic	0.12856	0.00515	−0.02811	0.07099
	(0.00071)	(0.00001)	(0.00023)	(0.00011)
Other race/ethnicity	0.09938	0.24597	−0.05971	0.10316
	(0.00059)	(0.00029)	(0.00051)	(0.00017)
Aged 16–18 to				
19–21	−0.02447	−0.14922	0.02848	−0.06538
	(0.00013)	(0.00014)	(0.00020)	(0.00006)
Single, never married to				
Married	−0.06715	0.28561	−0.03700	0.04882
	(0.00043)	(0.00023)	(0.00032)	(0.00007)
Div.-wid.-sep.	−0.08370	−0.18808	−0.02320	0.03693
	(0.00060)	(0.00048)	(0.00018)	(0.00006)

Highest grade = 12 to				
< 10	0.09339	0.00533	0.01010	0.03660
	(0.00051)	(0.00001)	(0.00007)	(0.00005)
10–11	0.07254	0.07497	0.01866	0.00780
	(0.00039)	(0.00009)	(0.00013)	(0.00001)
> 12	−0.00299	−0.09993	−0.01283	0.00333
	(0.00002)	(0.00013)	(0.00009)	(0.00000)
No child < 6 years of age to				
child < 6 years	0.06409	−0.03296	−0.03545	0.04130
	(0.00038)	(0.00006)	(0.00029)	(0.00006)
Family income < $3,000 to				
$3,000–$9,000	−0.13607	−0.10801	0.09427	−0.02889
	(0.00150)	(0.00018)	(0.00035)	(0.00003)
$9,000–$15,000	−0.17195	0.00445	−0.03412	−0.14599
	(0.00229)	(0.00001)	(0.00027)	(0.00013)
> $15,000	−0.57966	−0.08677	−0.05300	0.04362
	(0.00228)	(0.00010)	(0.00026)	(0.00006)

NOTE: Simulations use 1986 SIPP full panel data. Bootstrap standard errors appear in parentheses. The standard errors reflect variations due to the sample used to perform the simulation.
SOURCE: Heckman and Smith (2004).

Table 6.15 JTPA Participation Simulation Results—Weighted and Unweighted Effects of Changes in Characteristics on the Probability of Participation in JTPA 1986 SIPP Panel Sample of JTPA Eligibles: Female Youth (11,165 observations)

Change from:	Overall effect	Weighted eligibility term	Percent of overall	Weighted awareness term	Percent of overall	Weighted acceptance term	Percent of overall	Weighted enrollment term	Percent of overall
White to									
Black	0.60673	0.25958	42.78	0.15867	26.15	0.23113	38.09	−0.04265	−7.03
	(0.00343)	(0.00170)	(0.17)	(0.00122)	(0.08)	(0.00153)	(0.13)	(0.00043)	(0.04)
Hispanic	0.33973	0.13234	38.95	0.07296	21.48	0.03803	11.19	0.09640	28.38
	(0.00237)	(0.00086)	(0.18)	(0.00055)	(0.07)	(0.00031)	(0.04)	(0.00103)	(0.14)
Other race/ ethnicity	0.52914	0.21732	41.07	−0.15091	−28.52	0.39674	74.98	0.06597	12.47
	(0.00323)	(0.00135)	(0.24)	(0.00124)	(0.12)	(0.00309)	(0.24)	(0.00071)	(0.07)
Aged 16–18 to									
19–21	−0.13182	0.00600	−4.55	−0.04413	33.48	−0.09964	75.58	0.00594	−4.51
	(0.00103)	(0.00004)	(0.04)	(0.00033)	(0.09)	(0.00080)	(0.09)	(0.00006)	(0.02)
Single, never married to									
Married	−0.11438	0.04948	−43.26	0.02279	−19.93	−0.21716	189.86	0.03049	−26.66
	(0.00122)	(0.00031)	(0.52)	(0.00017)	(0.15)	(0.00170)	(0.81)	(0.00032)	(0.20)
Div.-wid.-sep.	0.43598	0.16794	38.52	−0.13812	−31.68	0.34108	78.23	0.06509	14.93
	(0.00272)	(0.00102)	(0.22)	(0.00113)	(0.13)	(0.00267)	(0.23)	(0.00070)	(0.08)

Highest grade = 12 to									
< 10	0.02402	0.10392	432.68	−0.13596	−566.07	0.03667	152.69	0.01939	80.72
	(0.00062)	(0.00064)	(10.15)	(0.00105)	(17.22)	(0.00030)	(4.69)	(0.00020)	(2.47)
10–11	−0.04111	0.00763	−18.55	−0.03043	74.01	−0.03857	93.82	0.02026	−49.28
	(0.00034)	(0.00005)	(0.16)	(0.00023)	(0.21)	(0.00032)	(0.27)	(0.00021)	(0.33)
> 12	−0.23797	−0.08057	33.86	−0.00592	2.49	−0.15552	65.35	0.00405	−1.70
	(0.00153)	(0.00052)	(0.16)	(0.00004)	(0.01)	(0.00120)	(0.16)	(0.00004)	(0.01)
No child < 6 years of age to child									
< 6 years	0.04561	0.16064	352.24	−0.01929	−42.29	−0.11019	−241.62	0.01445	31.68
	(0.00111)	(0.00095)	(7.62)	(0.00015)	(1.20)	(0.00094)	(7.36)	(0.00015)	(0.95)
Family income < $3,000 to									
$3,000–$9,000	−0.21200	−0.20549	96.93	0.04033	−19.02	−0.02672	12.60	−0.02013	9.49
	(0.00173)	(0.00166)	(0.09)	(0.00030)	(0.10)	(0.00022)	(0.08)	(0.00021)	(0.06)
$9,000–$15,000	−0.26501	−0.31212	117.78	−0.01785	6.73	0.05881	−22.19	0.00615	−2.32
	(0.00243)	(0.00277)	(0.12)	(0.00014)	(0.03)	(0.00049)	(0.11)	(0.00006)	(0.01)
> $15,000	−0.29814	−0.64432	216.11	−0.06660	22.34	0.43046	−144.38	−0.01767	5.93
	(0.00588)	(0.00390)	(3.51)	(0.00050)	(0.46)	(0.00460)	(4.09)	(0.00018)	(0.13)

(continued)

Table 6.15 (continued)

Change from:	Unweighted eligibility term	Unweighted awareness term	Unweighted acceptance term	Unweighted enrollment term
White to				
Black	0.07514	0.18894	0.08124	−0.06723
	(0.00020)	(0.00012)	(0.00038)	(0.00006)
Hispanic	0.03805	0.08826	0.01283	0.14839
	(0.00010)	(0.00004)	(0.00007)	(0.00011)
Other race/ethnicity	0.06344	−0.17801	0.13083	0.10252
	(0.00017)	(0.00019)	(0.00058)	(0.00011)
Aged 16–18 to				
19–21	0.00172	−0.05334	−0.03352	0.00931
	(0.00000)	(0.00000)	(0.00016)	(0.00001)
Single, never married to				
Married	0.01431	0.02747	−0.07153	0.04781
	(0.00004)	(0.00002)	(0.00036)	(0.00003)
Div.-wid.-sep.	0.04896	−0.16342	0.11298	0.10116
	(0.00013)	(0.00015)	(0.00052)	(0.00011)

Highest grade = 12 to				
< 10	0.03018	−0.16072	0.01233	0.03028
	(0.00008)	(0.00015)	(0.00006)	(0.00003)
10–11	0.00219	−0.03662	−0.01290	0.03163
	(0.00001)	(0.00002)	(0.00007)	(0.00003)
> 12	−0.02355	−0.00714	−0.05464	0.00635
	(0.00005)	(0.00000)	(0.00028)	(0.00001)
No child < 6 years of age to				
child < 6 years	0.04769	−0.02320	−0.03586	0.02259
	(0.00012)	(0.00002)	(0.00019)	(0.00002)
Family income < $3,000 to				
$3,000–$9,000	−0.05959	0.04868	−0.00894	−0.03154
	(0.00019)	(0.00002)	(0.00005)	(0.00002)
$9,000–$15,000	−0.09455	−0.02149	0.01981	0.00962
	(0.00035)	(0.00001)	(0.00010)	(0.00001)
> $15,000	−0.19203	−0.08038	0.11196	−0.02763
	(0.00017)	(0.00002)	(0.00045)	(0.00002)

NOTE: Simulations use 1986 SIPP full panel data. Bootstrap standard errors appear in parentheses. The standard errors reflect variations due to the sample used to perform the simulation.
SOURCE: Heckman and Smith (2004).

for the decomposition in Tables 6.12–6.15, the weighted eligibility term is given by the first term on the right-hand side of Equation (6.7), the weighted acceptance term by the second term, the weighted awareness term by the third term, and the weighted enrollment term by the fourth term. The third, fifth, seventh, and ninth columns present the percentage of the overall effect attributable to each of the four components. Thus, the third column indicates the percentage of the overall effect that results from the effect of the indicated change in x on the conditional probability of eligibility, which is given by the ratio of the weighted eligibility term to the overall effect multiplied by 100. The second panel of each table presents the *unweighted* effect of the indicated change in x on each of the conditional probabilities. This unweighted effect is just the average partial derivative (or finite difference) of the probability with respect to the characteristic.

The results for race and ethnicity are especially striking. Blacks consistently have an overall probability of participation higher than that of whites. For three of the four demographic groups, this higher overall probability decomposes into higher conditional probabilities of eligibility and awareness, but lower conditional probabilities of acceptance and enrollment. Decomposing the overall effect in this way makes it clear where blacks fall out of the participation process, and suggests that policy measures designed to increase their participation should likely focus relatively more attention on the stages of application, acceptance, and enrollment, rather than on changes in eligibility rules or on outreach efforts to increase awareness, although such measures may still bear fruit. This evidence indicates that the concerns expressed in GAO (1991) regarding minority participation may not have been misplaced. Administrative discretion may have played a role in reducing black participation in JTPA, and may continue to do so under WIA.

A different pattern emerges for the categorical age variables. For adults, older persons nearly always have lower conditional probabilities at every stage in the participation process relative to persons aged 22–29. The same is true of youth, where a modest overall negative effect for 19–21-year-olds relative to 16–18-year-olds is mirrored at each stage in the process except for the application/acceptance stage for male youth and the eligibility and enrollment stages for female youth.

Overall, being married rather than being single decreases the probability of participation in JTPA for all four demographic groups. The dominant factor lowering enrollment among married persons is a strong negative effect of marriage on the conditional probability of application/acceptance. For adult males, this negative term outweighs a positive effect of marriage on the conditional probabilities of eligibility, awareness, and enrollment. The probability of participation for divorced, widowed, or separated persons exceeds that for single persons in three of the four groups. For adult males, positive effects of having once been married on eligibility, awareness, and enrollment dominate the negative acceptance term, while all but the eligibility term are positive for adult females.

For adults, the relationship between the overall probability of participation in JTPA and years of completed schooling is roughly hill-shaped, with its peak occurring at 10–11 years of completed schooling for men and 13–15 years for women. The decompositions reveal that the overall relationship results from combining a negative relationship between years of schooling and eligibility, and generally hill-shaped relationships between schooling and awareness, application/acceptance, and enrollment. For youth, the overall relationship between participation and years of completed schooling peaks at 10–11 years for males and at less than 10 years for females.

For three of the four demographic groups, the overall effect of having an own child under six years of age in the home breaks down into a positive component due to increased conditional probabilities of eligibility and enrollment, and negative components due to decreased probabilities of awareness and acceptance. The overall effect is negative for men and positive for women.

The overall probability of participation in JTPA decreases monotonically in family income for adult males and male and female youth, and peaks in the $3,000–$9,000 category for adult females. The strong negative relationship between family income and the probability of eligibility described earlier in the chapter dominates the overall effect in almost every case. The exception is the peak for adult females, which results from the influence of a similarly peaked pattern in the relationship between family income and the conditional probabilities of awareness and of application/acceptance for that group.

Tables 6.16–6.19 present a second set of decompositions. In these tables, we decompose the probability of application/acceptance conditional on eligibility into components due to awareness and due to

Table 6.16 JTPA Simulation Results—Two-Step Decomposition Weighted Effects of Changes in Characteristics on the Probability of Acceptance into JTPA National JTPA Study Eligible Nonparticipant Sample: Adult Males (1,552 observations)

Change from:	Overall effect		Weighted awareness term		Percent of overall		Weighted acceptance term		Percent of overall	
White to										
Black	2.5149	(0.0675)	1.5521	(0.0495)	61.72	(0.66)	0.9628	(0.0257)	38.28	(0.66)
Hispanic	−2.9536	(0.0902)	−2.6335	(0.0844)	89.16	(0.25)	−0.3201	(0.0087)	10.84	(0.25)
Other race/ethnicity	5.8446	(0.1485)	−1.4193	(0.0457)	−24.28	(0.85)	7.2639	(0.1668)	124.28	(0.85)
Aged 22–29 to										
30–39	−3.7082	(0.0993)	−1.3499	(0.0433)	36.40	(0.62)	−2.3583	(0.0664)	63.60	(0.62)
40–49	−4.2680	(0.1146)	−1.2858	(0.0412)	30.13	(0.55)	−2.9822	(0.0838)	69.87	(0.55)
50–54	−2.5991	(0.0765)	0.1994	(0.0064)	−7.67	(0.22)	−2.7985	(0.0803)	107.67	(0.22)
Highest grade 12 to										
< 10	−6.5763	(0.1825)	−2.1992	(0.0693)	33.44	(0.54)	−4.3771	(0.1279)	66.56	(0.54)
10–11	−1.4067	(0.0380)	−0.7153	(0.0233)	50.85	(0.70)	−0.6914	(0.0193)	49.15	(0.70)
13–15	2.1957	(0.0557)	0.5977	(0.0192)	27.22	(0.57)	1.5980	(0.0430)	72.78	(0.58)
> 15	−7.3700	(0.2089)	−1.6050	(0.0516)	21.78	(0.40)	−5.7650	(0.1688)	78.22	(0.40)
Not receiving AFDC to										
Current AFDC receipt	−5.5477	(0.1714)	0.4306	(0.0138)	−7.76	(0.22)	−5.9783	(0.1800)	107.76	(0.23)
Not receiving Food Stamps to										
Current Food Stamp receipt	4.4612	(0.1165)	2.8726	(0.0897)	64.39	(0.68)	1.5886	(0.0424)	35.61	(0.68)
Two most recent labor force statuses from employed → employed to										

Unemployed → employed	11.1319	(0.2484)	2.8784	(0.0920)	25.86	(0.60)	8.2535	(0.1969)	74.14	(0.60)
OLF → employed	15.2249	(0.3061)	2.6670	(0.0845)	17.52	(0.45)	12.5578	(0.2646)	82.48	(0.44)
Employed → unemployed	23.9905	(0.4532)	2.8125	(0.0946)	11.72	(0.31)	21.1780	(0.3998)	88.28	(0.31)
Unemployed → unemployed	15.9797	(0.3196)	3.6041	(0.1122)	22.55	(0.55)	12.3756	(0.2652)	77.45	(0.55)
OLF → unemployed	28.6514	(0.4525)	6.4026	(0.2087)	22.35	(0.59)	22.2488	(0.3654)	77.65	(0.59)
Employed → OLF	25.9317	(0.3865)	−1.6591	(0.0530)	−6.40	(0.22)	27.5908	(0.3904)	106.40	(0.22)
Unemployed → OLF	30.8787	(0.4021)	−4.9403	(0.1627)	−16.00	(0.67)	35.8191	(0.3365)	116.00	(0.67)
OLF → OLF	6.8828	(0.1859)	−0.0298	(0.0009)	−0.43	(0.01)	6.9126	(0.1864)	100.43	(0.03)
No child < 6 years of age to										
child < 6 years	−0.9468	(0.0270)	−0.5962	(0.0190)	62.97	(0.71)	−0.3506	(0.0114)	37.03	(0.71)
Family income < $3,000 to										
$3,000–$9,000	−5.2227	(0.1744)	−0.1078	(0.0034)	2.06	(0.06)	−5.1149	(0.1725)	97.94	(0.04)
$9,000–$15,000	−2.4054	(0.0750)	−0.1520	(0.0048)	6.32	(0.18)	−2.2535	(0.0722)	93.68	(0.19)
> $15,000	−6.8375	(0.2571)	1.6230	(0.0511)	−23.74	(0.94)	−8.4605	(0.2804)	123.74	(0.94)
Corpus Christi site to										
Fort Wayne site	12.6473	(0.3162)	1.0828	(0.0346)	8.56	(0.22)	11.5644	(0.2958)	91.44	(0.23)
Jersey City site	6.3780	(0.1534)	0.3288	(0.0105)	5.16	(0.15)	6.0492	(0.1490)	94.84	(0.16)
Providence site	6.4292	(0.1691)	−1.5965	(0.0509)	−24.83	(0.95)	8.0257	(0.1824)	124.83	(0.95)
Never married to										
Currently married	−4.9098	(0.1401)	0.4562	(0.0145)	−9.29	(0.31)	−5.3660	(0.1467)	109.29	(0.31)
Married 1–24 months ago	4.3002	(0.1261)	4.2079	(0.1252)	97.85	(0.04)	0.0923	(0.0025)	2.15	(0.07)
Married > 24 months ago	5.3340	(0.1391)	3.6192	(0.1166)	67.85	(0.73)	1.7147	(0.0441)	32.15	(0.73)

NOTE: Simulations use National JTPA Study data. Bootstrap standard errors appear in parentheses. These standard errors reflect variation in the samples used to do the simulations.

SOURCE: Heckman and Smith (2004).

Table 6.17 JTPA Simulation Results—Two-Step Decomposition Weighted Effects of Changes in Characteristics on the Probability of Acceptance into JTPA National JTPA Study Eligible Nonparticipant Sample: Adult Females (2,438 observations)

Change from:	Overall effect		Weighted awareness term		Percent of overall		Weighted acceptance term		Percent of overall	
White to										
Black	0.3406	(0.0082)	0.5807	(0.0110)	170.49	(1.57)	−0.2401	(0.0044)	−70.49	(1.57)
Hispanic	2.5843	(0.0514)	−1.5509	(0.0312)	−60.01	(1.29)	4.1352	(0.0709)	160.01	(1.29)
Other race/ethnicity	−0.5642	(0.0140)	−0.9772	(0.0192)	173.22	(1.55)	0.4130	(0.0074)	−73.22	(1.55)
Aged 22–29 to										
30–39	−1.5293	(0.0272)	−0.2304	(0.0044)	15.07	(0.18)	−1.2989	(0.0238)	84.93	(0.17)
40–49	−1.0421	(0.0184)	−0.3973	(0.0075)	38.12	(0.30)	−0.6449	(0.0120)	61.88	(0.30)
50–54	−0.9142	(0.0163)	−0.3667	(0.0071)	40.12	(0.30)	−0.5474	(0.0102)	59.88	(0.30)
Highest grade 12 to										
< 10	−2.6424	(0.0495)	−2.0099	(0.0393)	76.06	(0.21)	−0.6325	(0.0119)	23.94	(0.21)
10–11	−0.8521	(0.0151)	−0.2605	(0.0050)	30.57	(0.27)	−0.5916	(0.0109)	69.43	(0.27)
13–15	1.4035	(0.0265)	−0.5493	(0.0103)	−39.14	(0.72)	1.9527	(0.0332)	139.14	(0.72)
> 15	−3.5102	(0.0668)	−1.4343	(0.0283)	40.86	(0.26)	−2.0760	(0.0410)	59.14	(0.26)
Not receiving AFDC to										
Current AFDC receipt	−3.9558	(0.0809)	−0.0051	(0.0001)	0.13	(0.00)	−3.9507	(0.0808)	99.87	(0.00)
Not receiving Food Stamps to										
Current Food Stamp receipt	2.4674	(0.0416)	1.3765	(0.0242)	55.79	(0.30)	1.0908	(0.0201)	44.21	(0.30)
Two most recent labor force statuses from employed → employed to										

Unemployed → employed	10.1978	(0.1374)	0.2336	(0.0044)	2.29	(0.04)	9.9642	(0.1353)	97.71	(0.00)
OLF → employed	6.0237	(0.0963)	−0.6424	(0.0123)	−10.66	(0.17)	6.6660	(0.1040)	110.66	(0.18)
Employed → unemployed	20.0536	(0.2370)	1.9825	(0.0363)	9.89	(0.15)	18.0711	(0.2195)	90.11	(0.15)
Unemployed → unemployed	19.1886	(0.2369)	1.1889	(0.0234)	6.20	(0.12)	17.9997	(0.2287)	93.80	(0.11)
OLF → unemployed	13.1690	(0.1825)	0.8147	(0.0151)	6.19	(0.09)	12.3543	(0.1737)	93.81	(0.09)
Employed → OLF	7.3442	(0.1160)	0.2988	(0.0056)	4.07	(0.06)	7.0454	(0.1125)	95.93	(0.04)
Unemployed → OLF	13.9890	(0.1926)	−0.6109	(0.0118)	−4.37	(0.08)	14.5999	(0.1989)	104.37	(0.05)
OLF → OLF	4.2671	(0.0845)	−0.9764	(0.0188)	−22.88	(0.45)	5.2435	(0.0952)	122.88	(0.46)
No child < 6 years of age to										
child < 6 years	−0.8987	(0.0173)	−0.1516	(0.0029)	16.87	(0.21)	−0.7471	(0.0151)	83.13	(0.20)
Family income < $,3000 to										
$3,000–$9,000	2.1865	(0.0390)	1.1198	(0.0208)	51.22	(0.38)	1.0667	(0.0215)	48.78	(0.38)
$9,000–$15,000	1.0367	(0.0183)	0.6227	(0.0117)	60.07	(0.38)	0.4140	(0.0083)	39.93	(0.37)
> $15,000	0.5172	(0.0107)	−0.0683	(0.0013)	−13.20	(0.22)	0.5855	(0.0116)	113.20	(0.23)
Corpus Christi site to										
Fort Wayne site	7.6811	(0.1556)	−0.6637	(0.0124)	−8.64	(0.19)	8.3448	(0.1608)	108.64	(0.18)
Jersey City site	5.4065	(0.0990)	−0.7513	(0.0147)	−13.90	(0.24)	6.1578	(0.1084)	113.90	(0.23)
Providence site	7.3382	(0.1506)	−2.0068	(0.0412)	−27.35	(0.62)	9.3450	(0.1711)	127.35	(0.62)
Never married to										
Currently married	−3.7900	(0.0758)	−0.3984	(0.0077)	10.51	(0.13)	−3.3915	(0.0697)	89.49	(0.12)
Married 1–24 months ago	3.1004	(0.0569)	−0.0496	(0.0009)	−1.60	(0.02)	3.1499	(0.0576)	101.60	(0.00)
Married > 24 months ago	6.3540	(0.1107)	0.5205	(0.0100)	8.19	(0.11)	5.8335	(0.1038)	91.81	(0.12)

NOTE: Simulations use National JTPA Study data. Bootstrap standard errors appear in parentheses. These standard errors reflect variation in the samples used to do the simulations.
SOURCE: Heckman and Smith (2004).

Table 6.18 JTPA Simulation Results—Two-Step Decomposition Weighted Effects of Changes in Characteristics on the Probability of Acceptance into JTPA National JTPA Study Eligible Nonparticipant Sample: Male Youth (530 observations)

Change from:	Overall effect		Weighted awareness term		Percent of overall		Weighted acceptance term		Percent of overall	
White to										
Black	4.8041	(0.2699)	6.6041	(0.2893)	137.47	(2.52)	−1.7999	(0.0720)	−37.47	(2.52)
Hispanic	5.9390	(0.2145)	0.2688	(0.0123)	4.53	(0.22)	5.6701	(0.2112)	95.47	(0.22)
Other race/ethnicity	−3.1888	(0.3835)	6.6837	(0.3157)	−209.60	(28.11)	−9.8724	(0.4783)	309.60	(28.11)
Aged 16–18 to										
19–21	−1.1238	(0.2264)	−5.3078	(0.2366)	472.32	(109.67)	4.1840	(0.1576)	−372.32	(109.67)
Never married to										
Currently married	2.1384	(0.3343)	7.4097	(0.3489)	346.50	(54.91)	−5.2712	(0.2273)	−246.50	(54.91)
Div.-wid.-sep.	−3.4641	(0.1330)	−2.0780	(0.0950)	59.99	(1.04)	−1.3862	(0.0561)	40.01	(1.04)
Highest grade 12 to										
< 10	−0.3731	(0.0267)	−0.6401	(0.0292)	171.56	(6.06)	0.2670	(0.0103)	−71.56	(6.06)
10–11	1.9636	(0.0810)	1.6799	(0.0760)	85.55	(0.59)	0.2837	(0.0110)	14.45	(0.59)
> 12	−1.8382	(0.0667)	−0.6697	(0.0305)	36.43	(1.04)	−1.1685	(0.0468)	63.57	(1.04)
Not receiving AFDC to										
Current AFDC receipt	−11.1117	(0.4965)	−4.2387	(0.1942)	38.15	(0.74)	−6.8730	(0.3298)	61.85	(0.74)
Not receiving Food Stamps to										
Current Food Stamp receipt	3.7423	(0.1253)	1.8386	(0.0835)	49.13	(1.20)	1.9037	(0.0692)	50.87	(1.20)

Two most recent labor force statuses from employed → employed to										
Unemployed → employed	14.4300	(0.3934)	1.1809	(0.0536)	8.18	(0.40)	13.2491	(0.3886)	91.82	(0.40)
OLF → employed	−4.5935	(0.2030)	0.5569	(0.0255)	−12.12	(0.57)	−5.1505	(0.2159)	112.12	(0.57)
Employed → unemployed	16.6120	(0.4569)	3.5322	(0.1670)	21.26	(0.93)	13.0798	(0.4174)	78.74	(0.93)
Unemployed → unemployed	10.3782	(0.2823)	3.2308	(0.1478)	31.13	(1.11)	7.1474	(0.2211)	68.87	(1.11)
OLF → unemployed	0.3517	(0.0666)	−1.2450	(0.0573)	−354.01	(72.52)	1.5967	(0.0634)	454.01	(72.52)
Employed → OLF	26.9129	(1.1099)	−8.8298	(0.4202)	−32.81	(2.70)	35.7427	(0.8344)	132.81	(2.70)
Unemployed → OLF	5.5548	(0.3447)	7.5616	(0.3597)	136.13	(2.89)	−2.0068	(0.0916)	−36.13	(2.89)
OLF → OLF	6.9113	(0.5004)	−6.8417	(0.3147)	−98.99	(10.08)	13.7529	(0.4157)	198.99	(10.08)
No child < 6 years of age to										
child < 6 years	−9.2754	(0.4498)	−1.9897	(0.0911)	21.45	(0.67)	−7.2856	(0.3823)	78.55	(0.67)
Family income < $,3000 to										
$3,000–$9,000	9.3512	(0.4811)	−4.6211	(0.2073)	−49.42	(3.64)	13.9722	(0.4734)	149.42	(3.64)
$9,000–$15,000	−2.6233	(0.1288)	−3.1610	(0.1402)	120.50	(1.17)	0.5377	(0.0256)	−20.50	(1.17)
> $15,000	−4.7303	(0.1979)	−3.8578	(0.1714)	81.56	(0.69)	−0.8725	(0.0425)	18.44	(0.69)
Corpus Christi site to										
Fort Wayne site	10.3470	(0.3620)	0.3657	(0.0169)	3.53	(0.17)	9.9813	(0.3578)	96.47	(0.17)
Jersey City site	3.0515	(0.1968)	−1.4890	(0.0675)	−48.80	(3.80)	4.5406	(0.2061)	148.80	(3.80)
Providence site	18.4090	(0.6361)	−2.3738	(0.1081)	−12.89	(0.76)	20.7827	(0.6359)	112.89	(0.75)

NOTE: Simulations use National JTPA Study data. Bootstrap standard errors appear in parentheses. These standard errors reflect variation in the samples used to do the simulations.
SOURCE: Heckman and Smith (2004).

Table 6.19 JTPA Simulation Results—Two-Step Decomposition Weighted Effects of Changes in Characteristics on the Probability of Acceptance into JTPA National JTPA Study Eligible Nonparticipant Sample: Female Youth (701 observations)

Change from:	Overall effect		Weighted awareness term		Percent of overall		Weighted acceptance term		Percent of overall	
White to										
Black	3.9275	(0.1724)	3.0290	(0.1451)	77.12	(0.49)	0.8985	(0.0322)	22.88	(0.49)
Hispanic	1.0273	(0.0415)	0.5037	(0.0249)	49.03	(0.75)	0.5236	(0.0189)	50.97	(0.75)
Other race/ethnicity	2.8539	(0.1085)	−2.4043	(0.1197)	−84.25	(5.34)	5.2582	(0.1592)	184.25	(5.34)
Aged 16–18 to										
19–21	−2.3024	(0.0867)	−0.5579	(0.0272)	24.23	(0.54)	−1.7445	(0.0634)	75.77	(0.54)
Never married to										
Currently married	−1.5024	(0.0587)	0.6539	(0.0321)	−43.52	(1.63)	−2.1563	(0.0833)	143.52	(1.63)
Div.-wid.-sep.	−1.1802	(0.0922)	−2.5635	(0.1267)	217.21	(7.55)	1.3833	(0.0481)	−117.21	(7.55)
Highest grade 12 to										
< 10	−2.0172	(0.0973)	−2.0554	(0.0984)	101.89	(0.00)	0.0381	(0.0014)	−1.89	(0.05)
10–11	−1.7373	(0.0661)	−0.4037	(0.0200)	23.24	(0.50)	−1.3336	(0.0487)	76.76	(0.51)
> 12	1.0272	(0.0355)	−0.0518	(0.0025)	−5.04	(0.16)	1.0790	(0.0375)	105.04	(0.15)
Not receiving AFDC to										
Current AFDC receipt	−2.3463	(0.0926)	1.2829	(0.0633)	−54.68	(2.33)	−3.6292	(0.1378)	154.68	(2.33)
Not receiving Food Stamps to										
Current Food Stamp receipt	6.5595	(0.2010)	0.1105	(0.0054)	1.68	(0.06)	6.4490	(0.1971)	98.32	(0.07)

Two most recent labor force statuses from employed → employed to										
Unemployed → employed	9.5744	(0.2550)	−0.4118	(0.0203)	−4.30	(0.18)	9.9862	(0.2662)	104.30	(0.18)
OLF → employed	11.3506	(0.2832)	−1.8182	(0.0898)	−16.02	(0.81)	13.1688	(0.3136)	116.02	(0.81)
Employed → unemployed	24.0502	(0.4336)	−1.4540	(0.0712)	−6.05	(0.31)	25.5041	(0.4422)	106.05	(0.32)
Unemployed → unemployed	17.0906	(0.4181)	1.2007	(0.0580)	7.03	(0.29)	15.8899	(0.3908)	92.97	(0.29)
OLF → unemployed	21.6456	(0.4132)	0.3991	(0.0197)	1.84	(0.09)	21.2465	(0.4105)	98.16	(0.08)
Employed → OLF	8.6803	(0.2773)	1.4078	(0.0686)	16.22	(0.52)	7.2725	(0.2306)	83.78	(0.53)
Unemployed → OLF	7.1564	(0.2625)	3.3152	(0.1614)	46.32	(0.97)	3.8412	(0.1313)	53.68	(0.97)
OLF → OLF	4.6998	(0.1774)	−1.0262	(0.0503)	−21.84	(0.98)	5.7260	(0.2065)	121.84	(0.99)
No child < 6 years of age to										
child < 6 years	−1.3768	(0.0594)	−0.8447	(0.0417)	61.36	(0.74)	−0.5320	(0.0210)	38.64	(0.74)
Family income < $3,000 to										
$3,000–$9,000	−0.8170	(0.0328)	0.1014	(0.0050)	−12.41	(0.43)	−0.9184	(0.0366)	112.41	(0.43)
$9,000–$15,000	−0.7310	(0.0416)	−0.9901	(0.0490)	135.45	(1.50)	0.2591	(0.0101)	−35.45	(1.50)
> $15,000	8.3821	(0.2512)	−1.1948	(0.0593)	−14.25	(0.59)	9.5768	(0.2877)	114.25	(0.59)
Corpus Christi site to										
Fort Wayne site	3.5282	(0.1269)	0.3522	(0.0173)	9.98	(0.30)	3.1761	(0.1138)	90.02	(0.30)
Jersey City site	0.3881	(0.0532)	−1.5274	(0.0769)	−393.62	(69.52)	1.9155	(0.0728)	493.62	(69.53)
Providence site	3.5378	(0.1675)	−2.1585	(0.1040)	−61.01	(3.86)	5.6963	(0.2075)	161.01	(3.86)

NOTE: Simulations use National JTPA Study data. Bootstrap standard errors appear in parentheses. These standard errors reflect variation in the samples used to do the simulations.
SOURCE: Heckman and Smith (2004).

application/acceptance given awareness. Omitting the stages of eligibility and enrollment allows us to simulate using the same ENP and control data from the National JTPA Study that we use to estimate the conditional probabilities of awareness and of application/acceptance. Omitting the enrollment stage allows us to include variables representing recent labor force status transitions, which are not available in the treatment group data we use to estimate the probability of enrollment. Otherwise, the format of the tables and the construction of the individual terms parallels that for the decompositions already discussed.

The basic patterns for those variables, such as age and schooling, included in the earlier decompositions remain essentially the same as for the decompositions previously discussed, so we do not dwell on them here. Of great interest are the decompositions of the overall effects of family receipt of AFDC and Food Stamps on the application/acceptance probabilities. The overall effect of AFDC receipt is negative for all four groups. For both groups of adults, the overall effect decomposes into a small effect due to awareness, combined with a large negative effect of living in a family receiving AFDC on the probability of application/acceptance conditional on awareness. For male youth, living in a family receiving AFDC has negative effects of equal size on awareness and on application/acceptance given awareness. For female youth positive awareness and negative application and acceptance effects cancel to yield a small overall effect.

All four demographic groups show a positive impact of living in a family receiving Food Stamps on the probability of application/acceptance. For all the groups except female youth, this effect decomposes into roughly equal positive effects of Food Stamp receipt on the probabilities of awareness and of application/acceptance conditional on awareness. For female youth, the contribution of the awareness term is negligible, leaving the impact of living in a family receiving Food Stamps on application/acceptance to dominate the overall effect. Interpreting the effect of AFDC receipt as measuring the difference between receiving both AFDC and Food Stamps and just Food Stamps, we find that AFDC receipt primarily discourages application/acceptance.

Finally, examination of the decompositions for the variables representing the two most recent labor force statuses at the time of random assignment or eligibility screening shows that in all cases it is the effect of these statuses on the probability of application/acceptance conditional on awareness that accounts for their large positive effects on the unconditional probability of application/acceptance. The estimated effects of labor force status transitions on awareness are small and are of mixed sign, with negative estimated effects usually associated with transitions out of the labor force.

These decompositions offer unique insights regarding the effects of characteristics such as race, age, education, transfer program participation, labor force status, and family income on the various stages of the process by which individuals select and are selected into the JTPA program. For many characteristics, such as race and ethnicity, the same characteristic has competing effects at different stages of the process. Other characteristics, such as age among adults, operate in the same direction on the conditional probabilities of program eligibility, awareness, application/acceptance, and formal enrollment. Sorting out the effects of particular characteristics at each step enriches our understanding of the overall participation process and demonstrates quite clearly that much of the action in terms of subgroup differences arises at stages in the participation process over which JTPA staff have little or no control.

SUMMARY AND CONCLUSIONS

This chapter lays out a framework for studying the determinants of participation in social programs using data on random samples of individuals at each stage in the participation process. We outline the evidence our framework can provide regarding cream skimming by program staff, perhaps motivated by the incentives resulting from administrative performance standards, in the context of what we call mutually voluntary programs. In such programs, participation depends on the choices of both potential participants and program staff. In that context, our framework can provide only suggestive evidence for or against cream skimming based on characteristics observed by both the researcher and the program staff, except in the special case where program staff completely control certain stages of the process. Except in that special case, our framework cannot provide the sort of definitive positive evidence of caseworker responses to performance incentives obtained by studies that rely on exogenous variation in the existence or nature of those incentives, such as Courty, Kim, and Marschke (forthcoming). When caseworkers (or other program staff) have little or no control over specific stages of the process, our framework also reveals the importance of factors other than cream skimming in generating differences in participation among groups.

We apply our framework to data from the JTPA program, which allows us to decompose participation into the stages of eligibility, awareness, application/acceptance, and enrollment. From the perspective of this volume, two major empirical findings emerge from this analysis. Although they arise from data on JTPA, the similarity between JTPA and other programs (including its successor WIA) documented in Chapter 2 suggests that they likely apply more broadly.

The first major finding is that much of the action in terms of differences in participation rates across groups occurs at stages in the participation process over which program staff have little or no control. This finding highlights the dangers of inferring cream skimming from simple comparisons of program participants and program eligibles.

The second major finding is that we find only modest evidence of cream skimming at the stages of the participation process where JTPA caseworkers arguably do have some influence, namely enrollment, and to a lesser extent, application and acceptance. Several factors may account for this lack of strong evidence, particularly relative to the amount of attention cream skimming receives in discussions of performance management systems for employment and training programs.

First, caseworkers may have goals that conflict with those of the performance management system. Given the relatively indirect and low-powered incentives offered by the system, they may choose to indulge those goals. Heckman, Smith, and Taber (1996) use data from Corpus Christi, the only site in the NJS to collect good data on applicants, to study the transition from application to enrollment. They find evidence that caseworkers prefer applicants with relatively weak, rather than relatively strong, expected labor market outcomes in the absence of the program. This suggests that caseworker preferences for serving the most disadvantaged may overcome the incentives provided by the performance standards system in some contexts.

Second, JTPA caseworkers faced many constraints other than the performance standards system. Local JTPA offices faced political constraints emanating from politicians, businesspeople, community groups, and service providers. For example, Smith (1992) shows that three of the four sites analyzed here underserve (relative to its representation in the eligible population) the race/ethnic group locally in the majority, even when that group is black. This may reflect political pressures to cater to marginal voting blocks. Some or all of these other pressures may weigh against the incentives for cream skimming provided by the performance measures. They may also lead program staff to focus on alternative forms of strategic behavior aimed at improving their measured performance, such as those discussed in Chapter 7.

Third, Courty, Kim, and Marschke (forthcoming) suggest a role for the regression model developed by the USDOL and used to adjust the performance standards faced by local JTPA offices for differences in participants' observed characteristics. Although optional for states at the time, all of the states with sites in the NJS used the regression adjustment model. The model relied on data from prior years on the relationship between participants' characteristics and their postprogram labor market outcomes. If the model worked as intended, it should have diminished or even eliminated the incentive sites faced to cream-skim based on the observed characteristics included in the adjustment model. Many of those same characteristics appear in our model, with the result that if the regression adjustment did its job, we should not expect to find much evidence of cream skimming in our analysis. Of course, program staff may still have tried very hard to select participants based on characteristics not included in the adjustment model.

Fourth, the empirical patterns generated by participant choices may simply overshadow the efforts of the caseworkers, even at the stages of the participation process where caseworkers have the most influence.

Overall, the results of our empirical analysis provide valuable insights into the importance of cream skimming under JTPA and suggest the value of a similar but richer analysis using data from the current WIA program.

Notes

1. In addition to issues related to the effects of performance standards, Heckman and Smith (2004) focus on how decomposing the participation process illuminates the causes of differences in program participation across groups more generally and how it contributes to the selection and specification of econometric evaluation estimators.
2. More recent work in this area includes Aizer (2007); Bitler, Currie, and Scholz (2003); Burton, Macher, and Mayo (2007); Dahan and Nisan (2009); and Kleven and Kopczuk (2008).
3. A related literature considers how participants get allocated to services within programs that provide more than one service. See Plesca and Smith (2007) and Mitnik (2009) and the references therein.
4. The act also specifies additional eligibility criteria for several small groups. In the Survey of Income and Program Participation (SIPP) data used in our analysis, we are not able to accurately measure foster child status, disability, or homelessness on a monthly basis, and so are unable to implement the special eligibility rules applicable to these groups in selecting our sample of eligibles. However, these groups represent a very small portion of the overall eligible population, and many of those eligible under the special provisions will also be eligible under the basic family income and program participation criteria described in the text.
5. Program year 1991 covers the period from July 1991 to June 1992.
6. Two other details regarding JTPA eligibility deserve note. First, the implementation of the rules varied somewhat across localities, as states and training centers had some discretion over exactly what did and did not constitute family income and what did and did not constitute a family for the purposes of the program. Devine and Heckman (1996) find these differences too small to affect the patterns discussed here. Second, the eligibility rules described here are those in place at the time our data were collected. Some small changes in rules took place after that time; see Devine and Heckman (1996) or USDOL (1993).
7. See Doolittle and Traeger (1990) for a discussion of the implementation of the NJS and Bloom et al. (1997) and Orr et al. (1996) for summaries of the impact estimates.
8. Appendices A and B in Heckman and Smith (2003) provide additional detail regarding the NJS and SIPP samples used in our analyses.
9. Doolittle and Traeger (1990), Kemple, Doolittle, and Wallace (1993), and Orr et al. (1996) all provide even more detail about the sites in the National JTPA Study.
10. We present mean derivatives and not derivatives evaluated at the mean of the x. That is, we calculate the derivative (or finite difference for binary variables) for each observation and report the (weighted) sample mean. The literature sometimes refers to these as mean marginal effects. The standard errors take account of the use of multiple observations on the same individuals.
11. The English language ability variable should be interpreted with caution as it arises from different underlying measures in the ENP and control group samples.

For the ENPs, lack of English ability is measured by the language in which the respondent chose to complete the baseline survey, while for the controls it is obtained from a question on language preference administered around the time of random assignment.

12. Appendix C of Heckman and Smith (2003) provides additional details regarding the methods used to obtain the reported results.
13. Heckman and Smith (1999) discuss the importance of these variables at greater length. See also Card and Sullivan (1988) and Dolton and Smith (2010).
14. Heckman, Smith and Taber (1998) discuss nonenrollment within the experimental treatment group and its implications for the evaluation of JTPA. See also the general discussions of treatment group dropout and control group substitution in Heckman et al. (2000) and Heckman, LaLonde, and Smith (1999).
15. Appendix C of Heckman and Smith (2003) contains a detailed discussion of the simulations.

References

Aizer, Anna. 2007. "Public Health Insurance, Program Take-Up and Child Health." *Review of Economics and Statistics* 89(3): 400–415.

Barnow, Burt. 1993. "Getting It Right: Thirty Years of Changing Federal, State, and Local Relationships in Employment and Training Programs." *Publius: The Journal of Federalism* 23(3): 75–94.

Becker, Gary. 1964. *Human Capital: A Theoretical and Empirical Analysis, with Special Reference to Education.* New York: Columbia University Press.

Bitler, Marianne, Janet Currie, and Karl Scholz. 2003. "WIC Eligibility and Participation." *Journal of Human Resources* 38(Supplement): 1139–1179.

Bloom, Howard, Larry Orr, Stephen Bell, George Cave, Fred Doolittle, Winston Lin, and Johannes Bos. 1997. "The Benefits and Costs of JTPA Title II-A Programs: Findings from the National Job Training Partnership Act Study." *Journal of Human Resources* 32(3): 549–576.

Burton, Mark, Jeffrey Macher, and John Mayo. 2007. "Understanding Participation in Social Programs: Why Don't Households Pick Up the Lifeline?" *B.E. Journal of Economic Analysis and Policy: Topics* 7(1): Article 57.

Card, David, and Daniel Sullivan. 1988. "Measuring the Effect of Subsidized Training Programs on Movements In and Out of Employment." *Econometrica* 56(3): 497–530.

Courty, Pascal, Do Han Kim, and Gerald Marschke. Forthcoming. "Curbing Cream Skimming: Evidence on Enrollment Incentives." *Labour Economics*.

Courty, Pascal, and Gerald Marschke. 2008. "A General Test for Distortions in Performance Measures." *Review of Economics and Statistics* 90(3): 428–441.

Cragg, Michael. 1997. "Performance Incentives in the Public Sector: Evidence from the Job Training Partnership Act." *Journal of Law, Economics, and Organization* 13(1): 147–168.

Currie, Janet. 1996. "The Take-Up of Social Benefits." In *Poverty, the Distribution of Income, and Public Policy*, Alan Auerbach, David Card, and John Quigley, eds. New York: Russell Sage, pp. 80–148.

Dahan, Momi, and Udi Nisan. 2009. "The Effect of Benefit Levels on Take-Up Rates: Evidence from a Natural Experiment." *International Tax and Public Finance* 17(2): 151–173.

Devine, Theresa, and James Heckman. 1996. "The Structure and Consequences of Eligibility Rules for a Social Program." In *Research in Labor Economics,* Vol. 15, Solomon Polachek, ed. Greenwich, CT: JAI Press, pp. 111–170.

Dolton, Peter, and Jeffrey Smith. 2010. "The Impact of the UK New Deal for Lone Parents on Benefit Receipt." Unpublished manuscript. University of Michigan, Ann Arbor, MI.

Doolittle, Fred, and Linda Traeger. 1990. *Implementing the National JTPA Study*. New York, NY: Manpower Demonstration Research Corporation.

Forsythe, Dall, ed. 2001. *Quicker, Better, Cheaper? Managing Performance in American Government*. Albany, NY: Rockefeller Institute Press.

General Accounting Office (GAO). 1991. *Job Training Partnership Act: Racial and Gender Disparities in Services*. Report to the Chairman, Legislation and National Security Subcommittee, Committee on Government Operations, House of Representatives. HRD-91-148. Washington, DC: GAO.

Heckman, James, Neil Hohmann, Jeffrey Smith, and Michael Khoo. 2000. "Substitution and Drop Out Bias in Social Experiments: A Study of an Influential Social Experiment." *Quarterly Journal of Economics* 115(2): 651–694.

Heckman, James, Robert LaLonde, and Jeffrey Smith. 1999. "The Economics and Econometrics of Active Labor Market Programs." In *Handbook of Labor Economics,* Vol. 3A, Orley Ashenfelter and David Card, eds. Amsterdam: North-Holland, pp. 1865–2097.

Heckman, James, and Jeffrey Smith. 1999. "The Pre-Programme Dip and the Determinants of Participation in a Social Programme: Implications for Simple Programme Evaluation Strategies." *Economic Journal* 109(457): 313–348.

———. 2003. "The Determinants of Participation in a Social Program: Evidence from a Prototypical Job Training Program." NBER Working Paper No. 9818. Cambridge, MA: National Bureau of Economic Research.

———. 2004. "The Determinants of Participation in a Social Program: Evidence from a Prototypical Job Training Program." *Journal of Labor Economics* 22(2): 243–298.

Heckman, James, Jeffrey Smith, and Christopher Taber. 1996. "What Do Bureaucrats Do? The Effects of Performance Standards and Bureaucratic Preferences on Acceptance into the JTPA Program." In *Advances in the Study of Entrepreneurship, Innovation, and Economic Growth,* Vol. 7: *Reinventing Government and the Problem of Bureaucracy,* Gary Libecap, ed. Greenwich, CT: JAI Press, pp. 191–217.

———. 1998. "Accounting for Dropouts in Evaluations of Social Programs." *Review of Economics and Statistics* 80(1): 1–14.

Heinrich, Carolyn, and Laurence Lynn, eds. 2000. *Governance and Performance: New Perspectives*. Washington, DC: Georgetown University Press.

Kemple, James, Fred Doolittle, and John Wallace. 1993. *The National JTPA Study: Site Characteristics and Participation Patterns*. New York: Manpower Demonstration Research Corporation.

Kleven, Henrik, and Wojciech Kopczuk. 2008. "Transfer Program Complexity and the Take-Up of Social Benefits." NBER Working Paper No. 14301. Cambridge, MA: National Bureau of Economic Research.

Leigh, Duane. 1995. *Assisting Workers Displaced by Structural Change*. Kalamazoo, MI: W.E. Upjohn Institute for Employment Research.

Meyer, Bruce, Wallace Mok, and James Sullivan. 2009. "The Under-Reporting of Transfers in Household Surveys: Its Nature and Consequences." NBER Working Paper No. 15181. Cambridge, MA: National Bureau of Economic Research.

Mitnik, Oscar. 2009. "How Do Training Programs Assign Participants to Training? Characterizing the Assignment Rules of Government Agencies for Welfare-to-Work Programs in California." IZA Discussion Paper No. 4024. Bonn, Germany: IZA.

Orr, Larry, Howard Bloom, Stephen Bell, Fred Doolittle, Winston Lin, and George Cave. 1996. *Does Training Work for the Disadvantaged? Evidence from the National JTPA Study*. Washington, DC: Urban Institute Press.

Osborne, David, and Ted Gaebler. 1992. *Reinventing Government: How the Entrepreneurial Spirit is Transforming the Public Sector*. New York: Basic Books.

Osborne, David, and Peter Plastrik. 1997. *Banishing Bureaucracy: The Five Strategies for Reinventing Government*. Reading, MA: Addison-Wesley.

O'Shea, Daniel, and Christopher King. 2001. *The Workforce Investment Act of 1998: Restructuring Workforce Development Initiatives in States and Localities*. Report No. 12. Albany, NY: Nelson Rockefeller Institute of Government.

Parsons, Donald. 1991. "Self-Screening in Targeted Public Transfer Programs." *Journal of Political Economy* 99(4): 859–876.

Plesca, Miana, and Jeffrey Smith. 2007. "Evaluating Multi-Treatment Programs: Theory and Evidence from the U.S. Job Training Partnership Act." *Empirical Economics* 32(2): 491–528.

Radin, Beryl. 2006. *Challenging the Performance Movement: Accountability, Complexity and Democratic Values*. Washington, DC: Georgetown University Press.

Skedinger, Per, and Barbro Widerstedt. 2007. "Cream Skimming in Employment Programmes for the Disabled? Evidence from Sweden." *International Journal of Manpower* 28(8): 694–714.

Smith, Jeffrey. 1992. *The JTPA Selection Process: A Descriptive Analysis*. Report prepared for the U.S. Department of Labor, Washington, DC.

Smith, Jeffrey, and Alexander Whalley. 2009. "How Well Do We Measure Public Job Training?" Unpublished manuscript. University of Michigan, Ann Arbor, MI.

Social Policy Research Associates. 2004. *The Workforce Investment Act after Five Years: Results from the National Evaluation of the Implementation of WIA*. Report prepared for the USDOL-ETA, Office of Policy Development, Evaluation and Research. Oakland, CA: SPRA.

Tienda, Marta, and Leif Jensen. 1988. "Poverty and Minorities: A Quarter-Century Profile of Color and Socioeconomic Disadvantage." In *Divided Opportunities: Minorities, Poverty and Social Policy*, Gary Sandefur and Marta Tienda, eds. New York: Plenum, pp. 25–33.

U.S. Department of Labor (USDOL). 1993. *Title II Eligibility Documentation*. Washington, DC: USDOL, Employment and Training Administration.

———. 1998. *Summary of Workforce Development Provisions of the Workforce Investment Act of 1998 (P.L. 105-220)*. Washington, DC: USDOL, Employment and Training Administration.

Weber, Andrea. 2008. "Individual Incentives in Program Participation: Splitting Up the Process in Assignment and Enrollment." IZA Discussion Paper No. 3404. Bonn, Germany: IZA.

7

Measuring Government Performance

An Overview of Dysfunctional Responses

Pascal Courty
Gerald Marschke

Explicit performance measurement systems may elicit unintended and dysfunctional responses, also known as gaming responses. Understanding when such responses take place, their extent and their nature, is essential for improving the design of measurement systems and the overall effectiveness of performance incentives. This concern is reflected in the recent growth in empirical studies focusing on unintended behavioral responses to explicit incentives. We review this literature and try to provide a unifying framework to put into perspective the various classes of dysfunctional responses that have been identified in practice. We use this framework to discuss implications for the design of performance measurement systems.

The performance measure is the rule used to collect and aggregate the data generated by the agent's actions. The performance outcome is the value generated when that rule is applied to specific data. The next section proposes a formal classification of dysfunctional responses based on the terminology of the multitasking literature. Dysfunctional responses occur when the performance measure does not communicate correctly the marginal impact of decision making on the true objective of the organization. We distinguish three kinds of dysfunctional responses: 1) accounting manipulations, which are responses that boost the performance outcome but have no other impact on the organization; 2) gaming responses, which boost the performance outcome and have a negative impact on the organization; and 3) marginal misallocations, which have a positive impact on the organization but are suboptimal in the sense that alternative allocations would have a higher impact.

This classification is useful because it can help guide the organization's response to different dysfunctional behaviors. In the case of accounting manipulation, for example, the organization only has to invert the performance inflation relation and appropriately discount the rewards to performance achievement. If this cannot be done satisfactorily, however, accounting manipulations will have an indirect negative impact on the organization because the information contained in performance outcomes may be misinterpreted. Gaming responses should unambiguously be eliminated as they have both a direct negative impact on the organization (misallocation of resources) and an indirect one (misinterpretation of outcomes). Marginal misallocations often originate from the fact that the performance measure is too coarse and does not capture some dimensions of value added. The typical remedy is to complement the performance measure with finer measures or with alternative evaluation methods (i.e., subjective performance evaluation).[1]

After that we summarize the empirical literature on dysfunctional responses to performance measurement systems in public and private sector organizations, with an emphasis on the former. We then review the evidence on dysfunctional responses in the JTPA organization. Our point of departure is the earlier discussion of the weaknesses of the JTPA incentive system presented in Chapter 4. We exploit the analytical framework introduced there to understand the sources and consequences of dysfunctional responses. We conclude that section with some thoughts on the implications of the JTPA experience for WIA and its new performance incentive system.

The chapter ends with an assessment of the extent to which dysfunctional responses may impede the performance of measurement systems and draws lessons for policymakers. An important lesson of this review is that much progress has been made in identifying dysfunctional responses. A growing literature has produced studies that go beyond anecdotal reports and impressionistic evidence and try to identify dysfunctional behavior and measure performance inflation. Still, we find that this literature typically focuses on a narrow set of responses. In addition, the evidence reviewed rarely addresses the fundamental efficiency question of measuring the welfare impact of the dysfunctional responses identified. These conclusions suggest that much work is still necessary to further our understanding of dysfunctional behavior.

Before proceeding, we should acknowledge that others have discussed the existence of problems with performance measurement in both private and public organizations. See in particular Prendergast (1999), Propper and Wilson (2003), and Smith (1995). Other chapters in this book also discuss problems with performance measurement in JTPA and WIA. The main contribution of this chapter is to focus exclusively on the issue of dysfunctional responses, leaving aside more general problems associated with performance measurement, and to try to provide a comprehensive overview of such responses. To achieve this goal, we provide a theoretical framework to develop a formal classification of dysfunctional responses. This classification is useful to understand the practical challenges of identifying dysfunctional responses, to evaluate the negative impact of such responses, and to formulate appropriate remedies. We hope that this formal framework will be helpful in understanding the difficulties organizations face to correctly measure and reward productivity, and ultimately that it will support the design of more effective models of performance measurement and incentive systems.

DEFINITIONS OF DYSFUNCTIONAL RESPONSES

A central assumption of the incentive literature is that performance measurement influences behavior, and most importantly, that it may be sometimes difficult to anticipate how it does so. Performance measures encourage the right kind of behavioral responses only if they successfully communicate the organization's true objectives. In an early discussion of the subject, Blau (1955) warns that if performance measures are not perfectly aligned with the organization's objective, they may generate, in addition to intended responses, what could be called unintended or dysfunctional responses.

A dysfunctional response is an action that increases the performance measure but is unsupported by the designer because it does not efficiently further the true objective of the organization (see, for example, Kerr [1975] and Jensen and Meckling [1992]). The multitasking framework captures the notion that the investment allocation that maximizes performance outcomes does not necessarily correspond to the allocation that maximizes value added (Baker 1992; Holmstrom and Milgrom 1991).[2]

Although all dysfunctional responses share the general property that they were not intended by the incentive designer, there are types of dysfunctional responses that correspond to different ways in which the measurement technology may be imperfect. To provide a more precise classification of dysfunctional responses, we borrow the language of the multitasking literature. The starting point of this literature is to assume that the agent invests in tasks. One could think of a task as a project. In the context of JTPA, for example, a task could be a single enrollee or a group of enrollees. The agent has to allocate resources across tasks and the issue is how the performance measure guides, or misguides, the agent's resource allocation. Each task is characterized by its type α. The agent privately observes the task's type α and invests in effort, e. The performance outcome for task α is

$$M_\alpha(e,g) = m_\alpha e.$$

We assume without loss of generality that $m_\alpha \geq 0$. Our specification ignores additive performance measurement noise.[3] This assumption is not restrictive for the analysis, which focuses on defining dysfunctional responses.[4] The principal's objective or social value added on task α is

$$V_\alpha(e) = v_\alpha e.$$

Finally, we assume that investment in effort is costly:

$$C_\alpha(e,g) = (½)c_\alpha e^2,$$

where $c_\alpha \geq 0$. The performance outcome is

$$M = \Sigma_\alpha M_\alpha(e).$$

The fundamental assumption of the multitasking literature is that the principal can observe only M. The performance measure, however, is an imperfect measure of the agent's effectiveness because it aggregates the outcome of multiple tasks. As a result, the performance measure may not be aligned with the true objective of the principal. Stated formally, this will be the case when the marginal return of effort on the measure is not the same as the marginal return of effort on the principal's objective, $m_{\alpha} \neq v_{\alpha}$.

Several comments are in order. First, this setup focuses exclusively on problems that are associated with the inadequacy of the measure to convey the true objective. It omits problems relating to the principal's ability to select the right measure and implement it properly and to the agent's willingness or capacity to respond to performance measurement. Although we briefly discuss the limitations imposed by these assumptions next, see Smith (1995) and Kravchuk and Schack (1996) for a more complete discussion of the problems that emerge when these assumptions do not hold. Some of these additional concerns regarding the implementation of performance measurement are also discussed in Chapters 3 and 4.

Second, the multitasking framework assumes that the principal's objective, $V_{\alpha}(e)$, is well defined. In practice, performance measurement sometimes fails because the principal's objective is poorly defined or because the principal must strike a compromise between potentially conflicting goals. Our analysis does not address these problems. Consider next our assumption that the agent chooses the resource allocation that achieves the highest outcome on the performance measures. This assumption rules out the possibility that the agent has his/her own preferences over resource allocation that conflict with performance measurement. It also rules out the possibility that the agent is actually an organizational unit composed of multiple decision makers with conflicting objectives, as is frequently the case in the real world. In addition, we assume that the agent understands the technology of production of the performance measure, $M_{\alpha}(e)$. Finally, our model abstracts from issues related to the dynamics of performance measurement. Here we consider a static model, ignoring the possibility that the principal may change the performance measure and the potential dysfunctional responses associated with such a possibility (Courty and Marschke 2003a).

Keeping these qualifications in mind, our setup suggests a formal definition of dysfunctional responses. A dysfunctional response is an investment choice that is different from the investment choice that maximizes the organizational goal. Formally, an agent who maximizes the performance outcome invests

$$e_\alpha = m_\alpha / c_\alpha$$

in task α, while the investment that maximizes the organizational objective is

$$\overset{*}{e}_\alpha = v_\alpha / c_\alpha .$$

A dysfunctional response occurs when $e_\alpha \neq \overset{*}{e}_\alpha$. We distinguish three types of dysfunctional responses:

1) Marginal misallocation: actions that enter the principal's objective but are distorted in the performance measure. Formally, $m_\alpha \neq v_\alpha > 0$ and $c_\alpha > 0$. To illustrate, consider the case of performance measurement in schools (Jacob 2005; Hannaway 1992). In recent years some policy analysts and public officials have advocated setting up performance measures for local school districts, possibly backed by educational subsidies as incentives (e.g., No Child Left Behind Act of 2002). Such performance measures are based on scores from standardized tests of reading, writing, and arithmetic. These tests do not measure the results of teaching citizenship, conflict resolution, and interpersonal skills—skills that are an important aim of primary schools. Because the tests do not measure citizenship, for example, the theory predicts that teachers will invest less, or possibly neglect altogether, this skill. Instituting performance measurement can produce distortions by causing agents to spend little time on activities that are productive but not fully taken into account in the performance measure.
2) Accounting manipulation: actions that increase the performance measure but do not enter the principal's objective and do not enter the cost function. Formally, $m_\alpha > 0$ and $v_\alpha = c_\alpha = 0$. Accounting manipulations are activities that boost the performance measure and do not waste resources. Such responses are informally known as "cooking the books" or "window dressing." Accounting manipulation increases the agent's chances of earning the rewards associated with higher perfor-

mance outcomes. They may not create welfare loss since the organization could, in principle, neutralize this behavior by appropriately discounting the rewards to higher performance outcomes (Courty and Marschke 2004). If such adjustment in rewards is possible, this class of dysfunctional responses does not have direct inefficiency implications (since $e_\alpha = e_\alpha$ on all tasks that actually enter the organization's objective). Often, however, the principal may not be aware of such responses. When this is the case, the informative power of the performance measure decreases and the principal may overreward those agents who invest more in accounting manipulation. Such dysfunctional manipulation would have indirect negative efficiency impacts on the organization.

3) Gaming: actions that increase the performance outcome negatively enhance the principal's objective and/or positively increase the cost function. Formally, $m_\alpha > 0$, $v_\alpha \leq 0$, and $c_\alpha \geq 0$, with at least one of the last two inequalities strict. The distinction between accounting manipulation and gaming is that the latter imposes a cost to the organization because the agent ends up wasting resources to boost performance. For example, if the activities involved in "cooking the books" waste resources, then they fall within the category of gaming. Gaming implies not only some kind of accounting manipulation but also a costly misallocation of resources.

This classification is useful because the organization's optimal response depends on the type of dysfunctional behavior under consideration. As mentioned earlier, the organization does not care about accounting manipulation if it can invert the performance inflation relation and appropriately discount the rewards to performance achievement. If this cannot be done satisfactorily, then accounting manipulations will have an indirect negative impact on the organization. Gaming responses should unambiguously be eliminated as they have both a direct negative impact ($e_\alpha \neq e_\alpha$) and an indirect impact on the organization. Marginal misallocations often originate from the fact that the performance measure is too coarse and does not capture some dimensions of value added. The typical remedy is to complement the performance measure with additional measures or with alternative evaluation methods (i.e., subjective performance evaluation).

REVIEW OF EVIDENCE OF DYSFUNCTIONAL RESPONSES IN PUBLIC AND PRIVATE SECTORS

Casual reports of dysfunctional responses to performance incentives abound. Although sometimes insightful, such accounts only give a very impressionistic view of the actual extent and impact of such responses. It is typically not possible to establish on the basis of such reports the amount of performance inflation that actually goes on, or to determine the existence of welfare loss. To draw relevant lessons for the design of performance measurement systems, one must develop systematic methods to identify and measure distortions. We start by discussing why it is difficult to systematically measure dysfunctional responses in practice. Next, we review different methods that have been successful at producing hard empirical evidence on dysfunctional responses.

Challenges in Identifying Dysfunctional Responses

Several difficulties arise when one tries to assess the extent of dysfunctional behavior. To start, demonstrating the existence of dysfunctional responses involves estimating relationships that are typically hidden from the researcher. One needs to identify actions that are not perfectly aligned with the principal's objective. Using the notation of the model, one needs to show that $m_\alpha \neq v_\alpha$, and also possibly that $c_\alpha > 0$, depending on the type of dysfunctional responses considered. But the researcher does not typically observe the marginal impacts of decision making on the production and cost functions.

To illustrate, consider the case of marginal misallocation. Researchers who study agent responses to performance measures often find evidence of actions that raise performance outcomes, but then find it difficult to demonstrate that these actions are suboptimal (i.e., to show that these responses are not the ones that maximize the stated objective of the organization). The difficulty lies in establishing the counterfactual of what the agent's value added would have been absent the agent's actions. Consider the cream skimming literature in job training programs that has studied enrollment responses to performance measurement in the JTPA organization (Chapters 6 and 9). Critics of JTPA's performance incentive system feared that the measures used, which focus on labor market success (e.g., employment status) at the end of training, would encourage managers to enroll only those participants likely to perform well on employment measures—the most "job ready"—irrespective of how much they might gain from the program (that is, increase their human capital). Some studies have found evidence that program managers prefer the job ready, but this alone is not evidence of dysfunctional responses. To demonstrate dysfunctional response, one must show that the job-ready applicants are also those who do not benefit the most from the program (see Chapters 5 and 8, and Heckman, Heinrich, and Smith [2002]). Using our notation, although it seems intuitive that m_α/c_α is high for the job ready, one needs to prove that v_α/c_α is low for this target population to establish the existence of marginal misallocation.

The literature has circumvented this challenge by focusing on incentive schemes where dysfunctional responses can be unambiguously identified from the specifics of the contract. A substantial fraction of the literature focuses on accounting manipulation responses where the agent uses its discretion over the timing and reporting of performance outcomes to meet performance thresholds (Asch 1990; Courty and Marschke 2004; Healy 1985; Jacob and Levitt 2003; Oettinger 2002; and Oyer 1998). The advantage of focusing on such timing and misreporting strategies is that the observed responses can only be consistent with the specifics of the contract. Using the notation introduced earlier, these actions are unambiguously dysfunctional since $m_\alpha > 0$ while $v_\alpha = 0$. The main shortcomings of this approach, however, are that it can be applied only to a narrow set of dysfunctional responses and requires detailed information on the contracts and behavior that is often hidden from the researcher. Another shortcoming of this approach is that it will work only to identify accounting manipulations, to the extent that $c_\alpha = 0$, and such responses are likely to have lower direct efficiency impact than the other two types of dysfunctional responses.

A final approach to identify dysfunctional responses focuses on changes in performance outcomes that follow the introduction of a new performance measure. We discuss this approach in more detail in the next section.

Evidence of Dysfunctional Responses

Propper and Wilson (2003) present some evidence of dysfunctional responses in their review of the empirical literature on the use and usefulness of performance measures in the public sector. In this section, we review some of this evidence, as well as new evidence, using the classification presented above.

Health sector

Dranove et al. (2003) study whether the introduction of report cards changes how health care providers select patients. Report cards provide information about the performance of hospitals. Skeptics argue that health report cards may encourage providers to game the system by cream skimming, that is, by avoiding sick and/or seeking healthy patients. Their evidence shows that report cards led to substantial selection by providers, with a decline in the illness severity of patients, a finding consistent with a cream skimming hypothesis. They conclude that the overall impact of the report card was to reduce welfare. This evidence is consistent with marginal misallocation, since performance measurement generates a reallocation of resources that reduces efficiency.

Goddard et al. (2000) present a general discussion of the difficulties in implementing performance measurement. They consider the impact of the "Performance Framework," an initiative by the UK National Health Service to increase the importance attached to formal performance indicators in the health sector. They present qualitative interview evidence consistent with the hypothesis that performance measurement may generate a wide range of unintended responses.

School and training program

Jacob and Levitt (2003) investigate teacher cheating, a behavioral response consistent with accounting manipulation. Some school districts allocate school budgets on the basis of schools' performance. A number of highly publicized incidents of teacher cheating have fueled the suspicion that teachers have responded by "teaching the test" and manipulating students' grade-to-grade promotions to boost scores. However, most of this evidence is anecdotal. Jacob and Levitt propose an innovative way to measure the extent of teacher cheating that combines measures on unexpected test score fluctuations and suspicious patterns of answers for students. They show that the joint distribution of these two variables should demonstrate systematic patterns if some teachers cheat and others do not.

Jacob (2005) presents some evidence of marginal misallocation. He examines the impact of an accountability policy implemented in the Chicago Public Schools in 1996–1997. He finds that math and reading achievement increased sharply following the introduction of the accountability policy. He also finds that teachers responded strategically to the incentives along a variety of dimensions—by increasing special education placements, preemptively retaining students, and substituting away from low-stakes subjects like science and social studies.

Oettinger (2002) presents a study of academic performance evaluations and shows that undergraduate students respond to nonlinear incentives. Due to the threshold effects implied by a discrete grade system, students tend to cluster slightly above grade boundaries. Using our terminology, this evidence is consistent with marginal misallocation because students strategically change effort decisions to meet performance thresholds, a behavior that is unlikely to be efficient. In fact, Oettinger's evidence suggests that the performance incentive generates allocations of effort over the duration of the term that depend on the realized grade history. The efficient allocation of effort, however, should not depend on grade history.

Burgess et al. (2003) evaluate the impact of a pilot incentive scheme in Jobcentre Plus, a large UK public job training agency, and present some evidence of marginal misallocation. The incentive scheme they consider gives team bonuses for five different targets that measure with varying degrees of precision the bureaucrats' effectiveness at placing the unemployed into jobs. The authors hypothesize that in such a multitasking environment, where different tasks are measured with different degrees of precision, workers may choose to exert effort on the tasks for which their actions are more easily verifiable. Consistent with this hypothesis, they find an impact on job placement (quantity measure) but little impact on less precise measures (quality measures).

Private sector: managers and salespeople

Explicit performance measures are commonly used in private sector occupations such as firm executives (using both accounting and stock market based measures) and salespeople.[5] Evidence of accounting manipulations from these occupations abounds. In an early contribution to the accounting manipulation literature, Healy (1985) documents that managers who are compensated for meeting annual income thresholds use their discretion over the timing of income reporting to smooth their compensation across accounting years. Similarly, Oyer (1998) uses differences in the date of the end of the fiscal year for companies that are otherwise similar to show that there is more variability in firms' sales at the end of the fiscal years—when salespersons' bonuses are computed—than in the middle. Oyer's evidence should be interpreted as accounting manipulation, if salespeople only manipulate sales reports. Alternatively, if salespeople reallocate effort over the accounting year, then the evidence should be interpreted as marginal misallocation.[6]

Gibbs et al. (2009) present some evidence that incentive designers are aware of marginal misallocations and actually structure measurement systems to address such problems. They use data on incentive contracts for auto dealership managers to investigate whether incentive designers internalize multitasking concerns. They show that incentive designers select pools of incentive measures that complement each other, and set the relative weights on the different measures selected to address multitasking concerns. For example, the extent to which a measure distorts incentives (by discouraging cooperation or encouraging a short-term focus) reduces the weight it receives. In addition, firms use additional performance bonuses, based on subjective performance evaluation, to balance multitasking and manipulation incentives.

EVIDENCE FROM JTPA

This section reviews the evidence of dysfunctional responses in the JTPA organization. Here we draw from our own work but also refer to the work of Heckman and Smith presented in Chapter 6 and Heinrich in Chapter 8 of this monograph. The evidence presented in this section builds upon the characteristics of the JTPA incentive system presented in Chapter 4 (see also Courty and Marschke [2003b]).

We present two kinds of evidence. The first summarizes the econometric evidence of behavioral responses to JTPA's attempts to evaluate organizational performance, as well as estimates of the costs that are incurred when performance measures lead to dysfunctional behavior. This evidence establishes a clear link between the specifics of the incentive policies faced by bureaucrats and their behavior. The second kind of evidence is based on survey data of self-reported behavior. This evidence reviews a wider set of hypotheses regarding the implications of the incentive system but because the evidence is based on self-reported behavior, the inference is more anecdotal in nature and sometimes subject to interpretation.

Timing Strategies

Using data from the National JTPA Study, we document how in the first decade of JTPA, agencies delayed terminating unemployed enrollees, even after their training concluded, to maximize the performance outcomes (Courty and Marschke 1997, 2004). This strategic termination behavior can be of two types. The first type takes advantage of the fact that training agencies do not need to report the employment status of the enrollees who have completed their training on the date training ends but have a 90-day window to do so. Because labor market outcomes vary over time naturally on their own, training agencies have an incentive to strategically choose the date they report enrollees' employment outcomes. At the end of an enrollee's training, training agencies face a decision: terminate the enrollee and report her labor market outcomes or postpone termination in hopes that the outcome improves. The optimal termination strategy leads the training agency to terminate enrollees who are employed within the 90-day period following training either on the last day of training or on the first day of employment, whichever occurs first, and all others on the 90th day following training end. Courty and Marschke (2004) report evidence consistent with this hypothesis. They find that this strategic reporting increases the overall employment rate at termination, which was the most important performance measure at the time, by 11.3 percentage points, from 47.0 percent to 58.3 percent. Stated differently, training agencies in their study would produce an employment rate outcome 20 percent lower if they were required to graduate enrollees (and report their performance outcomes) on the date they actually finish training.

The second type of strategic termination behavior takes place at the end of the fiscal year. Consider a stylized two-program-year incentive system where the training agency receives an award if the yearly labor market–based performance outcome exceeds a fixed performance standard. The training agency does not know its final aggregate performance outcome until the end of the program year because the labor market outcomes depend on random factors, such as the state of the local economy, which are outside its control. Because of the graduation strategy described above, the training agency reaches the end of the year with an inventory of enrollees who have finished training within the previous 90 days but are unemployed. At the end of the first program year, the training agency chooses how many from this inventory to graduate in the present program year, with the remainder to be graduated in the following program year. Assume there are n such persons, of whom n_1 will be graduated in the first program year and $n_2 = n - n_1$ in the next one. The training agency chooses n_1 to maximize the present value of the sum of the two awards.

The optimal graduation strategy on the last day of the first program year depends on the difference between the performance outcome and the standard as the last day arrives. Let $N = N_e + N_u$ be the number of persons who were graduated during the year (excluding the year's last day), where N_e and N_u and are the numbers of such persons graduated employed and unemployed, respectively. Let $\overline{S}$ be the performance standard. Three cases can be distinguished (see Figure 7.1). In case 1, on the last day of the year, the cumulative performance outcome exceeds the standard by so much that the training agency can graduate all unemployed enrollees. This corresponds to the *HIGH* region in Figure 7.1. In case 1, because $N_e/(N+n) \geq \overline{S}$, $n_1 = n$. In case 2, which corresponds to the *MED* region in Figure 7.1, the cumulative performance outcome exceeds the standard, but not by much. In case 2, because graduating all unemployed enrollees would push the outcome below the standard, it pays the training agency to graduate persons from its inventory only until the performance outcome equals the performance standard. That is, the training agency chooses n_1 such that $N_e/(N+n) = \bar{S}$. Rearranging yields

$$n_1 = \frac{N_e}{\bar{S}} - N.$$

This equation implies that n_1 lies between zero and n, approaching zero when the training agency just meets the standard and n when the training agency outperforms the standard by n/N percentage points or more. In case 3, corresponding to the *LOW* region in Figure 7.1, the training agency fails to meet the standard at the end of the year ($N_e/N \leq \bar{S}$). In this case, because it cannot win an award this year, the training agency "takes a bath," graduating all n persons from its inventory to maximize the probability of an award next year.

Courty and Marschke (2004) find evidence that training agencies pursued such a termination strategy. In particular, they found that JTPA training agencies delayed graduating idle, unemployed enrollees longer than idle, employed ones; graduated idle, unemployed enrollees sooner if they finished in the last three months of the program year than if they finished within the first nine months of the program year; and graduated

Figure 7.1 The Graduation Decision

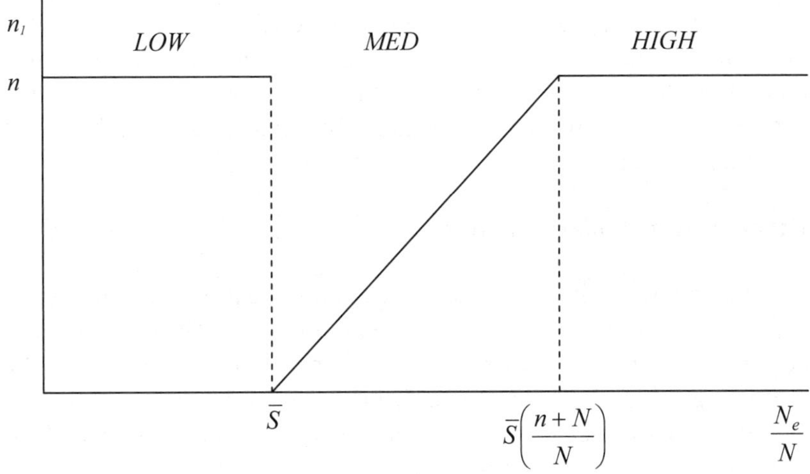

unemployed enrollees who finished training in the last three months of the program year sooner if the training agencies were doing either very well or poorly relative to the employment standard. These findings are consistent with the two-period graduation model. Thus the evidence suggests that by timing performance measurement in this way, training agencies boosted their performance and their awards without providing higher-quality services or providing services more efficiently.

Courty and Marschke (2004) make the important distinction between responses that divert resources (e.g., agents' time) from productive activities and responses that simply reflect an accounting phenomenon. Using our terminology, the former would be labeled gaming and the latter accounting manipulations. Others have documented timing strategies but have not shown any efficiency impact. Courty and Marschke, however, provide evidence that the responses they identify, by consuming programmatic resources, have a negative impact on the true goal of the organization and thus conclude that these responses are more than a mere accounting phenomenon. They are evidence of gaming. For example, they find that earnings impacts are lower in those training agencies that engage more in termination strategies, which is consistent with the hypothesis that graduation timing is inefficient. In addition, they find that year-end timing is inefficient on two counts. First, training agencies are more likely to suddenly truncate training in June, an input distortion that is a direct consequence of the strategic manipulation of yearly performance that takes place in the month of June. Second, they find that earnings impacts are lower for those enrollees who receive training in June. They interpret this finding as evidence that training agencies substitute time and effort away from training toward the end of the program year.

Other Dysfunctional Responses

We review additional evidence also consistent with dysfunctional behavior. To start, we show that accounting manipulation behavior is not limited to the employment at termination performance measure by presenting evidence from other performance measures. Then we present evidence that the incentive system may also distort the enrollment decision and the training allocation decision.

Manipulating the wage and earning measures

The graduation decision was also influenced by the other class of JTPA performance measures: the performance measures based on wages and earnings. Courty and Marschke (2004) focus on the optimal termination strategy for employed enrollees. They show that training agencies may choose to terminate employed enrollees who have little chance of experiencing a wage increase, but wait on those employed enrollees who have a high likelihood of experiencing a wage increase. The training agency does not wait on all enrollees because by doing so it might lose credit for some employment. This risk is significant because approximately one-quarter of the enrolled who were employed on their graduation date were not employed at the same job three months later. The refined strategy that takes the wage measure into account implies that some employed enrollees should be terminated later than is predicted under the simple strategy presented earlier. Focusing on the enrollees who were employed at the end of training and who experienced a second employment spell under a new employer before the close of the 90-day window, Courty and Marschke show that those enrollees who experience a wage decrease are more likely to be terminated during the first employment spell. They also show that those participants who are graduated after the start of their secondary employment spell should experience higher wage offers. They conclude that the covariation of graduation delay and the wages in secondary employment spells appear consistent with a graduation strategy that maximizes the wage and earnings performance outcomes. This behavior qualifies as accounting manipulation or gaming depending on its efficiency impact.

Manipulating the follow-up measures

The switch from termination-based follow-up measures may have provoked several kinds of responses by local decision makers. First, the follow-up measures may have encouraged training centers to emphasize intensive training services (as opposed to employment-focused services, such as job search) in the hopes of producing larger and longer-lasting impacts on earnings and employment. Second, the follow-up measures may have induced caseworkers to extend their contact with enrollees beyond their termination dates. Courty and Marschke (2007) present some evidence suggesting that the follow-up performance measures captured how effective training centers were at offering postprogram "quick fixes" (such as transportation allowances) to enable the enrollees to stay employed on the follow-up measurement date. These responses qualify as marginal misallocation because such quick fixes, although potentially productive, divert resources away from other activities that would have increased long-term earning and employment.

Manipulating the cost measure

In addition to employment and wage/earning measures, in the early years JTPA training centers faced a cost-based measure that judged the program's managers by how much they spent to produce an employment at termination. The incentives inherent in the cost and employment rate at termination measures were very similar (Courty and Marschke 2007). Thus, in time, JTPA officials came to believe that the cost measure also was encouraging short-run, "quick fix"–type job placement activities in lieu of longer-term activities with more training content. In 1990, when they replaced the termination-based measures with follow-up-based measures, they also phased out the cost measure because they believed "that the use of cost standards in the awarding of incentives [had] the *unintended effect* of constraining the provision of longer-term training programs" (italics ours) (*Federal Register* 1990). Such responses—if they indeed occurred—belong to the category of marginal misallocation.

Enrollment

Cream skimming—the use of the training center's considerable discretion to select enrollees on the basis of their expected effect on performance outcomes—is the core concern of most empirical analyses of JTPA's incentive system. The system judged training centers on the basis of postprogram employment and earnings levels, whereas the objective of training was skill development. Such performance outcomes induce training centers to choose persons with high levels of human capital at the expense of persons who would most benefit from training. The nature and evidence of cream skimming is discussed at length in Chapters 6 and 9.

Training selection

Researchers have also investigated the effects of JTPA performance incentives on training centers' training strategies. While training choice has received less attention than the cream skimming issue, its study is motivated by similar concerns—that short-term performance measures encourage training centers to emphasize "quick fixes," services that have no long-term impact on enrollee skills.

Marschke (2002) studies the effects of two performance measure reforms on the training strategies of JTPA training centers. In the early 1990s, the USDOL moved away from termination-based measures toward performance measured three months *after* termination. The USDOL also eliminated measures that rewarded training agencies that kept low the average cost of training an enrollee. Both reforms occurred in response to a growing perception that the training centers were relying heavily on job-placement-oriented services at the expense of more intensive kinds of training. Many policymakers also felt that the typical JTPA training spell was too short to be effective (average enrollment in the first decade of JTPA lasted only about five months).

Marschke (2002) finds that these performance reforms produced mixed results. The switch to performance measurement three months after training ends appeared to encourage agencies to offer the kinds of intensive training that raise the long-term earnings abilities of JTPA enrollees, but the impacts from this reform were offset by the elimination of the cost measure. Apparently the cost measure had been discouraging training agencies from offering classroom vocational training because it was the longest and most expensive of the major kinds of training. After the cost measure was removed, training agencies offered more classroom vocational training, but earnings impacts fell because classroom vocational training produced the smallest earnings impacts of the main kinds of training offered.[7]

In the context of the multitasking model, rewarding the employment rate at termination measure, for example, was leading the center to prescribe training activities that increased the training center's employment rate but reduced the earnings ability of JTPA enrollees. The employment rate at termination measure and earnings impacts are misaligned. The cost measure, on the other hand, was leading training centers to favor training types that increased both earnings impacts and the training center's award. Thus, the cost measure, insofar as it discouraged the use of vocational training, a relatively low-gain and high-cost activity, appears to have been aligned. To conclude, this discussion presents some evidence consistent with the hypothesis that the choice of performance measure influences the agent's choice of resource allocation, and that different performance measures are imperfect in different ways in the sense that each produces different patterns of marginal misallocation.

General Test of Dysfunctional Responses

Courty and Marschke (2008) propose a different approach to identify dysfunctional responses. They look at how the correlation between the objective of the organization and the performance measure changes after a measure is introduced. The multitasking model predicts that this correlation should decrease after a measure is introduced if the agent engages in any kind of dysfunctional response. Courty and Marschke conclude that one can identify dysfunctional responses by estimating the change in correlation between a performance measure and the true goal of the organization before and after the measure has been activated. Using data from the JTPA incentive system, they test the hypothesis for the introduction of the follow-up measures, which corresponds to one of the most important changes in the history of JTPA's incentive system. They find some evidence consistent with the hypothesis and draw implications for the choice of performance measures.

WIA

WIA's performance incentive system is still relatively new and therefore little studied. Nonetheless, the record on JTPA may allow us to draw some conclusions about the performance of WIA's system. As Chapters 2 and 5 show, there are many similarities and some differences between performance incentives under JTPA and performance incentives under WIA. As in JTPA, most of the performance measures in WIA are based on enrollees' labor market outcomes. All labor market outcomes are measured after training ceases (as opposed to on the date of termination), as in latter-day JTPA. Moreover, WIA focuses on outcomes six months after job placement. In JTPA, performance outcomes were far more short term. This may be an improvement over

JTPA in two ways. First, because labor market outcomes are measured six months after an enrollee leaves the program, outcomes are harder to manipulate in WIA by the strategic timing of graduation. Second, measuring outcomes six months after graduation reduces the return to "quick fix"–type training strategies. As the JTPA evidence seems to show, longer-term measures lead to greater earnings gains from training. WIA also reinstates cost measures, which the evidence seems to show also improve earnings gains.

Interestingly, in its early years WIA includes among the JTPA-style performance measures a before-after measure of enrollees' earnings. Conceptually, the difference between an enrollee's earnings before enrollment and after termination is more similar to an earnings or employment gain—and thus more similar to the objective of job training under JTPA and WIA—than is a posttraining labor outcome. While it is more similar to a job training impact, a before-after earnings measure also suffers from potential problems. For the average enrollee, earnings dip just before entering job training, suggesting that her earnings would eventually rise even if the job training program had no value. This phenomenon, the so-called Ashenfelter dip, means that before-after earnings differences are distorted measures of the true impact of job training (see Heckman and Smith [1999] for a discussion of this point.) Thus, whether before-after measures lead to less cream skimming is a question that must be answered with empirical studies.

CONCLUSIONS

This chapter offers a comprehensive overview of dysfunctional responses covering theoretical concepts, empirical evidence from both the public and private organizations, and summarizing studies of dysfunctional responses that focus on the JTPA organization. We assess the extent to which dysfunctional responses may impede the performance of the measurement system, and we draw lessons for policymakers.

Taken together, the evidence suggests that performance measures elicit unanticipated responses because line workers and their managers gain a superior understanding of how to influence these measures. Managers and workers acquire through their day-to-day operation of their programs an expert's knowledge of the levers available to manipulate performance outcomes. Because the designers of the performance measures are remote from the everyday operations of the agencies they oversee, they lack this knowledge. This information asymmetry means that the designers of performance measures cannot anticipate all behavioral responses *ex ante*. An implication is that dysfunctional responses can present substantial challenges to the design of performance measurement systems. At least three lessons can be drawn from the evidence.

1) Designers of performance measures should consider how local decision makers respond to the performance measures and accept that they cannot anticipate all responses. Most performance measures elicit unanticipated responses because agents gradually gain a superior understanding of how to influence them. Designers should encourage some of these unanticipated responses and discourage others.
2) Designers should respond differently to different types of dysfunctional behavior. In the case of accounting manipulation, for example, the organization only has to appropriately discount the rewards to performance achievement. Gaming responses should unambiguously be eliminated as they have both a direct negative impact on the organization (misallocation of resources) and an indirect one (misinterpretation of outcomes). Marginal misallocations often originate from the fact that the performance measure is too coarse and does not capture some dimensions of value added. The typical remedy is to complement the performance measure with finer measures.
3) The evidence reinforces the conjecture that explicit performance measures impose costs—monitoring and improvement consume resources (Prendergast 1999). Until performance measure designers discover them, the dysfunctional responses that imperfectly conceived performance measures engender can undermine the organization's mission. These costs make the use of performance measurement systems uneconomical for many public sector organizations because they raise more management problems than they solve. This may explain why such organizations rarely implement explicit performance measures.

In a separate line of research, we characterize a process by which the designers of performance measures learn about and respond to local decision maker responses (Courty and Marschke [2003a]; see also Heinrich and Marschke [2010]). This feedback loop suggests that performance measurement systems must be continuously monitored and improved. We conclude that implementation is not a static, one-time challenge but a dynamic one.

An important lesson of this review is that much progress has been made in identifying dysfunctional responses. A growing literature has produced studies that go beyond casual reports and anecdotal evidence and try to measure performance inflation and assess the impact of these responses on the organization. Still, we find that this literature typically focuses on a narrow set of responses. In addition, the evidence reviewed rarely compellingly addresses the fundamental efficiency question of measuring the welfare impact of the dysfunctional responses identified. This suggests that there is still much work to be done to further our understanding of dysfunctional behavior.

Notes

We would like to thank James Heckman and Carolyn Heinrich.

1. Subjective performance evaluation is based on judgment and is more qualitative and flexible than explicit performance incentives. Unlike explicit performance measures, subjective performance measures cannot be verified by outside parties and therefore organizations cannot contract upon them.
2. The theoretical literature on incentive provision is reviewed in Gibbons (1997) and Prendergast (1999). Marschke (2001), Courty and Marschke (2003a), and Propper and Wilson (2003) also review this literature and draw implications specific to government organizations. Dixit (2002) and Burgess and Ratto (2003) review the broader literature on organizational design and focus on issues that are specific to the public sector. Interestingly, this framework was introduced to explain why high-powered explicit incentives, whose canonical illustration is a piece rate system, appeared far less frequently in practice than is predicted by standard principal-agent models. The point of the theoretical literature on multitasking was to extend the principal-agent model to accommodate the possibility that high-powered explicit incentives may not be optimal when the principal cannot perfectly measure the objective she wants the agent to pursue.
3. Our specification is very similar to the specification in Baker (2002), who assumes that $V = f.a + \varepsilon$ and $P = g.a + \phi$, where f and g are vectors of marginal products

of actions, *a*, in the principal's objective and performance outcome equations. We ignore the error terms ε and ϕ as they do not influence the agent's action choice (see the following note).

4. In the standard principal-agent model, measurement noise plays a role in the determination of the optimal contract, but it does not directly influence the agent's investment decisions.
5. When output can be measured, manual work is another occupation where explicit performance measurement is common. In an unusual study, Lazear (2000), for example, discusses how an installer of automobile glass minimized the impact of potential dysfunctional responses to the introduction of piece rate rewards.
6. Asch (1990) also presents some evidence of reporting timing. She shows that navy recruiters who receive awards for meeting year-end recruitment quotas respond by reallocating their work efforts over the year.
7. This finding is consistent with the results of the National JTPA Study, which found that compared with job search assistance and on-the-job training, vocational classroom training produced the weakest earnings and employment gains (see Orr et al. 1994). One interpretation of Marschke's finding is that the deactivation of the cost measure in the early 1990s was misguided. The finding does not rule out, however, that at the same time it discouraged the use of vocational classroom training, the cost measure encouraged training centers to cut corners in the delivery of services, or to dilute or prematurely shorten training activities for enrollees.

References

Asch, B. J. 1990. "Do Incentives Matter? The Case of Navy Recruiters." *Industrial and Labor Relations Review* 43(3): S89–S106.

Baker, George P. 1992. "Incentive Contracts and Performance Measurement." *Journal of Political Economy* 100(3): 598–614.

———. 2002. "Distortion and Risk in Optimal Incentive Contracts." *Journal of Human Resources* 37(4): 728–751.

Blau, P. 1955. *The Dynamics of Bureaucracy: A Study of Interpersonal Relations in Two Governmental Agencies*. Chicago: University of Chicago Press.

Burgess, Simon, Carol Propper, Marisa Ratto, and Emma Tominey. 2003. "Incentives in the Public Sector: Evidence from a Government Agency." CMPO Working Paper No. 03/080. Bristol, UK: Centre for Market and Public Organisation, University of Bristol.

Burgess, Simon, and Marisa Ratto. 2003. "The Role of Incentives in the Public Sector: Issues and Evidence." *Oxford Review of Economic Policy* 19(2): 250–267.

Courty, Pascal, and Gerald Marschke. 1997. "Measuring Government Performance: Lessons from a Federal Job-Training Program." *American Economic Review* 87(2): 383–388.

———. 2003a. "Dynamics of Performance Measurement Systems." *Oxford Review of Economic Policy* 19(2): 268–284.

———. 2003b. "Performance Funding in Federal Agencies: A Case Study of a Federal Job Training Program." *Public Budgeting and Finance* 23(3): 22–48.

———. 2004. "An Empirical Investigation of Dysfunctional Responses to Explicit Performance Incentives." *Journal of Labor Economics* 22(1): 23–56.

———. 2007. "Making Government Accountable: Lessons from a Federal Job Training Program." *Public Administration Review* 67(5): 904–916.

———. 2008. "A General Test for Distortions in Performance Measures." *Review of Economics and Statistics* 90(3): 428–441.

Dixit, A. 2002. "Incentives and Organizations in the Public Sector." *Journal of Human Resources* 37(4): 696–727.

Dranove, David, Daniel Kessler, Mark McClellan, and Mark Satterthwaite. 2003. "Is More Information Better? The Effects of 'Report Cards' on Health Care Providers." *Journal of Political Economy* 111(3): 555–588.

Federal Register. 1990. 55(4). Washington, DC: U.S. Government Printing Office.

Gibbons, R. 1997. "Incentives and Careers in Organizations." In *Advances in Economics and Econometrics: Theory and Applications: Seventh World Congress*, David Kreps and Kenneth Frank Wallis, eds. New York: Cambridge University Press.

Gibbs, Michael, Kenneth Merchant, Wim Van der Stede, and Mark Vargus. 2009. "Performance Measure Properties and Incentive System Design." *Industrial Relations: A Journal of Economy and Society* 48(2): 237–264.

Goddard, Maria, Russell Mannion, and Peter C. Smith. 2000. "Enhancing Performance in Health Care: A Theoretical Perspective on Agency and the Role of Information." *Health Economics* 9(2): 95–107.

Hannaway, Jane. 1992. "Higher Order Skills, Job Design, and Incentives: An Analysis and Proposal." *American Educational Research Journal* 29(1): 3–21.

Healy, P. 1985. "The Effect of Bonus Schemes on Accounting Decisions." *Journal of Accounting and Economics* 7(1–3): 85–107.

Heckman, James J., Carolyn Heinrich, and Jeffrey Smith. 2002. "The Performance of Performance Standards." *Journal of Human Resources* 37(4): 778–811.

Heckman, James J., and Jeffrey Smith. 1999. "The Pre-Program Earnings Dip and the Determinents of Participation in a Social Program: Implications for Simple Evaluation Strategies." *Economic Journal* 109(457): 313–348.

Heinrich, Carolyn, and Gerald Marschke. 2010. "Incentives and Their Dynamics in Public Sector Performance Management Systems." *Journal of Policy Analysis and Management* 29(1): 183–208.

Holmstrom, B., and P. Milgrom. 1991. "Multitask Principal-Agent Analyses: Incentive Contracts, Asset Ownership, and Job Design." *Journal of Law, Economics, and Organization* 7(Special Issue): 24–52.

Jacob, Brian A. 2005. "Accountability, Incentives, and Behavior: The Impact of High-Stakes Testing in the Chicago Public Schools." *Journal of Public Economics* 89(5–6): 761–796.

Jacob, Brian A., and Steven D. Levitt. 2003. "Rotten Apples: An Investigation of the Prevalence and Predictors of Teacher Cheating." *Quarterly Journal of Economics* 118(3): 843–877.

Jensen, M. C., and W. H. Meckling. 1992. "Specific and General Knowledge and Organizational Structure." In *Contract Economics*, L. Werin and H. Wijkander, eds. Oxford, UK: Blackwell, pp. 252–271.

Kerr, Steven. 1975. "On the Folly of Rewarding for A While Hoping for B." *Academy of Management Executive* 18(4): 769–783.

Kravchuk, Robert, and Ronald Schack. 1996. "Designing Effective Performance-Measurement Systems under the Government Performance and Results Act of 1993." *Public Administration Review* 56(4): 348–358.

Lazear, Edward. 2000. "Performance Pay and Productivity." *American Economic Review* 90(5): 1346–1361.

Marschke, Gerald. 2001. "The Economics of Performance Incentives in Government with Evidence from a Federal Job Training Program." In *Quicker, Better, Cheaper? Managing Performance in American Government*, Dall W. Forsythe, ed. Albany, NY: Rockefeller Institute Press, pp. 61–97.

———. 2002. "Performance Incentives and Organizational Behavior: Evidence from a Federal Bureaucracy." Working paper. Albany, NY: University at Albany, State University of New York.

Oettinger, Gerald S. 2002. "The Effect of Nonlinear Incentives in Performance: Evidence from 'Econ 101.'" *Review of Economics and Statistics* 84(3): 509–517.

Orr, Larry L., Howard S. Bloom, Stephen H. Bell, Winston Lin, George Cave, and Fred Doolittle. March 1994. *The National JTPA Study: Impacts, Benefits, and Costs of Title II-A*. Bethesda, MD: Abt Associates Inc.

Oyer, P. 1998. "Fiscal Year Ends and Non-Linear Incentive Contracts: The Effect on Business Seasonality." *Quarterly Journal of Economics* 113(1): 149–185.

Prendergast, C. 1999. "The Provision of Incentives in Firms." *Journal of Economic Literature* 37(1): 7–63.

Propper, Carol, and Deborah Wilson. 2003. "The Use and Usefulness of Performance Measures in the Public Sector." *Oxford Review of Economic Policy* 19(2): 250–267.

Smith, Peter. 1995. "On the Unintended Consequences of Publishing Performance Data in the Public Sector." *International Journal of Public Administration* 18(2–3): 277–310.

8
Local Responses to Performance Incentives and Implications for Program Outcomes

Carolyn J. Heinrich

In his classic piece on "street-level" bureaucracy, Lipsky (1980) describes the critical position occupied by public employees engaged in social service delivery. These employees, he argues, constitute the scope and function of government services, and the individual decisions of these workers become agency policy. Street-level bureaucrats shape citizens' expectations of government services, determine who qualifies for services, and implement service delivery.

This chapter presents research that explores how local (street-level) bureaucrats in the JTPA program shaped or moderated the role and effects of performance standards in program administration and service delivery. A case-study approach is used to investigate these effects in a county-level agency (located in the Chicago metropolitan area), using data on subunits (contractors) and their staff and individual participants. The local JTPA participant selection and service assignment processes are modeled using quantitative and qualitative data to facilitate a more precise understanding of how and the extent to which performance standards and related administrative policies influence participant access to training and the types of services provided to participants.

Although WIA superseded the JTPA program, the WIA program preserves major elements of the JTPA performance standards system and extends its role in managing local program processes and service delivery. WIA requires states to institute a performance-based certification system for training service providers that establishes a minimum performance level for all providers receiving individual training account (voucher) dollars. Local workforce investment boards and service providers continue to be responsible for guiding service and funding allocations, performance data collection, and the management and use of this information at the local level.

In this research, unique access to information from and about the job training agency's program administration, service providers, and the terms of their contracts with the agency facilitated the in-depth study of local JTPA program processes. Detailed information on individual participants from management information system (MIS) records (1984–1994) and detailed case management records maintained by staff also make possible the analysis of factors that are sometimes overlooked or obscured in aggregate (e.g., state-level) studies of program operations.

The findings of this research show that program administrators and service provider staff in this agency were highly conscious of the agency's performance goals. A contractual and administrative focus on specific levels of (or standards for) performance outcomes had direct and indirect effects on participant selection and training service assignment decisions of program staff. Both deliberate screening on applicant characteristics to advance performance goals and indirect cream skimming grounded in contractual arrangements and program administrative decisions appeared to occur in this agency, with possible negative implications for the participants and net value added of the program.

The remaining sections of this chapter are organized as follows. First, local-level administrative and service delivery processes and concerns about the role and influence of performance standards in these processes are described. The goals of the case study of participant selection and service assignments and hypotheses that were tested in a simulation of these processes are then explained. The next section presents the findings of the simulation and other multivariate analyses, as well as a discussion of these findings. The final section summarizes the findings and their implications for current employment and training programs and policies.

Role of Performance Standards in Local-Level Program Administration and Service Delivery

The substantial discretion accorded to local-level program administrators in deciding how performance standards are used and the extent to which they are used has confounded efforts to fully understand their influence and implications. The design and institution of performance standards systems varies not only across states but also at the local level, where the main responsibility for making these systems function effectively lies. Along with their own target population and service goals, job training agencies transmit federal- and state-level goals and requirements to training professionals who serve clients and manage job training programs on a daily basis. As both Lipsky (1980) and Brodkin (1987) have pointed out, bureaucratic discretion of this type provides the means for administrative agencies and program managers to make policy by shaping it as they implement it.

The county job training agency in this study relied primarily on contracts with other public and private sector organizations to deliver program services.[1] Service providers acted, in effect, as agents of the administrative entity and entered into a competitive bidding process to obtain contracts with the agency for service provision. Through the contract awards and negotiation processes, job training agency officials attempted to exert control over who received services, the types of training services made available, and program outcomes.

Federal and state governments generally specified few guidelines or requirements for contracts between agencies and their service providers. Yet one would expect job training agencies to design contracts that facilitate satisfactory job training program outcomes as measured by state performance evaluation models. Contracts between this agency and its service providers contained detailed information about target population demographic characteristics; the types of training to be made available and anticipated wages-at-placement, estimated service costs, including tuition, wage subsidies, and supportive service costs; and performance-based payment benchmarks for reimbursement of program costs. Service providers were also required to establish detailed program budgets and service plans before contracts were finalized, and any subsequent modifications to the contracts had to be approved and documented by agency officials.

In the contract awards process, the largest weights were accorded to service providers' proposed placement rates, costs per placement, and average wage rates at placement. Secondary criteria used in this process included service provider experience with targeted population(s), labor market need for proposed services, private sector linkages and coordination with other agencies, and service provider in-kind contributions. Service providers' performance in the previous year also factored into the decision process. Service providers who attained at least 90 percent of their planned goals for enrollment, job placements, and expenditures were eligible for exemplary service points that increased their competitive point totals.

If, in fact, service providers who satisfied or exceeded contract requirements—ostensibly furthering the performance and target population goals of the job training agency—were more likely to secure future contracts, the system would likely establish strong incentives for service providers to achieve high placement rates and wages at placement. Some research, discussed below, suggests that this type of performance evaluation system is also likely to contribute to unintended, negative program effects.

Arguments and Evidence on the Role and Influence of Performance Standards in JTPA Programs

Two fundamental issues underlie concerns about the influence of performance standards on employment and training programs: 1) who should have access to these services, and 2) what types of program services should be provided to achieve program goals. JTPA program eligibility guidelines required 90 percent of all enrollees to be disadvantaged; an equitable distribution of services among substantial segments of the eligible population; and minimum levels of service to youth, high school dropouts, and welfare recipients. WIA, however, has introduced a new universal access approach to service delivery in which all adults are eligible for core workforce development services, although local workforce investment boards are still encouraged to give priority for skills training services to public aid recipients and other low-income persons when program funds are sparse. A universal access approach to service does not eliminate the possibility that access to varying *levels* of service might still be constrained locally.

A primary concern expressed by JTPA program administrators was that performance standards might encourage cream skimming, or the selection of participants who are expected to have good postprogram outcomes, regardless of what the program contributes. In cases where participants would do nearly as well or equally well in the labor market without receiving program services, the program's measured performance would be high, but its net impact would be small or zero. (In

Chapter 6, Heckman and Smith define and discuss the cream skimming problem more extensively.)

Research on JTPA operations has generated mixed findings on the influence of performance standards, depending on the types of performance standards used and the local-level practices adopted. In a review of this research, Heinrich (1999) notes the general finding that state and local agencies with policies that emphasized exceeding performance standards while minimizing training costs tended to discourage services to hard-to-serve eligible applicants and reduced the intensity and average length of services for adults. Changes in the legislated performance standards requirements in 1988 were designed to deemphasize the role of performance standards in federal and state JTPA program evaluations and to encourage agencies to focus more on providing higher-quality training as measured by earnings and employment *retention* rather than job placement rates.[2]

From the program administrator's point of view, there was little effect of these legislated changes on service provider performance incentives. The system still focused on employment and earnings *levels* rather than *gains* or net value added of training programs. In the case-study agency, cost-per-placement standards were still included in contracts and were one of the primary criteria for evaluating service provider performance in contract award decisions. The 1988 legislative amendments that changed the evaluation of placement and earnings outcomes to three months after termination did not affect retention measures in this agency's contracts until the 1992 program year. Even then, the changes affected less than one-fourth of the contracts. This suggests that it is important to know what incentives went into contracts between job training agencies and their services providers and were used to guide competition among service providers. The findings also suggest that despite legislative changes, incentives to "cream-skim" may still have been present at the local level.

Because one does not observe participant outcomes in the counterfactual state (in the absence of program services), it is difficult to determine if intake staff participant selection decisions are unduly influenced by applicants' probable labor market success. Most research focuses on direct cream skimming by intake staff, or cream skimming based on their observations of applicant characteristics during the participant selection process. For example, one intake worker observed in this study described an applicant who was laid off from a high-wage, high-skilled job and was hoping to be called back to this position. Anticipating an easy job placement, the worker enrolled the applicant and assigned him to job search assistance activities. When the participant was called back to his previous job, the service provider received credit for this placement. This is a relatively obvious case of cream skimming.

Cream skimming may also operate indirectly, however, through practices that may be more difficult to identify. Program managers may influence participant mix indirectly by offering certain types of training services that may or may not appeal to specific applicant groups. They may also establish intake and assessment procedures that favor one type of applicant over another. JTPA's restrictions on stipends and supportive services and the capabilities or willingness of service providers to make supportive services available, for example, may have influenced who applied and the level of motivation they needed to secure an opportunity to participate. In addition, the location of service offices and focus of outreach activities may also affect program awareness and the resulting applicant pool.

In this research, I distinguish between indirect cream skimming, which typically influences who is likely to apply for services and who is likely to follow through the application process (i.e., decisions made by the eligible persons), and direct cream skimming, which, alternatively, results from decisions made by intake staff based on their observations of and interactions with applicants during the selection process. I hypothesize that incentives created by JTPA performance standards (and continuing under WIA) likely encouraged a combination of direct cream skimming on participant characteristics and indirect cream skimming that was grounded in program administrative decisions and contractual arrangements at the local level.

CASE STUDY AND SIMULATION OF JTPA PARTICIPANT SELECTION AND SERVICE ASSIGNMENT PROCESSES

While JTPA legislation, state- and local-level program priorities, and terms of contracts between job training agencies and service providers all provided guidelines for participant selection and service assignment, these decisions were typically made by the agency's job training professionals or service provider staff under contract with the agency. A goal of this case study was to uncover the underlying structure of these judgments, model the participant selection and service assignment processes, and evaluate their implications for employment and training outcomes.

A number of different factors might influence the judgments of agency and service provider staff in participant selection and service assignment decisions, including external influences such as agency or contract target population goals, training service and expenditures plans, eligibility requirements, and application procedures. Judgments of intake staff would also be based on their own knowledge, experience, and preferences, and the observed or measured characteristics of the applicants. Controls for these factors are necessary to evaluate their relative influences in participant selection and service assignment processes.

This study makes use of detailed information from applicants to a job training program at all stages of the participant selection process. Participant selection and service assignment decision-making processes were observed, intake staff were interviewed about these decision processes, and final outcomes (i.e., intake staff judgments) were recorded. These observations aided the formulation of hypotheses about these processes. Next, an empirical strategy was developed to assess how different factors interact to produce the final decision outcomes.

Case-Study and Simulation Goals, Methodology, and Hypotheses

In studying the structural components of human judgments, Rossi and Nock (1982) note that there are a relatively small number of characteristics to which decision makers pay attention when making judgments about persons. In other words, only a small number of characteristics of the seemingly infinite number of ways in which job training program applicants may differ are actually important to the judgments at hand. Second, they argue that, for the most part, judgments are "socially structured," i.e., there is general agreement among persons on how much weight should be given to relevant characteristics and on how these characteristics should be combined to arrive at judgments. A third structural component of human judgments is that each decision maker tends toward consistency in his or her own judgments, departing in a regular way from the socially defined consensus on how such judgments should be made. If these structural components exist for a specific set of judgments, then the judgments can be modeled to determine what variables or characteristics are most relevant to the judgment, as well as the nature of their influence.

Using detailed data on intake staff decisions, I formulate an approach to evaluate the influences of external factors and applicant characteristics that used both "constructed" and actual program data. First, based on observations of participant selection and service assignment decisions and discussions with intake staff, I generate a list of factors examined by intake staff in these decision-making processes. Using actual data collected by program staff on these factors, I construct a simulation exercise of these processes. The exercise consisted of four main parts: 1) the selection of job training program participants from a pool of applicants constructed using actual program data; 2) the assignment of the selected "participants" to training activities; 3) the consideration of alternative scenarios of constraints on participant selection decisions, including different levels of performance standards and cost constraints; and 4) a review and open group discussion of the caseworkers' selection decisions, which included case comparisons chosen to probe the influences of external factors and applicant characteristics on their decisions. (See Heinrich [1995] for a detailed description of the simulation exercise design as well as a transcription of the postsimulation discussion.)

I subsequently analyze a number of hypotheses using these data. First, are there a relatively small number of observed applicant characteristics which emerge as important in intake staff selection decisions? What are these characteristics? The relative importance of characteristics associated with applicants' employability or their probability of placement was of particular interest, as they relate to analyses of cream skimming. Using information known about the actual placement outcomes of program applicants, I also evaluate the influence of applicants' probability of placement on intake staff selection decisions.

A second set of hypotheses posed the following questions: Do intake staff use the same decision function in selecting participants (as other staff members), and do they make the same participant selections? Another hypothesis pertains to the third structural component of human judgments: Are intake staff selection decisions consistent, i.e., do they depart in a regular way from the socially defined consensus? The intake staff's actual selections of participants for the job training program were compared to their simulation selections to evaluate consistency.

The simulation was designed to hold constant or eliminate constraints on decision making that may influence intake staff's actual selection decisions. For example, in the simulation, intake staff were given explicit verbal and written instructions that they should assume no restrictions on the availability of training service activities. After making participant selections, intake staff assigned the selected cases to training service activities based on applicant characteristics. I subsequently analyzed the relationship of observed applicant characteristics to their assignment to different training service activities.

Intake staff were also provided with a target job placement rate and approximate cost per participant that reflected job training center contract averages of these performance standards for optional use in the simulation. I use responses of intake staff to a questionnaire administered during the exercise and postsimulation discussion to uncover information about the influence of these performance standards during the simulation and in practice and their interaction with training services constraints in actual job training programs.

Two professional job training program caseworkers who were employees of a job training service provider under contract with the agency participated in the simulation.[3] These caseworkers were exclusively responsible for selecting program participants and assigning them to program activities for the job training program studied. Agency officials and program caseworkers provided copies of all records of applicants to the program, including caseworkers' comments written during case reviews and following meetings with program applicants. Caseworkers' participant selection and service assignment procedures were also observed. While it might have been useful to conduct the simulation with many intake staff across the job training center, complete access to other applicant records and observations of intake staff were not possible, so that similar hypothesis testing and data analyses would not have been feasible.

Description of JTPA Participant Selection and Service Assignment Processes

Similar to many job training agencies under JTPA, the number of applicants eligible for program services in this service delivery area tended to substantially exceed the number of program openings. There were 221 applicants to the specific job training program studied, and 50 of these persons were eventually selected to participate. In screening applicants for the program, intake staff met with them an average of four times before they made a decision to either enroll them or to refer them to another organization for services.

All intake staff in Illinois were required to screen applicants for employment barriers, including basic skills deficiencies, limited work histories, single head of household with dependent children, displaced homemaker, child care needs, limited English proficiency, handicapped, veteran, ex-offender, and substance abuse. Caseworkers conveyed the importance of identifying applicants' employment barriers and determining whether they could be overcome with the commitment of the applicant and the resources of the program.

Caseworkers indicated that they viewed the presence of employment barriers as an opportunity to serve persons who have a greater need for program services. Employment barriers that emerged as positive selection criteria included basic skills deficiencies, minimal work histories, single head of household, and the presence of children in a household. Persons with employment barriers that could not be addressed with program resources, such as serious medical or mental health conditions, were referred to other agencies for assistance. In addition, caseworkers did not view the receipt of public assistance as an employment barrier, noting that since the stipend provided under CETA was eliminated in JTPA, the receipt of public aid may have provided an essential source of income for some participants during their enrollment.

Caseworkers also evaluated applicants' levels of motivation and commitment to making the program work. While the average number of times applicants met with caseworkers was four, case records of program applicants showed a range of as few as one meeting to as many as eight scheduled appointments over four to six weeks. Applicants were typically required to come back for at least one additional meeting; those who did not return again were assumed to be less serious about participating. If the applicants kept their appointments, were punctual, and came prepared, caseworkers interpreted these as signs that they were capable and willing to make a serious program commitment. In effect, caseworkers attempted to distinguish between those people who were only interested in a "quick fix" (i.e., looking for the shortest way to get money in their hands) and those who had a serious interest in increasing their skills and finding employment.

The types of information caseworkers sought from applicants also aided their efforts to assess the applicants' ability or willingness to commit to the program. In evaluating employment histories, caseworkers not only sought basic information about employment status, job positions, and recent wages, but they also wanted to know how long applicants stayed with their jobs, the reasons they were no longer at the jobs, and whether absenteeism was ever a problem. They wanted to know the types of occupational or job training activities received in order to avoid duplication or to build upon previously acquired skills. They asked whether the training was completed, if the applicant obtained a job after training, and how long the individual then stayed with the job. If there were gaps in an applicant's employment history, the caseworkers wanted to find out if there were reasonable explanations for them, such as pregnancy, health problems, or family responsibilities. As with employment barriers, their concern was not necessarily how many problems there were, but rather how much effort the applicant was willing to put forth to overcome these difficulties.

Caseworkers claimed that they were less likely to select individuals with post–high school educations, since they believed they could do more to serve persons with relatively less education. Their ability to effectively serve the less educated, however, was also contingent on contract specifications for training service availability. Caseworkers indicated in the simulation questionnaire that the types of training services and available training "slots" were determined long before their initial screening sessions with applicants. In fact, the types of training services and corresponding number of training opportunities were typically set before the final approval of program funding in the JTPA program. The program director then told the caseworkers how many vocational training, on-the-job training (OJT), and other positions could be made available to participants. "[The program director] will tell us something like 'we have five slots for OJT, and we want to fill them with $8.00 per hour positions," explained one caseworker. Caseworkers could make a request to modify the original training service plan, but this was usually not done. The service assignment process actually began, therefore, when the caseworkers commenced the applicant screening process.

Caseworkers also frequently arranged specific training opportunities (e.g., a particular apprenticeship position in a manufacturing plant), and then looked for applicants who met the position requirements. In effect, they would first "fill the training slots" with appropriate positions to satisfy the service provider contract and then screen for applicants who were suitable to these positions. The responses of 110 JTPA applicants to follow-up survey questions about their screening sessions with intake staff also provided evidence of this practice. About 20 percent of the applicants discussed *specific* training opportunities and jobs with intake staff. Several were even set up for interviews and offered jobs before they began intake procedures or before they were notified of the staff's decision to either accept them into the program or refer them elsewhere. One respondent indicated that she was offered a job during the application process and was worried that if that particular job closed, she might not be accepted into the program.

Performance standards in service providers' contracts with the agency may also have influenced the training opportunities made available and final participant selections. In the simulation, caseworkers were given a target job placement rate and an approximate cost per placement to guide their decisions if they chose to use this information. The caseworkers indicated in the postsimulation questionnaire, however, that this information did not have any influence on their participant selection and service assignment decisions. They pointed out that their objective was to "place" the participants, not to worry about costs. "I work with the person, not the money," wrote one caseworker.

During a meeting with agency officials prior to the start of the program, one of the caseworkers had made the comment that it was difficult to get "numbers" out of his mind, that he was thinking "numbers, numbers, numbers." When asked about his comment in the open discussion, this caseworker indicated that it was the job placement rate number that concerned him. He clarified that the placement rate affects whether or not his organization will get comparable funding in the next program year. The director who supervises the caseworkers' work also indicated that the job placement rate achieved by the program would be a key factor in agency's evaluation of the service provider's performance. On the other hand, caseworkers also emphasized the separation of day-to-day operations "in the field" and issues of the budget that are the director's concern: " . . . we're not dealing directly with the budget. We are the implementers of the program."

The findings of an interview conducted with the agency's intake supervisor supported the caseworkers' assertion about the role and influence of performance standards (see Heinrich [1995] for the interview transcription). The intake supervisor indicated that participants were selected on the basis of the professional judgment of intake staff, and that the performance standards played no direct role in their decisions. Yet the intake supervisor also indicated that intake staff had little discretion in deciding what types of training services they could make available to clients. She said they were given strict, detailed guidelines to which they were expected to closely adhere in assigning participants to activities. This finding is consistent with the caseworkers' responses indicating they did not have a role in determining the *availability and number* of training service openings. These decisions were made by the program director in consideration of contract requirements and budget specifications negotiated with agency officials. Together, these findings suggest that the influence of performance standards in the participant selection and service assignment processes may have been more likely to operate indirectly, at the administrative or executive level, through decisions made about service availability by program directors and agency executives. The reported separation of performance standards considerations from intake staff duties appears to refute contentions that performance standards lead to direct cream skimming based on applicant characteristics at the caseworker level.

SIMULATION FINDINGS: JTPA PARTICIPANT SELECTION AND SERVICE ASSIGNMENTS

Figure 8.1 shows how simulated data were analyzed to evaluate the influence of various factors on participant selection and service assignment decisions. The columns show the decision of caseworker

Figure 8.1 Analysis of Counselors' Simulated Selection Decisions

		Counselor 1 selections	
		Choose applicant	Do not choose
Counselor 2 selections	Choose applicant	Both select applicant	Only counselor 2 chooses
	Do not choose	Only counselor 1 chooses	Neither select applicant

1 (e.g., choose or do not choose applicant), and the rows reflect the same decision of caseworker 2. Also shown are the four possible outcomes of caseworkers' decisions for a given applicant: both select the applicant, neither selects the applicant, caseworker 1 selects the applicant but caseworker 2 does not, and caseworker 2 chooses the applicant but caseworker 1 does not. The simulation data for all applicants were aggregated to form the following variables for analyses: 1) applicants selected by caseworker 1 (column 1 in the box); 2) applicants selected by caseworker 2 (row 1 in the box); 3) applicants selected by either caseworker 1 or caseworker 2 (upper right-hand cell, upper left-hand cell and lower left-hand cell); and 4) the selection decisions of caseworker 1 plus those of caseworker 2 (all four cells in the box), which factors in their decisions not to choose applicants as well. The fourth decision variable is used only in logit analyses of the simulation data.

Comparison of Simulation Selections and Actual Program Selections

Simple comparisons of the caseworkers' simulation and actual program selections (e.g., chi-square tests) suggested that the two caseworkers selected similar groups of participants and that they were generally consistent in their decision-making procedures. Twelve of the 25 cases selected by the caseworkers in the simulation (48 percent) were the same. However, these comparisons do not provide information about which applicant characteristics they emphasized in their selection decisions, how much weight was given to these characteristics, or how different characteristics might have interacted to influence their selection decisions. To learn more about caseworkers' decision functions and how they arrived at final selections, maximum likelihood logit models of their participant selections were estimated.

Logit models were used to estimate factors influencing participant selections.[4] Four of the dependent variables employed in the logit analyses were described in Figure 8.1: 1) the simulated participant selections of caseworker 1; 2) the simulated participant selections of caseworker 2; 3) the simulated selections of either caseworker 1 or caseworker 2; and 4) selections of caseworker 1 plus caseworker 2, where cases selected by neither caseworker have zero "weight." Cases selected by one but not the other are "weighted" by one, and cases selected by both are "weighted" by two. Errors in these simulated selection models may represent individual errors (e.g., deviations from the caseworkers' usual judgment processes), intrinsic uncertainty (e.g., reflecting that the caseworkers' judgments may naturally vary or not always be 100 percent consistent), and other possible decision errors.

The fifth dependent variable indicates which of the 50 applicant cases included in the simulation were actual program participants and was used to model the influence of applicant characteristics on caseworkers' actual participant selections. The error term in this model may reflect the influence of omitted variables (e.g., factors which caseworkers considered but were not incorporated in the simulation), such as the reasons applicants left their previous jobs. This type of information was not available for all applicants and therefore was not provided to caseworkers in the simulation.

A large number of possible explanatory variables was reduced through the modeling process to a core set of independent variables, including age, sex (male), single head of household, highest grade completed, previous training services, never married, welfare recipient, number of children, basic skills deficiency, limited work history, unemployed all of preprogram year, and most recent wage. All of the dependent and independent variables employed in the logit analyses are described in Appendix 8A.

The logistic regression model results for the five dependent variables are summarized in Table 8.1. The findings suggest that caseworkers emphasize different factors in their selection decisions, and the coefficient sizes and signs on many variables suggest that they weighed these factors differently as well. Four of the explanatory variables in the model of caseworker 2's selections attained statistical significance,

Table 8.1 Findings from Simulation and Actual Participant Selection Logit Models

	Dependent variables				
Independent variables	Caseworker 1 selections (N=46)	Caseworker 2 selections (N=46)	Selections of caseworker 1 or 2 (N=46)	Selections of caseworker 1 + caseworker 2 (N=96)	Actual participant selections (N=46)
Constant	45.473***	−13.098**	12.439	10.537**	−2.639
	(16.854)	(6.596)	(13.355)	(4.841)	(5.203)
Age	−0.088	0.260***	0.472	−0.021	0.044
	(0.086)	(0.099)	(0.291)	(0.038)	(0.069)
Sex (male)	1.332	−0.796	0.152	−0.012	0.979
	(1.512)	(1.161)	(0.865)	(0.698)	(1.103)
Single head of household	−0.220	−1.297	−6.275	−0.213	3.403***
	(1.496)	(1.472)	(4.392)	(0.744)	(1.383)
Highest grade completed	−3.503***	0.100	−2.887*	−0.910***	−0.111
	(1.341)	(0.469)	(1.551)	(0.374)	(0.370)
Previous training services	−0.156	−0.129	6.190	−0.100	0.501
	(1.016)	(1.034)	(4.256)	(0.603)	(0.855)
Never married	0.918	4.303***	10.909	2.013	−1.272
	(1.129)	(1.631)	(6.784)	(1.461)	(0.949)
Welfare recipient	2.200	1.559	1.978	0.456	−1.472
	(1.493)	(1.156)	(1.325)	(0.633)	(0.996)
Children	−0.412	0.635**	2.347*	−0.157	−0.027
	(0.274)	(0.324)	(1.349)	(0.167)	(0.210)

Basic skills deficiency	2.840**	8.054*	−0.586	−1.591	0.246
	(1.337)	(4.835)	(0.654)	(1.202)	(0.938)
Limited work history	−1.102	1.198	0.567	1.814	0.901
	(1.245)	(2.173)	(0.679)	(1.454)	(0.973)
Unemployed all of preprogram year	−0.661	−4.269	2.603***	−1.320	1.528*
	(0.995)	(3.111)	(0.682)	(1.326)	(0.919)
Most recent hourly wage	0.014	0.026	0.023	−0.163	0.098
	(0.246)	(0.115)	(0.142)	(0.308)	(0.191)
Log likelihood	−18.493	−8.464	−46.783	−16.963	−25.079
Pseudo R^2 (%)	37.2	15.6	84.5	36.9	48.2

NOTE: * significant at $\alpha = 0.100$; ** significant at $\alpha = 0.050$; *** significant at $\alpha = 0.010$. Standard errors are shown in parentheses below the coefficient values.

compared to only one independent variable in the model of caseworker 1's selections. Caseworker 2 was the older and more experienced intake staff member. It is possible that as intake staff gain more experience in this profession, they become more certain about which applicant characteristics are important and/or more consistent in their decision-making procedures.

A formal test of the hypothesis that the caseworkers employed the same decision function, a test for equality of the coefficients in the selection models, was performed.[5] The results of the likelihood ratio test rejected the null hypothesis (at $\alpha < 0.005$) that the caseworkers' decision functions were the same.[6] This finding suggests that there may not be a strong "social structure" or consensus as to how applicant characteristics should be evaluated in participant selection processes, at least for the characteristics measured and included in these models. I also calculated pseudo-R^2 values for the models (see Amemiya 1981) and found that when modeled separately, there is considerably more unexplained variance in the caseworkers' simulated selections. This seems to suggest that when combining the decisions made by both caseworkers and giving more weight to cases in which both agreed to either admit or reject applicants, we gain a better understanding of their decision-making processes.

The most consistent finding across the models in Table 8.1 was the negative coefficient on the highest grade completed variable, statistically significant in three of the five models. This finding implies that applicants with more education were less likely to be selected into the program and is consistent with caseworkers' indications that they favored applicants with lower education levels.

The two employment barriers mentioned most frequently in case reviews and in the postsimulation discussion were basic skills deficiencies and limited work histories. Being the most closely related (of the observed characteristics) to applicants' employability, one would expect that if intake staff were cream skimming based on these characteristics, they would be negatively related to the probability of selection. The coefficient for basic skills deficiency is positive in three models and is large and statistically significant in two of these. The limited work history variable also has a positive coefficient in four models but is not statistically significant in any model. These findings provide tentative evidence against the theory that intake staff cream-skim on observed characteristics related to employability. Long-term unemployment was also a statistically significant, *positive* selection factor in two models.

The variable coefficients in the model of the caseworkers' actual program participant selections, however, differed from those in the caseworkers' simulation models. These differences might be attributed to a number of factors, including unobserved and unmeasured factors (such as applicant motivation or constraints on training service assignments) and decision errors (including random deviations from their usual judgment processes or inconsistencies in their judgments).

With information about the caseworkers' actual program participant selections and the employment outcomes of program applicants, I further analyze the influence of applicants' probability of placement on participant selection decisions using a two-stage model. In the first-stage regression (shown in Table 8.2), a variable indicating whether or not employment was obtained following program application was regressed against applicants' demographic and employment and training history characteristics to obtain predicted probabilities of placement for the applicants. These predicted placement probabilities formed a new variable (the probability of placement) that was used as an explanatory variable in a second-stage regression with caseworkers' actual participant selections as the dependent variable (also shown in Table 8.2).

A striking finding of this second-stage regression is the relatively large, positive, and statistically significant coefficient on the probability of placement variable, more precisely estimated than any other explanatory variable in the regression. This finding suggests that in the actual participant selection process, caseworkers were likely influenced by factors related to applicants' probability of placement (or employment). It also indicates that direct cream skimming on applicant characteristics might have been occurring.

To further evaluate this argument, I also added the probability of placement variable to the caseworkers' simulated selection models and reestimated these logistic regressions (see Table 8.3). In estimating these models, I sought to test whether the probability of placement was some function of the observed applicant characteristics provided to caseworkers in the simulation, or a function of additional information the caseworkers acquire during the selection process, i.e., information not captured in the variables made available in the simulation.

Table 8.2 Two-Stage Logistic Regression Estimation of the Influence of Applicants' Probability of Placement on Participant Selection Decisions

Independent variables	First-stage logistic regression Dependent variable: Placed in employment (or employed) following program participation (or application)	Second-stage logistic regression Dependent variable: Actual participant selections
Constant	−34.547*	1.482
	(19.327)	(6.884)
Age	0.360**	−0.087
	(0.161)	(0.106)
Sex (male)	5.715	0.638
	(3.650)	(1.397)
Single head of household	2.835	3.960**
	(3.026)	(1.750)
Highest grade completed	1.171	−0.232
	(0.942)	(0.487)
Previous training services	0.576	0.615
	(0.898)	(1.092)
Never married	4.046*	−2.896**
	(2.398)	(1.375)
Welfare recipient	3.500	−2.358*
	(2.365)	(1.352)
Children	0.206	−0.148
	(0.669)	(0.284)
Basic skills deficiency	4.597	−0.297
	(3.027)	(1.316)
Limited work history	7.146*	0.070
	(3.983)	(1.217)
Unemployed all of preprogram year	−4.095*	2.365**
	(2.227)	(1.191)
Most recent hourly wage	−0.472	−0.126
	(0.354)	(0.260)
Probability of placement	n/a	6.392***
		(2.114)
Model log likelihood	−9.150	−18.360
Pseudo R^2 (%)	17.1	37.1

NOTE: * significant at $\alpha = 0.100$; ** significant at $\alpha = 0.050$; *** significant at $\alpha = 0.010$. Standard errors are shown in parentheses below the coefficient values.

The results presented in Table 8.3 indicate that the probability of placement was not a significant factor in the caseworkers' simulation selection decisions. There are several possible interpretations of these findings. One is that the caseworkers did evaluate and weigh applicants' observed characteristics to estimate their probability of placement, but that in the simulation (free of performance pressures and constraints), they did not use this information. A more plausible explanation, however, is that the probability of placement was judged mainly using information not made available in the simulation. For example, some of these unmeasured variables might include information that provides clues about the applicants' motivation (from details of employment history to physical appearance). Although this type of information is not systematically collected by employment and training program staff, in their actual participant selection decisions, caseworkers seemed to predict placement probabilities very well and to use this information to guide their decisions.

In his classic study on bureaucracy, Blau (1955) finds similar participant screening philosophies and practices among state employment agency staff. Like the JTPA intake workers, employment agency staff who exercised discretion in client selection indicated they derived satisfaction from helping those most in need and "welcomed the opportunity to assist them." However, in actual client selections, Blau finds the majority of agency staff favored "strivers," or persons who were most likely to be successful in society. He concluded that personal preferences for helping the most disadvantaged were set aside as a result of the orientation toward maximizing placements and in the interest of efficient performance. Forty years later, Blau's conclusions seem to garner support from this case study as well.

Multinomial Logit Analyses of Factors Influencing Participant Assignment to Training Activities

During the simulation, the caseworkers assigned each person they selected to a training service activity. They were given no guidelines as to the number of "participants" they could assign to each of four available program activities (vocational training, on-the-job training, remedial education, and job search assistance). In making these assignments, caseworkers were asked to consider only applicant characteristics.

Table 8.3 Logistic Regressions of Simulated Participant Selections from Caseworker 1 and Caseworker 2, Including Probability of Placement Variable

	Dependent variables	
Independent variables	Caseworker 1's simulated participant selections	Caseworker 2's simulated participant selections
Constant	45.367***	−18.037**
	(16.987)	(8.503)
Age	−0.105	0.362***
	(0.096)	(0.140)
Sex (male)	1.180	−0.860
	(1.545)	(1.220)
Single head of household	−0.432	−1.643
	(1.591)	(1.518)
Highest grade completed	−3.458***	0.239
	(1.347)	(0.500)
Previous training services	−0.136	−0.220
	(1.014)	(1.089)
Never married	0.753	5.884***
	(1.172)	(2.192)
Welfare recipient	2.125	1.806
	(1.484)	(1.191)
Number of children	−0.422	0.824**
	(0.274)	(0.375)
Basic skills deficiency	−1.610	4.045**
	(1.207)	(1.748)
Limited work history	1.557	−0.920
	(1.557)	(1.256)
Unemployed all of preprogram year	−1.223	−1.081
	(1.334)	(1.075)
Most recent hourly wage	−0.191	0.064
	(0.321)	(0.259)
Probability of placement	0.806	−2.816
	(1.886)	(2.224)
Model log likelihood	−16.726	−18.493
Pseudo R^2 (%)	36.8	37.2

NOTE: ** significant at $\alpha = 0.050$; *** significant at $\alpha = 0.010$. Standard errors are shown in parentheses below the coefficient values.

The multinomial logit analyses examine the factors that influenced intake staff service assignment decisions. The dependent variables are categorical variables for four main types of program activities made available in JTPA programs: vocational training, on-the-job training, basic or remedial education, and job search assistance. The independent variables in these models were the characteristics of the selected participants, i.e., the same core set of variables employed in the models of participant selection. Table 8.4 shows the multinomial logit estimation of participant service assignments using the simulation data. Despite the small sample of 38 simulation assignees (only those cases selected were assigned to services), there are a number of statistically significant findings among these results.

A multinomial logit regression of service assignment was also estimated for adult JTPA Title IIA program participants in the job training agency. The management information system (MIS) data provided by the agency for all JTPA program years was used, yielding a total of 18,120 observations. The dependent variable employed in the job training center multinomial logit model included assignment to the same four categories of training as the simulation model. The independent variables were also the same as those available for the simulation models, with a few exceptions.[7] The job training center multinomial logit model is shown in Table 8.5.

One of the more important findings of the multinomial logit models suggests that access to training opportunities for persons with basic skills deficiencies and low education levels may have been relatively limited. High school dropouts and persons with basic skills deficiencies were significantly more likely to be assigned to receive remedial education, while persons with more education were significantly less likely to receive these services. Persons with basic skills deficiencies were significantly less likely to be assigned to vocational training, on-the-job training, or job search assistance, while persons with post–high school educations were significantly more likely to receive job search assistance. These findings support the theory that individuals assigned to on-the-job training and job search assistance require basic education and skill levels that make them more "job-ready." Discussions with the program caseworkers and findings of the National JTPA Study also revealed that vocational training providers often have enrollment requirements that preclude the entry of persons with basic skills defi-

Table 8.4 Multinomial Logit Model of Training Activity Assignments Using Simulation Data

	Categorical dependent variable			
Independent variables	Vocational training	On-the-job training	Basic or remedial education	Job search assistance
Constant	−9.800	110.385	8.676	−4.052
	(13.93)	(258.1)	(5.799)	(15.53)
Age	0.121	−0.307*	−0.006	−0.579
	(0.114)	(0.179)	(0.060)	(0.460)
Sex (male)	0.427	0.324	0.301	−1.605
	(1.867)	(2.920)	(0.852)	(4.188)
Single head of household	3.618*	−3.555	0.725	−34.639
	(2.222)	(2.639)	(0.900)	(46.71)
Highest grade completed	−0.584	−8.869	−1.094**	0.724
	(0.887)	(20.93)	(0.483)	(1.991)
Welfare recipient	0.305	−1.049	0.562	7.679*
	(1.527)	(1.767)	(0.721)	(4.465)
Number of children	0.344	−0.571	−0.008	−1.801*
	(0.352)	(0.660)	(0.206)	(0.919)
Basic skills deficiency	1.169	−42.929**	1.828**	−1.203
	(1.664)	(20.15)	(0.926)	(3.050)
Limited work history	3.601**	0.571	0.539	−39.705**
	(1.782)	(3.122)	(1.045)	(16.40)
Unemployed all of preprogram year	0.500	10.278**	2.183***	20.488
	(1.288)	(4.167)	(0.761)	(14.47)

Never married	0.624	4.391	−0.514	0.117
	(1.386)	(2.768)	(0.753)	(0.116)
Most recent hourly wage	0.850**	0.546	0.114	0.010
	(0.431)	(0.322)	(0.182)	(0.008)
Model log likelihood	−61.396			

NOTE: * significant at $\alpha = 0.100$; ** significant at $\alpha = 0.050$; *** significant at $\alpha = 0.010$. Standard errors are shown in parentheses below the coefficient values.

Table 8.5 Multinomial Logit Model of Training Activity Assignments Using Service Records of 18,120 Adult JTPA Title IIA Participants, Program Years 1984–1993

	Categorical dependent variable			
Independent variables	Vocational training	On-the-job training	Basic or remedial education	Job search assistance
Constant	−0.297*	−0.303**	−4.899***	−2.951***
	(0.153)	(0.138)	(0.357)	(0.142)
Age	−0.016***	−0.029***	−0.033***	0.026***
	(0.003)	(0.003)	(0.006)	(0.002)
Sex (male)	−0.107*	0.571***	0.202	−0.007
	(0.064)	(0.058)	(0.130)	(0.054)
Single head of household	0.171**	0.155**	−0.120	0.188***
	(0.075)	(0.065)	(0.148)	(0.064)
High school dropout	0.098	−0.039	1.233***	0.169
	(0.076)	(0.068)	(0.129)	(0.704)
Post–high school education	0.016	−0.197***	−0.519***	0.152***
	(0.063)	(0.058)	(0.168)	(0.055)
Welfare recipient	0.147**	−0.573***	−0.466***	−0.023
	(0.069)	(0.067)	(0.123)	(0.061)
Household size	−0.013	0.029***	0.033*	−0.011
	(0.015)	(0.010)	(0.019)	(0.036)
Basic skills deficiency	−0.148***	−0.097*	0.593***	−0.087*
	(0.058)	(0.051)	(0.110)	(0.051)
Limited work history	0.067	−0.282***	0.346***	0.029
	(0.059)	(0.054)	(0.113)	(0.053)

Unemployed at application	−0.321	−0.135**	−0.029	0.027
	(0.338)	(0.060)	(0.138)	(0.063)
Unemployed all of preprogram year	−0.060	−0.293***	0.688***	0.234
	(0.076)	(0.069)	(0.151)	(0.157)
Employed–unemployed	−0.088	0.044	−0.160	0.031
	(0.074)	(0.060)	(0.148)	(0.065)
Unemployed–employed	−0.047	−0.092	0.145	0.249***
	(0.700)	(0.058)	(0.144)	(0.061)
African American	0.064	−0.340***	0.963***	−0.176***
	(0.061)	(0.052)	(0.145)	(0.054)
Program year 1989	0.806***	0.970***	2.177***	1.072***
	(0.096)	(0.078)	(0.205)	(0.090)
Program year 1990	0.993***	0.670***	2.496***	0.830***
	(0.082)	(0.077)	(0.184)	(0.089)
Program year 1991	0.930***	0.698***	2.030***	0.613***
	(0.093)	(0.079)	(0.093)	(0.099)
Program year 1992	−0.228**	−0.244***	0.308	0.354***
	(0.097)	(0.079)	(0.252)	(0.060)
Model log likelihood	−20,586.83			

NOTE: * significant at $\alpha = 0.100$; ** significant at $\alpha = 0.050$; *** significant at $\alpha = 0.010$. Standard errors are shown in parentheses below the coefficient values.

ciencies, e.g., requirements such as a high school diploma or minimum scores on tests of adult basic education.

Another noteworthy finding was that males were more likely to be assigned to on-the-job training, which has consistently been shown to be the most effective employment and training service (Barnow and Gubits 2002). During case reviews and the postsimulation discussion, the caseworkers pointed out that men tended to be more eager to get into training activities that generated a faster monetary payoff. Since on-the-job training participants received wages during the training period, males found these training opportunities more lucrative. In addition, male applicants were more likely to have had previous job experience that was expected to aid a successful outcome in on-the-job training activities. In general, women and welfare recipients were more likely to be assigned to vocational training activities, and welfare recipients were also significantly less likely to be assigned to on-the-job training activities. Also consistent with the above findings, persons with limited work histories (i.e., minimal job experience) were significantly less likely to be assigned to on-the-job training and job search assistance; they were significantly more likely to receive remedial education or vocational training services.

The coefficients for the program year indicators (Table 8.5) show a pattern of declining assignment probabilities in the 1990s, most likely reflecting the decline in JTPA program funding and reduced number of training opportunities during these years. Studies suggest that with fewer resources, job training agencies are more likely to allocate funds to less expensive, shorter-term training activities and to avoid serving those who require more intensive services to become job-ready (Dickinson and West 1988; Zornitsky et al. 1988; Orfield and Slessarev 1986). Table 8.6 shows that corresponding to funding declines in the 1990s, there was a noticeable shift in this agency toward less expensive services (e.g., job search assistance and job club activities). There was also a less definitive trend away from the provision of more expensive training such as remedial education services, on-the-job training and vocational training (with costs per placement ranging from $2,917.90 to $2,834.10). Job search assistance and job club activities (a less intensive form of job search) were much less expensive services (approximately $1700). (See Table 8.7 for job placement rates, wages at place-

Table 8.6 Number of Training Services Received by JTPA Title 2A Adult Participants, Program Years 1986–1993

		PY 1986	PY 1987	PY 1988	PY 1989	PY 1990	PY 1991	PY 1992	PY 1993
JTPA training service activity[a]		N=2,732	N=2,302	N=1,811	N=1,633	N=1,314	N=1,010	N=1,101	N=1,065
Vocational training	n	1,145	947	730	733	654	527	544	409
	%	(41.9)	(41.1)	(40.3)	(44.9)	(49.8)	(52.2)	(49.4)	(38.4)
On-the-job training	n	815	609	530	473	340	288	325	281
	%	(29.8)	(26.5)	(29.3)	(29.0)	(25.9)	(28.5)	(29.5)	(26.4)
Remedial education	n	n/a[b]	n/a	n/a	186	96	51	38	50
	%				(11.4)	(7.3)	(5.0)	(3.5)	(4.7)
Job search assistance	n	n/a	n/a	216	204	157	84	197	184
	%			(9.1)	(12.5)	(11.9)	(8.3)	(17.9)	(17.3)
Job club	n	n/a	n/a	135	189	127	51	170	151
	%			(7.5)	(11.6)	(9.7)	(5.0)	(15.4)	(14.2)
Counseling and	n	1,149	1,040	653	419	300	195	0	9
assessment	%	(42.1)	(45.2)	(36.1)	(25.7)	(22.8)	(19.3)	(0.0)	(0.8)
Case management	n	n/a	n/a	n/a	n/a	n/a	n/a	950	1,036
	%							(86.3)	(97.3)

[a] Supportive services were not shown in this table since the identifier codes were used inconsistently in the JTPA MIS system.

[b] For some of the early program years, these data were either not available or were coded inconsistently.

ment, and estimated service costs for adult JTPA Title IIA participants by program activity.)

In addition, Table 8.6 shows that counseling and assessment activities were replaced by case management services beginning in program year 1992. To generate an official record of the provision of case management services, program staff had to make contact with a participant at least once per month. This minimal case-management requirement made these services very inexpensive to provide. In program year 1993, 23.8 percent of JTPA Title IIA program participants received *only* case management services while enrolled. It is possible that as program resources continued to decline, job training agencies found that providing only case-management services was an inexpensive way to maintain participant numbers despite squeezed budgets.

It is also possible that agency officials were struggling to manage trade-offs among the costs of services, the benefits to participants as measured by performance standards, and the number of training opportunities they could make available. The job placement rate was accorded the highest weight in this agency's performance evaluation process. The provision of on-the-job training services, which were more costly to provide but generated higher average job placement rates (by a margin of 21–38 percent) than other training activities, was not declining over time. Vocational training, however, had a substantially lower average

Table 8.7 Job Placement Rates, Wages at Placement, and Estimated Costs of Service for Adult JTPA Title IIA Participants by Program Activity

Program activity	Mean job placement rate (%)	Mean wage at placement ($)	Estimated cost per placement ($)
Vocational training	58.3	5.87	2,834.10
On-the-job training	81.2	6.72	2,844.13
Remedial education services	43.0	5.73	2,917.90
Job search assistance	47.7	6.82	1,789.06
Job club	51.2	6.90	1,642.90
Counseling and assessment	59.9	6.17	2,541.46
Case management	58.4	7.03	n/a[a]

[a] For most service provider contracts and participant records, the costs of case management activities are not specified separately from other service costs.

job placement rate (58.3 percent) that is about the same as the placement rate for counseling/case management activities, but is considerably more expensive to provide than counseling and case management. In a 1992 review of job training program evaluations, LaLonde finds that less expensive services provided to a larger segment of the eligible population yielded higher returns for each training dollar invested. It is also important to remember that costs per placement continued to be a primary factor in this agency's performance reviews and contract award decisions long after the federal government eliminated cost-per-placement standards.

Synthesis of Findings on Participant Selection, Service Assignment, and Program Management

The analyses of participant selection and service assignment decisions, in conjunction with the implications of declining program resources in this job training agency, suggest that declining program funds may have compelled the provision of cheaper training services. This, in turn, may have required the recruitment of more job-ready persons to attain successful outcomes (i.e., job placements). For example, given budgetary pressures due to declining federal program resources, service providers may have been led in competitive bidding and contract negotiations to increase the number of job search assistance (i.e., less expensive) positions budgeted for their programs. As intake staff typically worked with fixed numbers of available training positions when they began the applicant screening process, they may have been required to recruit more individuals suitable to job search assistance activities.

One of the most consistent findings in the simulated and actual participant selection models was the negative relationship of years of schooling completed to the probability of selection. On the other hand, Tables 8.4 and 8.5 showed that the number of years of schooling completed was positively related to assignment to job search assistance activities. Therefore, given a specific and growing number of job search assistance positions they were required to fill, intake staff may have been induced to select more applicants with higher education levels.

The participant selection models also indicated that applicants with basic skills deficiencies were more likely to be selected, and the service assignment models showed these persons were significantly more likely to receive remedial education services. However, remedial education was one of the more expensive training activities, and provision of these services declined over time under JTPA. Nonprofit agencies (independent of the JTPA program) were likewise under increasing performance accountability pressures and less likely to offer remedial education on their "menu" of services. As fewer remedial education opportunities were made available, it is possible that caseworkers were less likely to enroll persons with basic skill deficiencies. In addition, the findings also showed that participants with basic skills deficiencies were significantly less likely to be assigned to vocational training, on-the-job training, and job search assistance, suggesting that more disadvantaged participants might not have had access to the full range of training services if remedial education services were not made available to them.

Other case study findings generally supported these assertions about the effects of budgetary constraints on the availability of training opportunities and the selection of program participants. Service provider managers indicated that contract cost-per-placement standards discouraged the provision of multiple services (e.g., remedial education followed by vocational training), since these services raised average cost per placement figures and could negatively affect future contract awards. Even though intake staff asserted that they are not influenced by performance standards, the continued emphasis on placement rates and costs per placement in local-level service provider contracts seemed to be a pervasive force. A separate study (Heinrich 1999) of this agency's administrative and service provider contracting practices showed that service providers' performance relative to cost standards established in their contracts with the local JTPA agency was the most important factor influencing the agency's contract renewal and funding level decisions.

In conclusion, the strong emphasis on placement rates and costs per placement in the local-level performance evaluation system seemed to inevitably pervade intake staff participant selection and service assignment decisions, contributing to both direct and indirect creaming practices. Other factors affecting program administration and service delivery decisions exacerbated the pressures generated by performance standards. These factors included declining program resources (relative to a large job-training-eligible population), the absence of performance standard adjustments in service provider contracts for services to more disadvantaged applicants, and minimum qualifications required for entry to more intensive skill-building program activities.

CONCLUSION

While the findings of this case study are not generalizable to all job training programs, some basic policy conclusions emerge that have implications for the administration of current job training programs under WIA and other programs (e.g., public welfare). This research produced evidence that "street-level bureaucrats" engaged in job training program service delivery were responsive to incentives generated by the performance standards system. The local job training agency designed its own performance-based contracting and provider performance evaluation system, and program administrators and service provider staff demonstrated that they were highly conscious of the agency's emphasis on placement rate and cost-per-placement outcomes.

The agency's contractual and administrative focus on placement rates and cost-per-placement appeared to have both direct and indirect effects on the participant selection and training service assignment decisions of program staff. Both direct cream skimming on applicant characteristics during the participant selection process and indirect cream skimming grounded in contractual arrangements and program administrative decisions were likely occurring in this service delivery area, with potentially negative implications for the achievement of basic program objectives.

The research findings also suggest that the main sources of indirect cream skimming were contractual and administrative constraints on the types of training services that could be made available to program participants. The study of the JTPA service assignment processes showed that participant selection decisions and service assignment decisions were most often made concurrently, and that the numbers and types of available training positions were typically fixed before the intake process began. Therefore, intake staff were required to find persons suitable to the available training positions, rather than selecting participants based primarily on their relative need for and interest in training services and then assigning them to appropriate activities. This practice by itself does not constitute cream skimming. However, as job training program funds declined over time, the availability of remedial education services decreased substantially, and the provision of relatively less-expensive program services, such as job search assistance and job club activities, increased. As a result, access to training for persons with basic skills deficiencies and low education levels appears to be declining, while access for more able, job-ready applicants (better suited to job search activities) was likely increasing.

In the WIA program, concerns have again been raised about the influence of performance standards on individuals' access to program services. The WIA performance standards, like those in JTPA, still focus on shorter-term outcome levels, and budgetary constraints likewise limit the types of services that are made available to participants. In addition, WIA introduced a sequential process of service access, from core (basic and self-directed job search services) to intensive (job readiness and job search seminars) to substantive job skills training services. While local programs have adapted different approaches to sequencing, early studies show that few clients are receiving the more expensive intensive or training services (D'Amico et al. 2001). Barnow and Gubits (2002) note that in one site, the level of training provided under WIA was reduced by 75 percent.

As discussed in the introductory chapter, a 2002 GAO report suggests that history may be repeating itself. The GAO interviewed WIA program administrators in 50 states and visited five sites to assess the effectiveness of the WIA performance management system and reported that many states have indicated that the need to meet performance standards is a driving factor in who receives WIA-funded services at the local level. It also described how some local areas were limiting access to services for individuals who they perceive are less likely to get and retain a job. Observing the serious challenges that states and localities have faced in implementing the system, the GAO suggested that "even when fully implemented, WIA performance measures may still not provide a true picture of WIA-funded program performance" (GAO 2002, p. 3). In a summary report to the USDOL on the implementation of WIA, Barnow and Gubits (2002, Note 12) also find, based on meetings with officials from about 20 states, that "the greatest dissatisfaction in every instance has been with the way the performance management system has been implemented."

This study presents evidence of strong links between the types of services made available in public training programs and who gets access to these services, and the role and effects of performance standards on key decisions made by program administrators and street-level bureaucrats in implementing the program. More generally, the collective empirical findings of this book demonstrate the responsiveness of public organizations and their employees to performance standards, and suggest that in designing or refining performance standards systems for public programs, careful consideration should be given to both direct and indirect potential consequences of these systems for those served or seeking services.

Notes

1. While this administrative structure was common to many JTPA service delivery areas, WIA now prohibits these local agencies from directly providing training services, and the only contract or agreement for service provision that may be established (with few exceptions) is between the workforce investment boards and One-Stop center operators. The local workforce investment boards are required to select One-Stop operators through a competitive process or designation of a consortium that includes at least three of the federal programs providing services at the One-Stop.
2. The principal 1988 changes included an end to mandatory use of cost-per-placement standards and a shift toward the evaluation of placement and earnings outcomes three months after participant termination rather than at the time of termination.
3. The job training program service provider I closely studied has been operating in this job training center since the CETA years (i.e., before JTPA). It is one of the primary vendors and has accounted for approximately 7 percent of all service provider contracts since the start of JTPA. One of the two program caseworkers had approximately 5 years of experience working in this profession, and the other was employed as a caseworker for 16 years. Both had worked for this particular service provider for about 5 years.
4. The logit model estimated was: $P_i = E(Y{=}1 \mid X_i) = 1 / 1 + e^{-(b1 + b2Xi1 + \ldots + b_k X_{ik})}$, where P_i is the probability an applicant is selected, Y is the program caseworker's decision, taking on the value "1" if a given applicant is selected, and the X_{ik} are characteristics of the program applicants. The betas (b_k) measure the influence of applicant characteristics on caseworkers' judgments.

5. First, an *unrestricted* model of the caseworkers' simulation selections was estimated. This model included two sets of explanatory variables (i.e., the demographic characteristics and employment and training history variables included in the logit models)—one set interacted with caseworker 1's simulation selections and the other interacted with caseworker 2's selections. This model allowed different estimates of the variable coefficients for each caseworker. The restricted model used the dependent variable "caseworker 1 *plus* caseworker 2 selections."
6. Likelihood ratio statistic = $-2 \ln \lambda$, where $\ln \lambda = \ln L(\Omega_r) - \ln L(\Omega) = -56.376 - -33.492 = -22.884$. The observed value of $-2 \ln \lambda$ is very large (45.768). With 11 degrees of freedom, it is much greater than $\chi^2_{0.005}$, which leads me to strongly reject H_o.
7. In the job training center multinomial logit model: 1) education is represented by indicator variables (high school dropout, post–high school education, and college graduate, where the omitted category is high school graduate); 2) household size is used as a proxy for the number of children; 3) employment status and history are represented by an indicator variable for employment status at application (unemployed at application) and variables indicating employment history in the year prior to application (no preprogram year earnings, employed–unemployed transition, unemployed–employed transition); 4) an indicator variable for race (African American) is included in the model; 5) there were no variable measures available in the MIS data for marital status or previous training activities, and 6) program year indicators are included to capture the influence of changes in the availability of different training activities across program years.

References

Amemiya, T. 1981. "Qualitative Response Models: A Survey." *Journal of Economic Literature* 19(4): 483–536.

Barnow, Burt S., and Daniel B. Gubits. 2002. "Review of Recent Pilot, Demonstration, Research, and Evaluation Initiatives to Assist in the Implementation of Programs under the Workforce Investment Act." ETA Occasional Paper No. 2003-10. Washington, DC: USDOL.

Blau, Peter M. 1955. *The Dynamics of Bureaucracy: A Study of Interpersonal Relations in Two Government Agencies*. Chicago: University of Chicago Press.

Brodkin, Evelyn Z. 1987. "Policy Politics: If We Can't Govern, Can We Manage?" *Political Science Quarterly* 102(4): 571–587.

D'Amico, Ron, Deborah Kogan, Suzanne Kreutzer, Andrew Wiegand, and Alberta Baker. 2001. *A Report on Early State and Local Progress Towards WIA Implementation*. Submitted to U.S. Department of Labor, Employment and Training Administration, USDOL Contract No. G-7681-9-00-87-30. Washington, DC: USDOL.

Dickinson, Katherine P., and Richard W. West. 1988. *Evaluation of the Effects of JTPA Performance Standards on Clients, Services, and Costs*. Report No. 88-17. Washington, DC: National Commission for Employment Policy Research.

General Accounting Office (GAO). 2002. *Improvements Needed in Performance Measures to Provide a More Accurate Picture of WIA's Effectiveness*. Report to Congressional Requesters. GAO-02-275. Washington, DC: GAO.

Heinrich, Carolyn J. 1995. "Public Policy and Methodological Issues in the Design and Evaluation of Employment and Training Programs at the Service Delivery Area Level." PhD diss. Harris School of Public Policy Studies, University of Chicago.

———. 1999. "Do Government Bureaucrats Make Effective Use of Performance Management Information?" *Journal of Public Administration Research and Theory* 9(3): 363–393.

LaLonde, Robert J. 1992. "The Earnings Impact of U.S. Employment and Training Programs." Unpublished manuscript. University of Chicago.

Lipsky, Michael. 1980. *Street-Level Bureaucracy*. New York: Russell Sage.

Orfield, Gary, and Helene Slessarev. 1986. *Job Training under the New Federalism*. Chicago: University of Chicago Press.

Rossi, Peter H., and Steven L. Nock. 1982. *Measuring Social Judgements*. Beverly Hills: Sage Publications.

Zornitsky, Jeffrey, and Mary Rubin. 1988. *Establishing a Performance Management System for Target Welfare Programs*. Report No. 88-14. Washington, DC: National Commission for Employment Policy Research.

Appendix 8A
Variable Descriptions

DEPENDENT VARIABLES

Actual participant selections = 1 if actual program participant, 0 if applicant, nonparticipant.
Counselor 1 selections = 1 if selected by counselor 1 during the simulation, 0 if not selected by counselor 1.
Counselor 2 selections = 1 if selected by counselor 2 during the simulation, 0 if not selected by counselor 2.
Counselor 1 or counselor 2 selections = 1 if selected by either counselor 1 or counselor 2 during the simulation, 0 if not selected by either counselor 1 or counselor 2.
Counselor 1 plus counselor 2 selections: based on 100 evaluated exercise cases (50 by counselor 1 and 50 by counselor 2) = 1 if selected by either counselor 1 or counselor 2 during the simulation, 0 if not selected by either counselor 1 or counselor 2.
Service category = 0 if not selected nor assigned to a training activity, 1 if selected case was assigned to vocational training, 2 if selected case was assigned to on-the-job training, 3 if selected case was assigned to remedial education, and 4 if selected case was assigned to job search assistance.
Wage at placement = JTPA program participants' wage at placement (i.e., at the time of their termination from the program, if placed in a job), in dollars.

INDEPENDENT VARIABLES

Sex = 1 if male, 0 if female.

Age Variables

Age: (continuous, range 19–51).
Age less than 30 years = 1 if under 30 years old, 0 otherwise.
Age 30 to 39 years = 1 if 30 to 39 years old, 0 otherwise.
Age over 39 years = 1 if over 39 years old, 0 otherwise.

Ethnicity

White = 1 if white (Caucasian), 0 otherwise.
African American = 1 if African American, 0 otherwise.
Hispanic = 1 if of Hispanic origin (including South or Central Americans, Mexicans, Puerto Ricans, and others), 0 otherwise.
Other race = 1 if American Indian, Asian, or any other race excluded in other categories, 0 otherwise.

Education Variables

Highest grade completed: (continuous, range 10–16).
Dropout = 1 if high school dropout, 0 otherwise.
Graduated high school = 1 if high school graduate with no post–high school education, 0 otherwise.
Post–high school education = 1 if has post–high school education, 0 otherwise.
Any training = 1 if previously received vocational, on-the-job, or other training services, 0 otherwise.
GED = 1 if has GED, 0 otherwise.

Labor Force Status and Employment History Variables

Employed at application = 1 if employed at application, 0 otherwise.
Unemployed at application = 1 if unemployed at application, 0 otherwise.
Not in labor force at application = 1 if not in labor force, 0 otherwise.
Employed–unemployed transition = 1 if employed in 7–12 months prior to application and unemployed in 6 months prior to application, 0 otherwise.
Employed–not in labor force transition = 1 if employed in 7–12 months prior to application and not in labor force in 6 months prior to application, 0 otherwise.
Employed all of preprogram year = 1 if employed in 7–12 months prior to application and employed in 6 months prior to application, 0 otherwise.
Unemployed–employed transition = 1 if unemployed in 7–12 months prior to application and employed in 6 months prior to application, 0 otherwise.
Unemployed–not in labor force transition = 1 if unemployed in 7–12 months prior to application and not in labor force in 6 months prior to application, 0 otherwise.
Unemployed all of preprogram year = 1 if unemployed in 7–12 months prior to application and unemployed in 6 months prior to application, 0 otherwise.
Not in labor force–employed transition = 1 if not in labor force in 7–12 months prior to application and employed in 6 months prior to application, 0 otherwise.

Not in labor force–unemployed transition = 1 if not in labor force in 7–12 months prior to application and unemployed in 6 months prior to application, 0 otherwise.
Not in labor force all of preprogram year = 1 if not in labor force in 7–12 months prior to application and not in labor force in 6 months prior to application, 0 otherwise.
Ever worked full time = 1 if ever worked full time, 0 otherwise.
Most recent wage: (continuous, range $4.25– $10.40).
Zero earnings in year prior to enrollment = 1 if no earnings in employment security records in the four quarters prior to the individual's enrollment in JTPA, 0 otherwise.

Employment Barriers

Single head of household = 1 if single head of household, 0 otherwise.
Displaced homemaker = 1 if displaced homemaker, 0 otherwise.
Veteran = 1 if veteran of any war, 0 otherwise.
Vietnam veteran = 1 if veteran of Vietnam War, 0 otherwise.
Limited work history = 1 if limited work history, 0 otherwise.
Transportation = 1 if transportation is a barrier, 0 otherwise.
Basic skills deficiency = 1 if basic skills deficiency, 0 otherwise.
Child care = 1 if child care is a barrier, 0 otherwise.
Medical problem = 1 if medical problem, 0 otherwise.
Welfare recipient = 1 if receiving any public assistance (AFDC, food stamps, or general assistance), 0 otherwise.
Handicapped = 1 if physically handicapped, 0 otherwise.
Limited English proficiency = 1 if tested and found to have limited ability to speak English, 0 otherwise.
Ex-offender = 1 if convicted of criminal offense prior to time of application, 0 otherwise.
Substance abuse problem = 1 if determined by intake staff or medical doctor to be chemically dependent (i.e., a substance abuser), 0 otherwise.

Marital Status Variables

Never married = 1 if never married, 0 otherwise.
Married = 1 if married, 0 otherwise.
Married, not living with spouse = 1 if married, not living with spouse, 0 otherwise.
Divorced = 1 if separated, divorced, or widowed, 0 otherwise.

Family Composition

Number of children: (continuous, range 0–7).
Household size: (continuous variable).

Training History Variable

Previous training services = 1 if any vocational, occupational, or on-the-job training services were received by program applicant prior to his/her application to JTPA, 0 otherwise.

Program Year Indicator Variables

Program year 1985 through Program year 1993: Each of these indicators takes on the value 1 if the JTPA participant was enrolled during that program year (beginning July 1, ending June 30), 0 otherwise.

9
Do Short-Run Performance Measures Predict Long-Run Impacts?

James J. Heckman
Carolyn J. Heinrich
Jeffrey Smith

This chapter culminates the analysis in this volume by examining two closely related questions.[1] The first of these is posed in the title: Do performance measures based on short-run outcomes predict long-run program impacts? If they do, then performance management systems like those in JTPA and WIA will provide incentives that enhance the economic efficiency of program operations. Put differently, if existing performance measures predict long-term impacts, then their use provides some benefits to weigh against the costs documented in earlier chapters. The second question concerns the efficiency costs of cream skimming induced by the performance standards. As noted in Chapter 3, depending on the relationship between the performance measures and net program impacts, cream skimming may be efficiency increasing (a positive relationship), efficiency decreasing (a negative relationship), or neutral (no relationship).

We address these questions in two different ways. The two analyses build on different identifying assumptions but both utilize the experimental data from the National JTPA Study (NJS) introduced in Chapter 6. The two analyses represent different ways of dealing with the fact that, absent additional assumptions, experimental data do not provide impacts for individuals, only average impacts for groups. Both strategies have important limitations, which we discuss in detail later on in the chapter.

Both methods yield the same basic findings. First, the short-run labor market outcomes commonly used as performance measures do not predict long-run impacts. Indeed, in some cases we find a perverse relationship, indicating that the performance measures actually provide an incentive for program staff to move away from, rather than toward, economic efficiency. Second, we find little evidence of an efficiency cost associated with cream skimming; if anything, it may provide a small efficiency gain.

NJS DATA

We use data gathered as part of the NJS, an experimental evaluation of the JTPA program described in Chapters 2 and 4, for the analyses in this chapter. The experiment was conducted at 16 of the more than 600 JTPA training centers (which we will also refer to as sites). Table 9.1 lists the sites that volunteered to participate in the experiment and provides some descriptive statistics. Columns one through three indicate the racial/ethnic composition of the adult participant population during the study, while the fourth column indicates adult participants' average years of schooling. The fifth and sixth columns display unemployment and poverty rates.

The final three columns indicate the fraction of participants assigned to each of the three experimental treatment streams, based on the services recommended for them prior to random assignment. The classroom training in occupational skills (CT-OS) stream includes individuals who were recommended to receive CT-OS and possibly other services not including subsidized on-the-job training (OJT) at private firms. The OJT treatment stream includes individuals recommended to receive OJT and possibly other services not including CT-OS. The other services stream is a residual category that, with only a few exceptions, includes individuals not recommended to receive either CT-OS or OJT. As illustrated in Exhibit 3.17 of Orr et al. (1996), individuals in the CT-OS stream usually received classroom training whether in the form of basic education or CT-OS or both. Those in the OJT stream often did not enroll; when they did enroll they tended to receive OJT or, somewhat less often, job search assistance. Individuals in the "other" treatment stream received a wide variety of services.

Table 9.1 Descriptive Statistics for the 16 Sites in the National JTPA Study

	Fraction of participants that are:			Avg. yrs. of			Fraction of participants assigned to:		
Site	White	Black	Hispanic	schooling for participants	Unemp. rate	Poverty rate	CT-OS stream	OJT stream	Other services stream
Corpus Christi, TX	23.3	10.4	65.5	11.2	10.2	13.4	34.3	51.5	14.1
Cedar Rapids, IA	87.8	7.6	1.3	11.6	3.6	6.0	60.0	35.4	4.6
Coosa Valley, GA	82.1	17.1	0.6	10.7	6.5	10.7	36.1	38.1	25.7
Heartland of FL	50.2	45.7	2.8	11.4	8.5	11.3	28.9	27.1	44.0
Fort Wayne, IN	72.3	23.7	2.8	11.5	4.7	5.9	6.4	66.2	27.3
Jersey City, NJ	6.3	68.6	20.3	11.5	7.3	18.9	46.0	35.7	18.3
Jackson, MS	13.9	85.5	0.3	12.2	6.1	12.8	57.9	35.5	6.6
Larimer County, CO	77.9	1.8	17.0	12.2	6.5	5.9	29.6	7.1	63.3
Decatur, IL	68.1	31.9	0.0	11.8	9.2	7.8	14.4	79.1	6.5
Northwest MN	81.3	1.8	10.9	11.4	8.0	11.1	25.6	74.0	0.4
Butte, MT	86.6	0.3	5.0	11.7	6.8	7.5	26.6	40.1	33.3
Omaha, NE	38.6	53.4	4.2	11.7	4.3	6.7	77.4	18.9	3.7
Marion, OH	95.6	2.3	0.9	11.3	7.0	7.2	48.8	41.8	9.4
Oakland, CA	8.0	68.3	6.8	12.4	6.8	16.0	49.6	7.9	42.6
Providence, RI	33.6	33.9	24.6	11.3	3.8	12.1	32.3	13.0	54.7
Springfield, MO	96.1	1.8	0.0	11.9	5.5	10.1	17.7	74.6	7.7

SOURCE: Race/ethnicity and years of schooling for adult participants come from calculations by the authors using the National JTPA Study data. Race/ethnicity categories do not necessarily sum to one due to the omission of "other." Unemployment rates are from Orr et al. (1996, Exhibit 3.3) and are unweighted annual averages for 1987–1989. Poverty rates come from Orr et al. (1996, Exhibit 3.2) and are for 1979. The treatment stream recommendation fractions for adults come from Kemple, Doolittle, and Wallace (1993, Table 7.1).

The site selection strategy for the evaluation excluded sites with small enrollments for cost reasons. Attempts to gain external validity among larger sites by selecting sites at random failed due to high refusal rates, as described by Doolittle and Traeger (1990) and Hotz (1992). Without random site selection, external validity in the strict sense clearly fails. At the same time, Table 9.1 makes clear that the 16 sites represent a diverse mix in terms of participant demographics, local economic conditions, and service mix. Doolittle and Traeger (1990, Section 5) compare the 16 experimental sites to the population of all JTPA sites and find that, on average, the two groups look much alike. In our view, these patterns make our results suggestive, rather than either definitive or irrelevant, when generalized to the JTPA program more broadly.

At the experimental centers, persons who applied to and were accepted into the program were randomly assigned to either a treatment group allowed access to JTPA services or to a control group denied access to JTPA services for the next 18 months. A short survey at the time of random assignment collected background information on demographic characteristics, educational attainment, work history, past training receipt, current and past transfer program participation, and family income and composition. This survey was self-administered with assistance from program staff; it achieved a response rate well over 90 percent as well as only modest item nonresponse conditional on survey response. We use variables from this baseline survey to define our subgroups (and for the participant descriptive statistics in Table 9.1).

In addition, follow-up surveys collected information on employment and earnings around 18 months after random assignment and, for a random subsample, at around 30 months after random assignment. The response rates for the two surveys were 83 and 77 percent, respectively, with little difference between the experimental treatment and control groups (see Appendix A of Orr et al. [1994]). Both the program and the experimental analysis divided participants into four groups based on age and sex: adult males and females aged 22 and above and male and female out-of-school youth aged 16–21 (the NJS did not examine the component of JTPA serving in-school youth). We examine only adult males and females in this chapter due to the small samples available for the two youth groups.

We use the data on wages, earnings, and employment from the follow-up surveys to construct the performance measures and outcome variables. Our outcome variables consist of earnings and employment for 18 or 30 months after random assignment. For our analyses using percentiles, we use all observations with valid values of earnings over the 18 months after random assignment. For the analyses using subgroup variation in experimental impacts, we trim the top 1 percent of the earnings values. The employment variables measure the fraction of months employed, where we code an individual as employed in a month if they have positive earnings in that month.

The JTPA performance measures we analyze are hourly wage and employment at termination from the program and weekly earnings and employment 13 weeks after termination. In most states at this time, program staff members obtained these outcomes via telephone surveys of participants. We do not have access to the telephone survey data for our sample and instead use program termination dates from JTPA administrative data combined with data from the follow-up surveys on job spells to construct the performance measures. Because program administrators did not necessarily contact participants on the exact date of termination or follow-up (and to allow for some measurement error in the timing of the self-reported job spells), we count all job spells within 30 days on either side of the termination date (or 13 weeks after termination, as appropriate) in constructing the performance measures. We measure employment based on the presence or absence of a job spell within this window. For the wage measure, we use the highest hourly wage within the window for persons holding more than one job. For the earnings measure, we take the average weekly earnings on all jobs over the 61-day window. Following the definition of the corresponding official performance measures, we calculate hourly wages and weekly earnings for employed persons only.

For more information on the NJS experimental data, see the official impact reports in Bloom et al. (1997) and Orr et al. (1996), the official implementation reports in Doolittle and Traeger (1990) and Kemple, Doolittle, and Wallace (1993), and related papers on the design and the data by Hotz (1992), Smith (1997), Kornfeld and Bloom (1999), and Heckman and Smith (2000). For discussions of interpretational issues see Heckman, Smith, and Clements (1997), Heckman, Smith, and Taber (1998) and Heckman et al. (2000).

ECONOMETRIC ANALYSIS STRATEGIES: NOTATION AND MOTIVATION

Ideally, we would like to relate individual program impacts to individual values of the performance measures. Unfortunately, as discussed in, e.g., Heckman (1992); Heckman, Smith, and Clements (1997); Heckman and Smith (1998); and Djebbari and Smith (2008), without additional assumptions, even experimental data do not allow us to generate individual-level impact estimates.

To consider this issue more carefully, we return to the notation defined in Chapter 3. Recall that $Y^1_{a,i}$ denotes a labor market outcome for person i in some period a given treatment, where the 1 superscript denotes treatment. Similarly, $Y^0_{a,i}$ denotes a labor market outcome in the same period given no treatment, implying that the impact for individual i in period a equals $Y^1_{a,i} - Y^0_{a,i} = \Delta_{a,i}$. In this chapter, we distinguish between two periods: the short run, denoted by s, and the long run, denoted by l. Both periods begin at the time the individual decides to participate or not. In terms of this notation, we would ideally like to relate $Y^1_{s,i}$ and $\Delta_{l,i}$. Finally, recall that S denotes the set of individuals treated.

Experimental data consist of the marginal distributions of outcomes in the treated and untreated states, that is, $f(Y^0_a)$ and $f(Y^1_a)$. Experimental data to not identify the joint distribution of outcomes, $f(Y^0_a, Y^1_a)$, and therefore do not identify individual impacts. Experimental data do identify mean impacts for subgroups of individuals defined by characteristics not affected by the treatment (which usually means those observed prior to random assignment). Letting g denote some particular subgroup (such as those with exactly 12 years of schooling) out of a set G, we can construct the impact estimate for the subgroup by taking a mean difference between the treated and untreated units in subgroup g. More formally, we estimate the subgroup impact $\Delta_{a,g} = E(Y^1_a \mid G = g) - E(Y^0_a \mid G = g)$ by replacing the conditional expectations with the corresponding sample means.[2]

The next two sections describe the strategies we employ to deal with the lack of individual impact estimates. The first strategy imposes additional, nonexperimental, assumptions on the data that allow us to construct individual impact estimates. The second strategy relies solely on subgroup variation in the experimental impacts and, as such, requires no additional assumptions.

ECONOMETRIC ANALYSIS STRATEGIES: RANK PRESERVATION

Our first econometric strategy builds on the assumption of rank preservation outlined in Heckman, Smith, and Clements (1997).[3] We assume that the joint distribution of treated and untreated outcomes takes a very simple form: the counterfactual for each quantile of the treated outcome distribution consists of the corresponding quantile of the untreated outcome distribution. Thus, for example, the counterfactual outcome for the median treated person consists of the outcome of the median untreated person. Note that under this assumption, cream skimming on Y_a^0 implies the same choices as cream skimming on Y_a^1. We can think of the simple world defined by the rank preservation assumption as a "one factor" world in which those who do well in the treated state also do well in the untreated state and those who do poorly in the treated state also do poorly in the untreated state.

This assumption may seem quite unusual, but in fact it nests the widely (though often implicitly) used common effect model in which $\Delta_{a,i} = \Delta_a$. In the common effect world, the treatment has the same effect on all participants. In this world, the treated outcome distribution has the same shape as the untreated outcome distribution but its location differs by the common treatment effect. For example, if the untreated outcomes have a normal distribution with mean 100 and variance 20, and the common treatment effect equals 10, then the treated outcomes have a normal distribution with mean 110 and variance 20. Moreover, in the common effect world, quantiles of the treated and untreated outcome distributions again form counterfactuals for one another. The rank preservation assumption relaxes the assumption of an equal treatment effect for all participants while keeping the link between the quantiles of the two outcome distributions. It therefore nests the common effect model as a special case.

More formally, following Heckman, Smith, and Clements (1997), if each individual has the same rank in the distributions of Y_a^0 and Y_a^1, then we can associate a Y_a^0 with each Y_a^1; continuity of the two distributions implies a unique association. The assumptions of rank preservation plus continuity allow us to construct Δ_a as a function of Y_a^0 (or, what is the same thing, of Y_a^1). We operationalize this idea by taking percentile differences across the treated and untreated outcome distributions.[4] Let $Y_a^{0,j}$ denote the *j*th percentile of the Y_a^0 distribution, with $Y_a^{1,j}$ the corresponding percentile in the Y_a^1 distribution. Thus, we estimate $\Delta_a(Y_a^{0,j}) = Y_a^{1,j} - Y_a^{0,j}$. Our data include mass points at zero earnings in both the treated and untreated distributions. For the corresponding percentiles we simply assign an impact of zero; because all of the outcomes equal zero in the lower percentiles of the two distributions, order does not matter. Thus, the lack of a unique association in this part of the distribution poses no problems in our application.

ECONOMETRIC ANALYSIS STRATEGIES: SUBGROUP VARIATION IN EXPERIMENTAL IMPACTS

Our second identification strategy relies solely on the exogenous variation in treatment status induced by the experiment. As noted above, as a result of random assignment, we can construct unbiased mean impact estimates for subgroups defined by variables observed prior to random assignment.

To implement this strategy, we form 43 subgroups based on the following characteristics measured at the time of random assignment: race, age, education, marital status, time since most recent employment, receipt of Aid to Families with Dependent Children (AFDC—the predecessor to the current Temporary Aid to Needy Families program), receipt of Food Stamps, and training center. Individuals with complete data belong to eight subgroups, while we include those with incomplete data in as many subgroups as their data allow. Using a regression framework, we construct mean-difference experimental impact estimates for each subgroup.[5] We adjust these estimates by dividing through by the fraction enrolled in each subgroup to reflect the fact that a substantial fraction of persons (41 percent of adult males and 37 percent of adult females) in the treatment group dropped out and did not participate in JTPA.[6] We construct the subgroup average performance measures by simply averaging the individual performance measures over the members in each subgroup.

RESULTS BASED ON THE RANK PRESERVATION ASSUMPTION

Figures 9.1 and 9.2 present estimates of $\Delta_a(Y_a^{0,j})$ constructed under the rank preservation assumption. Self-reported earnings in the 18 months after random assignment constitute the outcome variable. The horizontal axis in each figure indicates percentiles of the treated and untreated (i.e., control) outcome distributions. The vertical axis indicates the difference in outcomes at each percentile.

We begin with the estimates for adult women in Figure 9.1, for whom the sample size is the largest. First, we observe zero impacts through the 20th percentile. This region corresponds to persons with zero earnings in the 18 months after random assignment in both the treated and untreated states under the rank preservation assumption. Second, we observe a relatively constant positive treatment effect of around $800 over the interval from thc 20th to the 90th percentile. Third, we note a discernible increase in the estimated impact in the final decile. Assuming roughly equal costs among participants at different percentiles, the pattern in Figure 9.1 suggests that cream skimming beyond the 20th percentile has little effect on the economic efficiency of JTPA. However, a policy of targeting services at the bottom two deciles entails clear costs. To the extent that the untreated outcome proxies for the performance measures, Figure 9.1 suggests only a very modest (and very nonlinear) positive relationship between the performance measures and the impacts.

Figure 9.2 for adult men tells a similar tale. We observe a relatively flat relationship over the range from the 10th to the 50th percentile, after which it dips and then rises again. Given the wide standard errors (and the smaller region of zero impacts at the lowest percentiles) we can say with some (but not overwhelming) confidence that cream skimming, in regard to adult males, also likely has little effect, either positive or negative, on efficiency. And, to the extent that the untreated outcomes

Figure 9.1 Quantile Treatment Effects, Adult Males

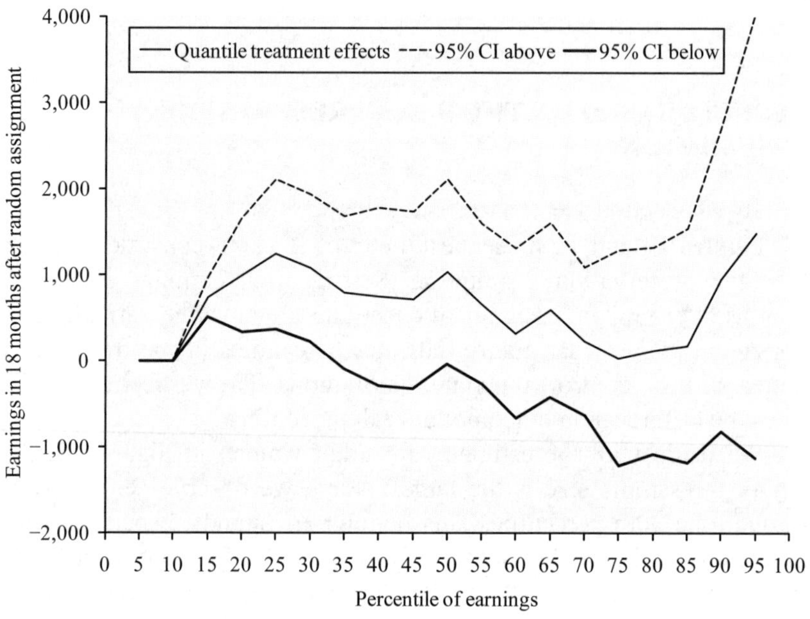

Figure 9.2 Quantile Treatment Effects, Adult Females

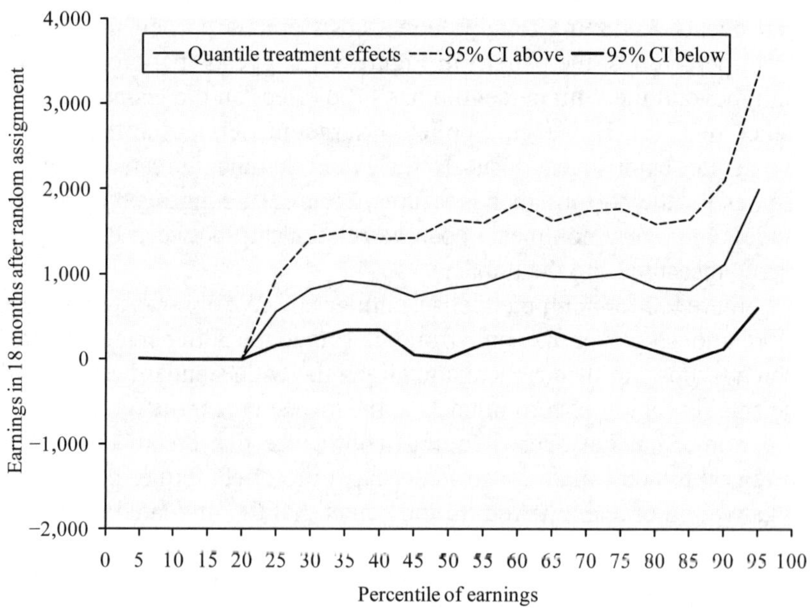

proxy for the performance measures, we see little relationship between the two for adult males under the rank preservation assumption.

RESULTS BASED ON SUBGROUP VARIATION: UNIVARIATE

In this section we examine the experimental impact estimates for subgroups defined by individual baseline characteristics. Put differently, we examine the correlation between predictors of Y_a^1 and impacts conditional on values of those predictors. Caseworkers may use specific variables, such as labor force status, to help them forecast short-run outcomes as part of a strategy to select as participants individuals likely to do well on the performance measures. Moreover, the relationship between such characteristics and Δ_a is of interest in its own right.

Tables 9.2 and 9.3 summarize subgroup estimates of the impact of JTPA on the earnings and employment of adult females and adult males in the JTPA experiment, respectively. The first column in each table lists the values of each subgroup variable. Columns two through five present impacts on earnings in the 18 and 30 months after random assignment and on the fraction of months employed in the 18 and 30 months after random assignment. Note that the samples differ for the 18 and 30 month outcomes due to survey nonresponse in the second follow-up survey. We also present p-values from tests of the null of equal impacts among the subgroups defined by each variable. We present subgroup impacts conditional on labor force status (employed, unemployed, and out of the labor force), highest grade completed, AFDC receipt and month of last employment (if any), all measured at the time of random assignment. All of these variables predict the level of the 18-month and 30-month outcomes for participants.

For adult females, we reject the null of equal impacts among subgroups in 4 of the 16 possible cases. Two of the rejections (at the 5 percent level) occur for employment over 18 months and earnings over 30 months conditional on AFDC receipt, with larger impacts in each case for women receiving AFDC. As AFDC receipt is negatively related to Y_a^1, this finding suggests that cream skimming may be somewhat inefficient for adult women. The other two rejections occur for earnings and employment over 30 months conditional on month of last employment.

Table 9.2 Experimental Impact Estimates by Subgroup, Adult Females

Subgroup	Earnings impacts ($)		Employment impacts	
	18 months	30 months	18 months	30 months
	Labor force status			
P-value for equal impacts	0.3919	0.5745	0.4715	0.2286
Employed	1,223.78	1,487.38	0.0017	−0.0158
	(651.64)	(2,461.08)	(0.0135)	(0.0168)
Unemployed	507.42	428.84	0.0112	0.0184
	(507.92)	(1,715.10)	(0.0112)	(0.0128)
Out of the labor force	1,543.72	3,274.29	0.0274	0.0184
	(601.48)	(2,089.21)	(0.0160)	(0.0188)
	Education			
P-value for equal impacts	0.6890	0.4641	0.8149	0.4646
Highest grade completed < 10	1,029.22	−2227.56	0.0135	0.0175
	(643.40)	(2,577.38)	(0.0164)	(0.0182)
Highest grade completed 10–11	1,341.37	3,088.46	0.0289	0.0246
	(592.06)	(2,179.51)	(0.0147)	(0.0171)
Highest grade completed 12	460.29	1503.23	0.0129	−0.0053
	(469.73)	(1,711.16)	(0.0109)	(0.0129)
Highest grade completed > 12	971.20	795.14	0.0115	0.0209
	(816.54)	(2,997.34)	(0.0172)	(0.0211)
	AFDC receipt			
P-value for equal impacts	0.7224	0.0371	0.0277	0.2607
Not receiving AFDC	712.26	−947.01	0.0028	0.0026
	(392.05)	(1,462.17)	(0.0087)	(0.0105)
Receiving AFDC	924.57	3,624.35	0.0343	0.0211
	(451.07)	(1,631.02)	(0.0113)	(0.0127)
	Recent employment			
P-value for equal impacts	0.8614	0.0492	0.5708	0.0139
Currently employed	1,104.08	396.24	0.0138	0.0056
	(721.42)	(2,851.27)	(0.0151)	(0.0197)
Last employed 0–2 months ago	594.01	979.22	0.0099	0.0060
	(713.69)	(2,485.38)	(0.0161)	(0.0181)
Last employed 3–5 months ago	171.44	−7,677.17	−0.0063	−0.0589
	(953.91)	(3,485.31)	(0.0199)	(0.0220)
Last employed 6–8 months ago	1,874.38	975.22	0.0451	0.0502
	(1,175.53)	(3,721.12)	(0.0263)	(0.0305)

Table 9.2 (continued)

Subgroup	Earnings impacts ($)		Employment impacts	
	18 months	30 months	18 months	30 months
	Recent employment			
Last employed 9–11 months ago	1,679.73	5,244.59	0.0310	0.0636
	(1,311.91)	(4,437.63)	(0.0305)	(0.0382)
Last employed ≥ 12 months ago	1,304.36	4,919.73	0.0341	0.0347
	(587.15)	(2,020.46)	(0.0155)	(0.0180)
Never employed	610.59	−2,490.44	0.0335	−0.0059
	(609.42)	(2,736.46)	(0.0168)	(0.0191)

NOTE: Monthly earnings are based on self-reports with top 1 percent trimming. Estimates are adjusted for program dropouts in the treatment group. Earnings impacts are calculated using all sample members with valid observations for self-reported monthly earnings during each period. The sample includes 4,886 valid observations for the 18-month period after random assignment and 1,147 valid observations for the 30-month period after random assignment. Heteroskedasticity-consistent standard errors appear in parentheses.
SOURCE: Heckman, Heinrich, and Smith (2002).

We have trouble interpreting these estimates, which do not reveal any obvious systematic pattern.

Considering the estimates in Table 9.2 more broadly, we see three patterns. First, we lack the data to precisely estimate most of the subgroup impacts. Second, the point estimates often suggest very different impacts by subgroup. Third, the subgroup impact estimates often change substantially between 18 and 30 months. Taken together, these findings leave us with a lot of uncertainty about the efficiency effects of cream skimming. At the same time, it seems unlikely that caseworkers, who receive little feedback about the long-run labor market outcomes of participants at either the individual or aggregate level, have more information about these patterns than we do. Thus, any efforts to select participants based on these observed variables will likely have little systematic relationship to impacts, a conclusion quite consistent with the finding in Bell and Orr (2002) and Lechner and Smith (2007) that caseworkers cannot predict impacts.

For adult males, statistically significant differences in impacts among subgroups defined by our set of characteristics emerge only once, for impacts on 18-month earnings conditional on labor force sta-

Table 9.3 Experimental Impact Estimates by Subgroup, Adult Males

Subgroup	Earnings impacts ($)		Employment impacts	
	18 months	30 months	18 months	30 months
	Labor force status			
P-value for equal impacts	0.0407	0.3469	0.2679	0.6517
Employed	2,839.24	6,328.20	0.0300	0.0005
	(1,145.51)	(4,143.22)	(0.0166)	(0.0194)
Unemployed	718.84	3,021.68	0.0056	0.0180
	(710.16)	(2,339.51)	(0.0105)	(0.0125)
Out of the labor force	−2,193.85	−2,725.72	−0.0163	0.0289
	(1,658.81)	(4,693.28)	(0.0262)	(0.0281)
	Education			
P-value for equal impacts	0.6077	0.7939	0.9587	0.7206
Highest grade completed	680.26	1,713.46	0.0114	0.0403
< 10	(1,193.62)	(3,935.62)	(0.0203)	(0.0225)
Highest grade completed	−64.77	−270.18	0.0120	0.0134
10–11	(1,020.79)	(3,516.67)	(0.0163)	(0.0188)
Highest grade completed	1,438.13	552.70	0.0030	0.0105
12	(793.68)	(2,729.26)	(0.0119)	(0.0141)
Highest grade completed	−92.00	4,886.81	0.0116	0.0201
> 12	(1,238.21)	(4,155.34)	(0.0172)	(0.0221)
	AFDC receipt			
P-value for equal impacts	0.5948	0.5794	0.3813	0.6678
Not receiving AFDC	722.73	2,933.22	0.0122	0.0161
	(556.43)	(1,810.58)	(0.0085)	(0.0099)
Receiving AFDC	−232.18	−274.82	−0.0132	0.0306
	(1,706.56)	(5,495.50)	(0.0278)	(0.0322)
	Recent employment			
P-value for equal impacts	0.5995	0.6193	0.9112	0.7010
Currently employed	2,668.20	3,053.96	0.0176	−0.0134
	(1,230.61)	(4,174.11)	(0.0178)	(0.0212)
Last employed 0–2 months ago	816.36	6,126.54	0.0168	0.0205
	(1,091.14)	(3,637.23)	(0.0152)	(0.0180)
Last employed 3–5 months ago	−425.61	1,248.64	0.0037	0.0119
	(1,162.99)	(3,794.83)	(0.0176)	(0.0209)
Last employed 6–8 months ago	−5.65	−790.27	−0.0135	0.0312
	(1,824.51)	(5,453.91)	(0.0256)	(0.0296)

Table 9.3 (continued)

Subgroup	Earnings impacts ($)		Employment impacts	
	18 months	30 months	18 months	30 months
	Recent employment			
Last employed 9–11 months ago	1,191.58	−4,914.81	0.0163	0.0098
	(2,328.58)	(7,657.02)	(0.0384)	(0.0478)
Last employed ≥ 12 months ago	525.44	3,885.63	0.0284	0.0475
	(1,333.79)	(4,722.38)	(0.0224)	(0.0257)
Never employed	−799.52	−6,377.68	0.0017	0.0145
	(1,606.04)	(6,242.27)	(0.0295)	(0.0319)

NOTE: Monthly earnings are based on self-reports with top 1 percent trimming. Estimates are adjusted for program dropouts in the treatment group. Earnings impacts are calculated using all sample members with valid observations for self-reported monthly earnings during each period. The sample includes 4,886 valid observations for the 18-month period after random assignment and 1,147 valid observations for the 30-month period after random assignment. Heteroskedasticity-consistent standard errors appear in parentheses.

SOURCE: Heckman, Heinrich, and Smith (2002).

tus. In this case, the largest impacts appear for men employed at the time of random assignment. Employment at random assignment correlates positively with Y_a^1. As for adult women, the insignificant coefficients vary substantially among subgroups, and exhibit patterns that are difficult to interpret, such as nonmonotonicity as a function of months since last employment or years of schooling, as well as substantial changes from 18 to 30 months. Combined with the general lack of statistically significant subgroup impacts, the pattern of estimates represents weak evidence of at most a modest efficiency gain to cream skimming for adult males. For both men and women, of course, the costs of service provision may vary among subgroups as well, so that the net impacts may differ in either direction from the gross impacts reported here.

Other results in the literature that make use of the experimental data from the NJS echo the findings in Tables 9.2 and 9.3. Bloom et al. (1993, Exhibits 4.15 and 5.14) present subgroup impact estimates on earnings in the 18 months after random assignment. Orr et al. (1996, Exhibits 5.8 and 5.9) present similar estimates for 30-month earnings using a somewhat different earnings measure than we use here.[7] Both consider a different set of subgroups than we do. Only a couple of significant subgroup impacts appear at 18 months. At 30 months, the only significant subgroup differences found by Orr et al. (1996) among adults are for adult men, where men with a spouse present have higher impacts.[8] Overall, the absence of many statistically significant subgroup differences, combined with the pattern of point estimates, makes the findings in Bloom et al. (1993) and Orr et al. (1996) consistent with our own findings. There exists little evidence of substantial efficiency gains or losses from picking participants on the basis of *X* and, even if such potential gains or losses exist, neither we nor, in all probability, the caseworkers, have any real knowledge of them.

RESULTS BASED ON SUBGROUP VARIATION IN EXPERIMENTAL IMPACTS: REGRESSION

We now turn to our multivariate regression analysis of the relationship between subgroup impacts and subgroup average performance measures. Table 9.4 presents estimates of the relationship between experimental impacts on earnings and on employment and various performance measures based on short-term labor market outcomes. We estimate separate regressions for each outcome (earnings and employment for 18 and 30 months) and for each performance measure.[9]

The four columns of estimates in Table 9.4 correspond to cumulated earnings and employment impacts for 18 and 30 months after random assignment. Each cell in the table presents the regression coefficient associated with the column's dependent variable and the row's independent variable, the estimated (robust) standard error of the coefficient, the p-value from a test of the null hypothesis that the population coefficient equals zero and the R^2 for the regression. We do not report the estimated constant terms from the regressions to reduce clutter. For example, the first row of the first column reveals that a regression of subgroup earnings impacts for the 18 months after random assignment on the subgroup average hourly wage at termination from the JTPA program yields an estimated coefficient of −\$577.61 on the hourly wage, with a standard error of \$304.00, a p-value of 0.0645, and an overall R^2 of 0.0809.

Four striking findings emerge from Table 9.4. First, and most important, we find many negative relationships between short-run performance indicators and experimental impact estimates at the subgroup level. In many cases the short-run outcome measures utilized in the JTPA performance standards system have a perverse relationship with the longer-run earnings and employment impacts that constitute the program's goals. The only evidence supporting the efficacy of short-run outcome measures comes from the employment-based performance measures for adult men, which are positive and statistically significant at the 10 percent level in three cases. These same performance measures have negative coefficients in seven out of eight cases for adult women.

Second, we find low R^2 values throughout. The short-term performance measures have only a very weak relationship with impacts on earnings and employment for 18 or 30 months. Third, moving from performance measures based on outcomes at termination from the program to longer-term measures based on outcomes three months after termination usually weakens the relationship between the performance measure and program impacts. In particular, the R^2 values nearly always decline and the estimated coefficients sometimes become less positive or more negative. Fourth, the performance measures often do worse (in terms of the fraction of variance explained) at predicting impacts for 30 months after random assignment than at predicting impacts for 18 months after random assignment. This indicates that the low predictive power of the performance measures in our analysis does not result from reductions in work activity during the periods of program participation (the so-called lock-in effect), which for some participants constitutes a nontrivial chunk of the 18 months after random assignment.

In sum, the regression analysis yields three clear conclusions. First, short-run performance measures do a very poor job of predicting long-run impacts, in terms of explained variation. In general, performance measures only weakly related to program goals accomplish little as rewards and punishments often get assigned based on noise. In terms of the discussion in Chapter 3, the JTPA performance measures do not solve the principal-agent problem by providing incentives for impact maximization. Moreover, they clearly fail to provide cheap, quick proxies for econometric impact evaluations. Second, the point estimates often suggest a negative relationship, indicating that the JTPA performance standards system may have provided an incentive for reduced

Table 9.4 Relationship between Δ and Y_1^1 in JTPA: Earnings and Employment Impacts

Performance standard measure	Earnings impact ($) measured over: 18 months after random assignment	Earnings impact ($) measured over: 30 months after random assignment	Employment impact measured over: 18 months after random assignment	Employment impact measured over: 30 months after random assignment
	Adult females			
Hourly wage at time of termination	−577.61	−1,729.66	−0.018	−0.010
	(304.00)	(1,280.64)	(0.008)	(0.011)
	$p = 0.0645$	$p = 0.1842$	$p = 0.0202$	$p = 0.3559$
	$R^2 = 0.0809$	$R^2 = 0.0426$	$R^2 = 0.1246$	$R^2 = 0.0208$
Weekly earnings at time of follow-up	−3.74	−12.05	−0.000	−0.000
	(8.78)	(36.54)	(0.000)	(0.000)
	$p = 0.6726$	$p = 0.7432$	$p = 0.2728$	$p = 0.3277$
	$R^2 = 0.0044$	$R^2 = 0.0026$	$R^2 = 0.0293$	$R^2 = 0.0234$
Employment at time of termination	−117.72	−2,065.61	−0.023	−0.029
	(941.92)	(3,928.63)	(0.023)	(0.033)
	$p = 0.9012$	$p = 0.6019$	$p = 0.3213$	$p = 0.3767$
	$R^2 = 0.0004$	$R^2 = 0.0069$	$R^2 = 0.0246$	$R^2 = 0.0196$
Employment at time of follow-up	1,513.28	−1,873.03	−0.067	−0.024
	(1,482.04)	(6,236.83)	(0.037)	(0.053)
	$p = 0.3132$	$p = 0.7655$	$p = 0.0767$	$p = 0.6521$
	$R^2 = 0.0248$	$R^2 = 0.0022$	$R^2 = 0.0745$	$R^2 = 0.0050$

	Adult males			
Hourly wage at time of termination	465.41	−1,405.68	0.003	−0.005
	(394.76)	(1,653.30)	(0.005)	(0.010)
	$p = 0.2452$	$p = 0.4001$	$p = 0.4914$	$p = 0.6230$
	$R^2 = 0.0328$	$R^2 = 0.0173$	$R^2 = 0.0116$	$R^2 = 0.0059$
Weekly earnings at time of follow-up	6.74	−20.76	0.000	−0.000
	(7.42)	(31.79)	(0.000)	(0.000)
	$p = 0.3690$	$p = 0.5174$	$p = 0.9921$	$p = 0.3274$
	$R^2 = 0.0197$	$R^2 = 0.0103$	$R^2 = 0.0000$	$R^2 = 0.0234$
Employment at time of termination	2,542.99	3,673.71	0.005	−0.059
	(1,384.72)	(5,869.08)	(0.017)	(0.034)
	$p = 0.0737$	$p = 0.5349$	$p = 0.7559$	$p = 0.0850$
	$R^2 = 0.0778$	$R^2 = 0.0097$	$R^2 = 0.0024$	$R^2 = 0.0723$
Employment at time of follow-up	2,579.24	18,716.00	0.050	0.021
	(2,486.91)	(9,842.28)	(0.028)	(0.061)
	$p = 0.3058$	$p = 0.0643$	$p = 0.0848$	$p = 0.7338$
	$R^2 = 0.0256$	$R^2 = 0.0810$	$R^2 = 0.0707$	$R^2 = 0.0029$

NOTE: The actual JTPA performance measures are defined as follows: "Hourly wage at placement" is the average wage at program termination for employed adults. "Weekly earnings at follow-up" are the average weekly wage of adults employed 13 weeks after program termination. "Employment rate at termination" is the fraction of adults employed at program termination. "Employment rate at follow-up" is the fraction of adults who were employed 13 weeks after program termination. In our analysis, employment rates were calculated based on the presence or absence of a job spell within 30 days before or after each reference date (termination or follow-up). Hourly wages were calculated based on the highest reported hourly wage for all job spells reported within 30 days before or after each reference date. Weekly earnings were calculated by averaging the product of hourly wages and hours worked per week across all reported job spells within 30 days before or after each reference date weighted by the fraction of the 61-day window spanned by each job spell.

SOURCE: Heckman, Heinrich, and Smith (2002).

efficiency. Third, we can say little about the efficiency cost to cream skimming other than that the data do not make a loud statement in either direction given our sample size and subgroups.

PUTTING THE RESULTS IN CONTEXT

The findings presented in this chapter do not represent an anomaly in the literature, but rather tell much the same story as the other studies that perform similar analyses. Table 9.5 summarizes six other studies that examine the relationship between performance standards measures based on short-run outcome levels and long-run program impacts; these six studies include, to the best of our knowledge, all of the published studies of this type as well as two that appeared only as government reports.[10] For each study, the table provides the citation, the particular employment and training program considered, the data used for the analysis, the impact measure used (for example, earnings from 18 to 36 months after random assignment), the impact estimator used (for example, random assignment), the particular performance measures considered (for example, employment at termination), and the findings.

Four studies, Gay and Borus (1980), Cragg (1997), Barnow (1999), and Burghardt and Schochet (2001), reach conclusions very similar to our own. The other two studies, Friedlander (1988) and Zornitsky et al. (1988), obtain more mixed results. The most positive of the studies, Zornitsky et al. (1988), examines the AFDC Homemaker/Home Health Aide Demonstration, which provided a homogeneous treatment to relatively homogeneous clients. This program represents a very different context from multitreatment programs serving heterogeneous populations such as JTPA and WIA. Moreover, this demonstration program, with its focus on the skills for a particular high-demand occupation, most likely did not lead to much postprogram human capital investment. As noted in Chapter 3, such investments tend to weaken the relationship between the short-run performance measures and long-run impacts. Taken together, these studies generally support our finding from the JTPA data that performance standards based on short-run outcome levels likely do little to encourage the provision of services to those who benefit most from them in employment and training programs.

LIMITATIONS OF OUR ANALYSIS

The analysis in this chapter focuses on one particular caseworker response to the imposition of a performance management system based on short-run outcomes: changes in who gets accepted into the program. In a model similar to the one presented in Chapter 3, caseworkers attempt to forecast both impacts and performance outcomes using the information available at the time of the acceptance decisions. In the case of the subgroup regression analysis, our interpretation assumes that caseworkers use observed characteristics to forecast both impacts and performance outcomes and then act on those forecasts. The performance management system causes them to put more weight onto the performance outcome forecast in making decisions about whom to serve.

Two important assumptions lurk in the shadows behind this interpretation. First, we must assume that mean impacts and mean performance at the subgroup level do not differ between a world with performance standards and a world without them. This assumption could easily fail if, for example, service allocations conditional on characteristics change with the introduction of performance management.[11] Second, we must also assume that mean impacts and mean performance at the subgroup level do not differ between applicants and participants.[12] Caseworkers see and make choices about applicants, while we have data only on individuals accepted into the program, as indicated by their reaching random assignment. The data from the Corpus Christi site in the NJS considered in Heckman, Smith, and Taber (1996) indicate that only about one-third of applicants reach random assignment, which leaves plenty of scope for differences between applicants and participants in the relationship that we estimate.

A final and very important limitation resides in the inability of our analyses in this chapter (or indeed, in this book) to say anything about the effect of the performance standards on the technical efficiency (or productivity) of the local JTPA training centers. By way of illustration, consider the subgroup regression analysis and suppose that having a performance standards system increases both the mental and physical effort levels (more "working smart" and less on-the-job leisure) of program staff. Suppose that this extra effort increases the impact of the

Table 9.5 Evidence on the Correlation Between Y_1 and Δ from Several Studies

Study	Program	Data	Measure of impact
Gay and Borus (1980)	Manpower Development and Training Act (MDTA), Job Opportunities in the Business Sector (JOBS), Neighborhood Youth Corps Out-of-School Program (NYC/OS), and the Job Corps	Randomly selected program participants entering programs from December 1968 to June 1970 and matched (on age, race, city, and sometimes neighborhood) comparison sample of eligible nonparticipants.	Impact on Social Security earnings in 1973 (from 18 to 36 months after program exit).
Zornitsky et al. (1988)	AFDC Homemaker-Home Health Aid Demonstration	Volunteers in the seven states in which the demonstration projects were conducted. To be eligible, volunteers had to have been on AFDC continuously for at least 90 days.	Mean monthly earnings in the 32 months after random assignment and mean monthly combined AFDC and food stamp benefits in the 29 months after random assignment.
Friedlander (1988)	Mandatory welfare-to-work programs in San Diego, Baltimore, Virginia, Arkansas, and Cook County	Applicants and recipients of AFDC (varies across programs). Data collected as part of MDRC's experimental evaluations of these programs.	Postrandom assignment earnings (from UI earnings records) and welfare receipt (from administrative data).

Impact estimator	Performance measures	Findings
Nonexperimental "kitchen sink" Tobit model	Employment in quarter after program, before-after (four quarters before to one quarter after) changes in weeks worked, weeks not in the labor force, wage rate, hours worked, income, amount of unemployment insurance received, and amount of public assistance received.	No measure has a consistent, positive, and statistically significant relationship to the estimated impacts across subgroups and programs. The before-after measures, particularly weeks worked and wages, do much better than employment in the quarter after the program.
Experimental impact estimates	Employment and wages at termination. Employment and welfare receipt three and six months after termination. Mean weekly earnings and welfare benefits in the three and six month periods after termination. These measures are examined both adjusted and not adjusted for observable factors including trainee demographics and welfare and employment histories and local labor markets.	All measures have the correct sign on their correlation with earnings impacts, whether adjusted or not. The employment and earnings measures are all statistically significant (or close to it). The welfare measures are correctly correlated with welfare impacts but the employment measures are not unless adjusted. The measures at three and six months do better than those at termination, but there is little gain from going from three to six.
Experimental impact estimates	Employment (nonzero quarterly earnings) in quarters 2 and 3 (short term) or quarters 4 to 6 (long term) after random assignment. Welfare receipt in quarter 3 (short-term) or quarter 6 (long-term) after random assignment.	Employment measure is positively correlated with earnings gains but not welfare savings for most programs. Welfare indicator is always positively correlated with earnings impacts, but rarely significantly so. It is not related to welfare savings. Long-term performance measures do little better (and sometimes worse) than short-term measures.

Table 9.5 (continued)

Study	Program	Data	Measure of impact
Cragg (1997)	JTPA (1983–87)	NLSY	Before-after change in participant earnings.
Barnow (1999)	JTPA (1987–89)	NJS	Earnings and hours worked in month 10 after random assignment.
Burghardt and Schochet (2001)	Job Corps	Experimental data from the National Job Corps Study	The outcome measures include receipt of education or training, weeks of education or training, hours per week of education or training, receipt of a high school diploma or GED, receipt of a vocational certificate, earnings, and being arrested. All are measured over the 48 months following random assignment.

Impact estimator	Performance measures	Findings
Generalized bivariate Tobit model of preprogram and postprogram annual earnings	Fraction of time spent working since leaving school in the preprogram period. This variable is strongly correlated with postprogram employment levels.	Negative relationship between work experience and before-after earnings changes.
Experimental impact estimates	Regression-adjusted levels of earnings and hours worked in month 10 after random assignment.	At best a weak relationship between performance measures and program impacts.
Experimental impact estimates	Job Corps centers divided into three groups: high performers, medium performers, and low performers based on their overall performance rankings in program years 1994, 1995, and 1996. High and low centers were in the top and bottom third nationally in all three years, respectively.	No systematic relationship between the performance groups and the experimental impact estimates.

SOURCE: Heckman, Heinrich, and Smith (2002); Barnow and Smith (2004).

program for all participants by $100 over 18 months. In our regressions of estimated subgroup mean impacts on estimated subgroup mean performance levels, this extra $100 shows up in the intercept, not in the slope coefficient, with the result that we do not interpret it as the effect of the performance standards. To our knowledge, the only evidence of the effect of performance management on technical efficiency in the context of an active labor market program comes from the United Kingdom, where Burgess et al. (2004) find evidence of such effects for small work teams but not for large ones. This lack of evidence comes as a real surprise, given that the literature on performance incentives in private firms, well summarized in Prendergast (1999), focuses almost exclusively on productivity effects.

SUMMARY AND CONCLUSIONS

This chapter presents several empirical analyses designed to address the questions laid out in the introduction: First, do short-run performance measures predict long-run impacts? Second, what are the efficiency costs of cream skimming? We describe the identifying assumptions underlying our analyses as well as their limitations.

Taken as a whole, our empirical analysis reaches two important conclusions. First, the limited evidence we have suggests that whatever cream skimming occurs in JTPA produces only modest efficiency gains or losses. In other words, though we must acknowledge the noisiness of the evidence, our results suggest at most a modest efficiency cost associated with eschewing cream skimming in favor of a focus on the most hard-to-serve among those applying to the program. Second, the JTPA performance standards do not promote efficiency because the short-run outcomes they rely on have essentially a zero correlation with long-run impacts on employment and earnings. This surprising result comports with the findings in several other studies that have estimated this relationship.

Notes

1. This chapter presents results from Heckman, Heinrich, and Smith (2002) and borrows in places from their text.
2. In addition to simple mean differences, we can also use regression analysis to obtain experimental impact estimates. Doing so may generate more precise estimates if the exogenous conditioning variables included in the regression soak up a lot of the residual variance.
3. This concept has a variety of names in the published literature, including "perfect positive dependence" and "perfect positive rank correlation." We use "rank preservation" here because it is short and seems to be gaining ground in the most recent literature.
4. See, e.g., Heckman, Smith, and Clements (1997); Bitler, Gelbach, and Hoynes (2008); and Djebbari and Smith (2008) for more details on this estimator, including the construction of the standard errors.
5. This correction amounts to using the simple Wald instrumental variables estimator with treatment status as an instrument for enrollment. See, e.g., the discussions in Heckman, Smith, and Taber (1998) and Heckman, LaLonde, and Smith (1999, Section 5.2) on the properties and origin of this estimator.
6. An alternative strategy would generate predicted individual impacts by including interaction terms between baseline covariates and the treatment group dummy in an impact regression; see Barnow (1999) for an application.
7. Their earnings measure combines self-report data with data from Unemployment Insurance earnings records. For more details, see the discussion in Orr et al. (1996).
8. Orr et al. (1996, Exhibits 5.19 and 5.20) also present subgroup impact estimates for male and female youth. As expected given the small sample sizes, they find no statistically significant differences in estimated impacts among the subgroups.
9. To improve statistical efficiency, we use the inverse of the robust standard errors from the corresponding impact estimation as weights in each regression. Recall that the dependent variable here is the impact; its estimated standard error is thus an estimate of the variance of the error term for that impact, which represents one observation in our regression. Viewed in this way, the procedure amounts to doing weighted least squares in the presence of heteroskedasticity, where the extent of the heteroskedasticity is indicated by differences among subgroups in the estimated standard errors of the impacts.
10. We thank Tim Bartik of the W.E. Upjohn Institute for Employment Research for providing us with copies of two of the unpublished papers.
11. To see this, consider a simple case with two groups, A and B, two services, Classroom Training (CT) and Job Search Assistance (JSA), and one short-run performance measure, P. For group A, CT yields impact 100 and performance 20 while JSA yields impact 40 and performance 40. In contrast, for group B, CT yields impact 30 and performance 10 while JSA yields impact 40 and performance 40. Suppose further that without the performance management system, program staff

would maximize impacts by assigning group A to CT and group B to JSA. In contrast, with the performance management system, they maximize performance by assigning both A and B to JSA. Thus, the introduction of the performance standards system induces a substantial efficiency loss. Unfortunately, our regression analysis applied to data collected from this imaginary program after the introduction of performance standards would not reveal the efficiency loss. This follows from the fact that in the world with the performance standards system, the correlation between subgroup mean impacts and subgroup performance equals zero.

12. To see the issue, consider a simple example. In this example our program has just one service: CT. Among the applicants, some individuals have a (H)igh impact of CT because they get along well with the instructor, others would have a (L)ow impact because they do not. At the same time, applicants also differ in their job search behavior following CT. Some individuals, call them (F)ast, take the first job they find after completing CT while other individuals, call them (S)low, search longer but find a higher paying job in the end, as standard search theory would predict. Together H/L and F/S define four groups. Assume that these four groups each constitute one-quarter of the applicants and that the program has sufficient resources to serve half of the applicants. To make the example concrete, we assign the following values: H-F individuals have impact 100 and performance 50, H-S individuals have impact 120 and performance 20, L-F individuals have impact 50 and performance 50, and L-S applicants have impact 80 and performance 10. In a world without performance standards, caseworkers serve only H individuals, while in a world with performance standards, caseworkers serve only F individuals. In the applicant population, impact and performance outcomes have a negative correlation, indicating an efficiency loss from selection into the program based on performance rather than impacts. In the participant population, impact and performance have a zero correlation because, by construction, performance equals 50 for all the participants regardless of their impact. This example clearly violates the assumption of the same relationship between impacts and performance among participants and applicants. It also demonstrates that failure of this assumption can lead to a misleading conclusion about the efficiency effects of cream skimming and about whether short-term outcomes predict long-term impacts.

References

Barnow, Burt. 1999. "Exploring the Relationship between Performance Management and Program Impact: A Case Study of the Job Training Partnership Act." *Journal of Policy Analysis and Management* 19(1): 118–141.

Barnow, Burt, and Jeffrey Smith. 2004. "Performance Management of U.S. Job Training Programs." In *Job Training Policy in the United States*, Christopher O'Leary, Robert Straits, and Stephen Wandner, eds. Kalamazoo, MI: W.E. Upjohn Institute for Employment Research, pp. 21–56.

Bell, Stephen, and Larry Orr. 2002. "Screening (and Creaming?) Applicants to Job Training Programs: The AFDC Homemaker–Home Health Aide Demonstrations." *Labour Economics* 9(2): 279–301.

Bitler, Marianne, Jonah Gelbach, and Hilary Hoynes. 2008. "Distributional Impacts of the Self-Sufficiency Project." *Journal of Public Economics* 92(3–4): 748–765.

Bloom, Howard, Larry Orr, Stephen Bell, George Cave, Fred Doolittle, Winston Lin, and Johannes Bos. 1997. "The Benefits and Costs of JTPA Title II-A Programs: Key Findings from the National Job Training Partnership Act Study." *Journal of Human Resources* 32(3): 549–576.

Bloom, Howard, Larry Orr, George Cave, Stephen Bell, and Fred Doolittle. 1993. *The National JTPA Study: Title IIA Impacts on Earnings and Employment at 18 Months*. Bethesda, MD: Abt Associates.

Burgess, Simon, Carol Propper, Marisa Ratto, and Emma Tominey. 2004. "Incentives in the Public Sector: Evidence from a Government Agency." CMPO Working Paper No. 04/103. Bristol, UK: Centre for Market and Public Organisation, Bristol Institute of Public Affairs, University of Bristol.

Burghardt, John, and Peter Schochet. 2001. *National Job Corps Study: Impacts by Center Characteristics*. Princeton, NJ: Mathematica Policy Research.

Cragg, Michael. 1997. "Performance Incentives in the Public Sector: Evidence from the Job Training Partnership Act." *Journal of Law, Economics, and Organization* 13(1): 147–168.

Djebbari, Habiba, and Jeffrey Smith. 2008. "Heterogeneous Program Impacts: Experimental Evidence from the PROGRESA Program." *Journal of Econometrics* 145(1–2): 64–80.

Doolittle, Fred, and Linda Traeger. 1990. *Implementing the National JTPA Study*. New York: Manpower Demonstration Research Corporation.

Friedlander, Daniel. 1988. *Subgroup Impacts and Performance Indicators for Selected Welfare Employment Programs*. New York: Manpower Demonstration Research Corporation.

Gay, Robert, and Michael Borus. 1980. "Validating Performance Indicators for Employment and Training Programs." *Journal of Human Resources* 15(1): 29–48.

Heckman, James. 1992. "Randomization and Social Program Evaluation." In *Evaluating Welfare and Training Programs*, Charles Manski and Irwin Garfinkel, eds. Cambridge, MA: Harvard University Press, pp. 201–230.

Heckman, James, Carolyn Heinrich, and Jeffrey Smith. 2002. "The Performance of Performance Standards." *Journal of Human Resources* 37(4): 778–811.

Heckman, James, Neil Hohmann, Jeffrey Smith, and Michael Khoo. 2000. "Substitution and Dropout Bias in Social Experiments: A Study of an Influential Social Experiment." *Quarterly Journal of Economics* 105(2): 651–694.

Heckman, James, Robert LaLonde, and Jeffrey Smith. 1999. "The Economics and Econometrics of Active Labor Market Programs." In *Handbook of Labor Economics,* Vol. 3A, Orley Ashenfelter and David Card, eds. Amsterdam: North-Holland, pp. 1865–2097.

Heckman, James, and Jeffrey Smith. 1998. "Evaluating the Welfare State." In *Econometrics and Economic Theory in the 20th Century: The Ragnar Frisch Centennial*, Steinar Strøm, ed. Econometric Society Monograph No. 31. Cambridge: Cambridge University Press, pp. 241–318.

———. 2000. "The Sensitivity of Experimental Impact Estimates: Evidence from the National JTPA Study." In *Youth Employment and Joblessness in Advanced Countries*, David Blanchflower and Richard Freeman, eds. NBER Comparative Labor Markets Series. Chicago: University of Chicago Press, pp. 331–356.

Heckman, James, Jeffrey Smith, and Nancy Clements. 1997. "Making the Most Out of Programme Evaluations and Social Experiments: Accounting for Heterogeneity in Programme Impacts." *Review of Economic Studies* 64(4): 487–535.

Heckman, James, Jeffrey Smith, and Christopher Taber. 1996. "What Do Bureaucrats Do? The Effects of Performance Standards and Bureaucratic Preferences on Acceptance into the JTPA Program." In *Advances in the Study of Entrepreneurship, Innovation, and Economic Growth,* Vol. 7: *Reinventing Government and the Problem of Bureaucracy*, Gary Libecap, ed. Greenwich, CT: JAI Press, pp. 191–218.

———. 1998. "Accounting for Dropouts in Evaluations of Social Programs." *Review of Economics and Statistics* 80(1): 1–14.

Hotz, V. Joseph. 1992. "Designing an Evaluation of the Job Training Partnership Act." In *Evaluating Welfare and Training Programs*, Charles Manski and Irwin Garfinkel, eds. Cambridge, MA: Harvard University Press, pp. 76–114.

Kemple, James, Fred Doolittle, and John Wallace. 1993. *The National JTPA Study: Site Characteristics and Participation Patterns*. New York: Manpower Demonstration Research Corporation.

Kornfeld, Robert, and Howard Bloom. 1999. "Measuring Program Impacts on Earnings and Employment: Do Unemployment Insurance Wage Reports from Employers Agree with Surveys of Individuals." *Journal of Labor Economics* 17(1): 168–197.

Lechner, Michael, and Jeffrey Smith. 2007. "What Is the Value Added by Case Workers?" *Labour Economics* 14(2): 135–151.

Orr, Larry, Howard Bloom, Stephen Bell, Fred Doolittle, Winston Lin, and George Cave. 1996. *Does Training for the Disadvantaged Work? Evidence from the National JTPA Study*. Washington, DC: Urban Institute Press.

Orr, Larry, Howard Bloom, Stephen Bell, Winston Lin, George Cave, and Fred Doolittle. 1994. *The National JTPA Study: Impacts, Benefits, and Costs of Title II-A*. Bethesda, MD: Abt Associates.

Prendergast, Canice. 1999. "The Provision of Incentives in Firms." *Journal of Economic Literature* 37(1): 7–63.

Smith, Jeffrey. 1997. "Measuring Earnings Levels among the Poor: Evidence from Two Samples of JTPA Eligibles." Working paper. London, Ontario, Canada: University of Western Ontario.

Zornitsky, Jeffrey, and Mary Rubin. 1988. *Establishing a Performance Management System for Targeted Welfare Programs*. Report No. 88-14. Washington, DC: National Commission for Employment Policy.

10
Lessons for Advancing Future Performance Standards Systems

James J. Heckman
Carolyn J. Heinrich
Jeffrey Smith

The economic recession that started in 2007 led to renewed interest in public employment and training services. At the same time, the accompanying financial crises also elevated concern for how dwindling government budgets could be spent more efficiently and effectively to maximize returns to public investments in training. As discussed in the introductory chapter, revamping incentive systems in government is a critical step toward improving government performance and our future economic outlook.

The chapters in this volume marshal some of the most detailed evidence available on how performance standards and incentives influence the behavior of program administrators and staff and contribute to program outcomes or unintended consequences. Since each chapter presents a self-contained summary of its main findings, we do not review the details of each one. Instead, this conclusion presents three main lessons learned from these essays and discusses some of their policy implications.

LESSON 1: AGENCIES RESPOND TO INCENTIVES

Concerns that performance incentives are disregarded by government employees because award levels are low or because benefits are diffused are not justified. Low-powered cash incentives may, in fact, be high-powered because of the value of the budgetary awards in establishing the reputation of bureaucrats and the recognition that comes with them. Bonuses and award money create leverage in the social services community and are thus frequently highly prized (Heinrich 2007). The evidence reported by Courty and Marschke in Chapter 7 demonstrates that agencies made placement, enrollment, and termination decisions in ways that were consistent with maximizing their performance as measured by the JTPA performance standards system. The evidence presented by Heinrich in Chapter 8 reveals that although caseworkers claimed to discount performance standards in decision making, they nevertheless selectively enrolled into JTPA people who were likely to contribute to the placement goals rewarded under the performance standards system.

Courty and Marschke and Heinrich also present a dark side to the behavior elicited by the JTPA performance standards system. Training centers showed remarkable ingenuity in manipulating the JTPA accounting system and reporting requirements in their efforts to boost their measured performance. Practices included enrolling persons receiving job search assistance or on-the-job training only after they found a job, using short-term training arrangements in order to maximize the probability of counting a successful placement, holding persons who did not find jobs in dead-end job clubs, and releasing poorly performing trainees from the program at strategic accounting dates when it did least damage to training center performance records. These all represent behaviors that make perfect sense in terms of the performance standards, but they do nothing to raise participant earnings or increase the equity with which program services are distributed.

The problem of regulating job-training programs—or any government agency—is that enforceable regulations cannot be written too finely, and simple rules can and will, as shown in this volume, be subverted. Along these lines, performance standards systems designers also need to grasp the dynamic properties of performance incentive systems, as discussed in Chapter 5 and illustrated throughout this volume. An incentive system designer's understanding of how individuals will respond to performance standards will inevitably be imperfect prior to their introduction, and it is only as performance measures and targets are tried, evaluated, modified, and/or discarded that their responses become known (Courty and Marschke 2007). Of course, this type of monitoring to assess a measure's effectiveness and possible distortion requires a considerable investment on the part of incentive system designers, one that has probably been underestimated in the past. And as Heinrich and Marschke (2010) point out, learning on the part of bureaucrats will advance over time as well, as they come to better know the distinct weaknesses of performance measures and how they can be exploited through their day-to-day experiences. Incentive system designers will have to expect to regularly review and revise the rules and incentives they create if they want to avoid the inefficient behavior documented in the chapters in this volume.

LESSON 2: CURRENT PERFORMANCE STANDARDS DO NOT PREDICT LONG-RUN GAINS

While the chapters by Courty and Marschke and Heinrich indicate that the JTPA performance standards system effectively motivated agency staff and service providers to meet short-run performance standards, they do not indicate whether the measures themselves are appropriate to induce the achievement of the primary program goals, i.e., increasing the earnings of program participants (or the value added of the program). Chapter 9 demonstrates that the short-run performance measures featured by the JTPA performance standards system were weakly and often perversely related to the long-term effects of the program on the earnings and employment of participants. Yet it is these long-term effects that constituted the true goal of the program's services. The analysis also reveals that the measurement of wages and employment at a later point following termination represented no improvement in the performance monitoring system. Neither set of measures was strongly positively related to long-run program impacts on earnings and employment, suggesting that the performance standards system did not promote the program's key objectives of long-run gains in earnings and employment for participants. We see no reason to expect that the relationships between the performance measures and programs have changed under WIA and thus no reason to think that this problem has gone away.

From the perspective of policymakers and taxpayers who would like to maximize the value from government dollars spent on public programs, the goal of incentive system designers should be to choose performance measures so that the effects of bureaucratic actions on measured performance are aligned with the effects of those same actions on value added. However, we frequently lack the information required to realize this objective in practice. Empirical research, as Heckman and Smith suggest, has focused primarily on estimating measures of statistical association between performance and value added, where the value added of programs has been assessed through the use of randomized experiments or through sophisticated statistical modeling. The dynamics of performance standards systems, however, may limit the usefulness even of these estimates, as the alignment between a performance measure and value added may decrease after a performance measure is introduced and bureaucrats respond by exploring *all* strategies for raising it, not just those that also increase program value added. Clearly, this will continue to be one of the most vexing issues for performance standards system designers for some time to come.

LESSON 3: THE CREAM SKIMMING PROBLEM IS OVERSTATED

The charge of cream skimming has arisen frequently in public job training programs, including the Workforce Investment Act program. In Chapters 3, 6, and 9, we define various uses of this term and present evidence that fears about cream skimming are overstated. For most demographic groups, experimental estimates of the earnings impacts of participation in JTPA are uniform over broad skill levels. Only at the lowest skill levels is there any evidence that impacts were smaller than at higher levels of the skill distribution. While there is some evidence of a trade-off between serving the most disadvantaged within eligible populations and allocating program resources most efficiently, it appears to be a modest one given the modest benefits realized by program participants.

Cream skimming is usually defined as arising from purposive screening behavior by bureaucrats. Chapters 6 and 8 present information about disparities in program participation rates among different demographic groups. Even among eligible persons, there are substantial differences in program participation rates. It is not enough to compare participation rates among the eligible to determine if cream skimming is an important factor. At issue is how much of the difference in participation rates conditional on eligibility is due to the voluntary choices of individuals, how much is due to their lack of information about the program, and how much is due to the decisions of bureaucrats. The decompositions of participation rates into components due to eligibility, awareness, and acceptance that are presented in Chapter 6 reveal that personal choices and lack of information play the major role in accounting for demographic disparities in participation. Administrative discretion also has some role to play in determining the participation rates of different groups in public job training programs, but it is not the dominant factor.

The evidence in Chapters 6 and 8 indicates that those whose characteristics make them more employable and more easily placed were more likely to be screened into the JTPA system. However, the analysis of Chapter 6 reveals that the same characteristics that make a person more attractive in terms of achieving objectives within the job placement system also made that person more aware of the program and more willing to apply to it. Thus, if resources are going to be used to improve equity in access to programs with voluntary enrollment, incentive system designers and program administrators should consider investing more in (or providing incentives for) increasing awareness of the program among the eligible population.

We realize that there will be some limits to the generalizability of these findings and the lessons of this collection of studies to other public program contexts, and that there is inherent variability in the potential of performance standards systems for improving government performance in the many different contexts in which they have been introduced or considered. At the same time, it is clear that there is no diminishing of demand on the part of policymakers or the public for greater accountability and a results-oriented focus of government. The research in this volume suggests that there is considerable work to do in addressing the flaws of current public sector performance standards systems as well as investing in research that will guide improvements and advancements to these systems as their use expands in the public sector.

References

Courty, Pascal, and Gerald Marschke. 2007. "A General Test for Distortions in Performance Measures." *Review of Economics and Statistics* 90(3): 428–441.

Heinrich, Carolyn J. 2007. "False or Fitting Recognition? The Use of High Performance Bonuses in Motivating Organizational Achievements." *Journal of Policy Analysis and Management* 26(2): 281–304.

Heinrich, Carolyn J., and Gerald R. Marschke. 2010. "Incentives and Their Dynamics in Public Sector Performance Management Systems." *Journal of Policy Analysis and Management* 29(1): 183–208.

Authors

Pascal Courty is a research fellow of the Centre for Economic Policy Research. In 2009 he joined the University of Victoria from the European University Institute, where he was a professor of economics. He was previously associate professor at the London Business School, and assistant professor at University Pompeu Fabra. He has taught at the University of Chicago GSB, Universitat Autònoma de Barcelona, and the Hong Kong School of Business. He received a PhD from the University of Chicago. Professor Courty has contributed to the fields of industrial organization, labor economics, personnel economics, and law and economics. His work is applied, and he has contributed to questions related to congestion pricing, resale markets for tickets, pop concert pricing, the design of incentives in government organizations, gaming in performance measurement systems, and the sorting of physicians in medical specialties. His work has been published in leading academic journals such as the *American Economic Review, Review of Economics Studies, Journal of Economics and Statistics, Journal of Labor Economics, Journal of Law and Economics, Journal of Economic Perspective, Economic Journal,* and *Journal of Human Resources*.

James J. Heckman is the Henry Schultz Distinguished Service Professor of Economics at the University of Chicago, where he has served since 1973. In 2000, he shared the Sveriges Riksbank Prize in Economic Sciences in Memory of Alfred Nobel with Daniel McFadden. Heckman directs the Economics Research Center and the Center for Social Program Evaluation at the Harris School for Public Policy. In addition, he is professor of science and society in University College Dublin and a senior research fellow at the American Bar Foundation. Heckman received a BA in mathematics from Colorado College in 1965 and a PhD in economics from Princeton University in 1971. His work has been devoted to the development of a scientific basis for economic policy evaluation, with special emphasis on models of individuals and disaggregated groups, and to the problems and possibilities created by heterogeneity, diversity, and unobserved counterfactual states. He developed a body of new econometric tools that address these issues. His research has given policymakers important new insights into areas such as education, job training, the importance of accounting for general equilibrium in the analysis of labor markets, antidiscrimination law, and civil rights. His recent research focuses on inequality, human development, and life cycle skill formation, with a special emphasis on the economics of early childhood. He is currently conducting new social experiments on early childhood interventions and reanalyzing old experiments. He is also studying the emergence of the underclass in the United States and Western Europe.

Carolyn J. Heinrich is the Director of the La Follette School of Public Affairs, Professor of Public Affairs and Affiliated Professor of Economics, and a Regina Loughlin Scholar at the University of Wisconsin–Madison. She earned a PhD at the University of Chicago in 1995. In August 2011, she will assume the Sid Richardson Chair in Public Affairs and the Directorship of the Center for Health and Social Policy at the Lyndon B. Johnson School of Public Affairs at the University of Texas at Austin. Her research focuses on public management and performance management and the implementation and evaluation of education, employment and training, and other human capital development and social welfare programs and policies. She is the author of more than 50 peer-reviewed publications, including articles in the *Journal of Human Resources, Journal of Labor Economics, American Economic Review, Review of Economics and Statistics, Review of Economics of the Household, World Development, Journal of Policy Analysis and Management, Journal of Public Administration Research and Theory, Public Administration Review*, and four coauthored/edited books. In 2004, she received the David N. Kershaw Award for distinguished contributions to the field of public policy analysis and management by a person under the age of 40.

Gerald Marschke is associate professor of economics at the University at Albany, SUNY. He has also taught at Harvard University and the University at Buffalo, State University of New York. Marschke is a faculty research fellow of the National Bureau of Economic Research and a research fellow at the Institute for the Study of Labor. From 2008 to 2010, he was a Wertheim Fellow with the Labor and Worklife Program at Harvard Law School. He received a PhD in economics in 1997 from the University of Chicago, where he had also been a research associate at the Center for Social Program Evaluation (directed by James J. Heckman). Marschke's research has spanned the fields of labor economics, industrial organization, public economics, organizational economics, and the economics of science. His recent work has examined how performance-based incentives in (primarily public) organizations affect organizational productivity and worker behavior. Much of his current work focuses on the economics of science and technology. Some of this work attempts to econometrically measure the importance of U.S. scientific and engineering labor markets in determining and directing technological progress; other work investigates the organization of science and R&D, including the evolution and life cycle of innovating teams and recent trends in scientific collaboration and their impacts on science. In another project, he examines the impact of federal science and research and development funding on scientific, technological, and economic growth. His work has been supported by the National Science Foundation, the National Institutes of Health, and the Sloan Foundation. He has published in leading economics and policy journals including the *American Economic Review, Journal of Human Resources, Journal of Labor Economics, Journal of Policy Analysis and Management, Labour Economics, The RAND Journal of Economics,* and *The Review of Economics and Statistics*.

Jeffrey Smith is professor of economics at the University of Michigan. He received a PhD in economics from the University of Chicago in 1996. From 1994 to 2001 he was on the faculty at the University of Western Ontario, and from 2001 to 2005 he was on the faculty at the University of Maryland. His research centers on experimental and nonexperimental methods for the evaluation of interventions, with particular application to social and educational programs. He has also written papers examining the labor market effects of university quality and the use of statistical treatment rules to assign persons to government programs. Important publications include "Is the Threat of Reemployment Services More Effective than the Services Themselves?" (with Dan Black, Mark Berger, and Brett Noel) in the *American Economic Review* (2003), "The Economics and Econometrics of Active Labor Market Programmes" (with James Heckman and Robert LaLonde) in the *Handbook of Labor Economics, Volume 3A* (1999), "Does Matching Overcome LaLonde's Critique of Nonexperimental Mcthods?" (with Petra Todd), *Journal of Econometrics* (2005), and "Heterogeneous Program Impacts: Experimental Evidence from the PROGRESA Program" (with Habiba Djebbari), *Journal of Econometrics* (2008). He has consulted on evaluation issues to governments in the United States, Canada, the United Kingdom, and Australia.

Index

The italic letters *f, n,* and *t* following a page number indicate that the subject information of the heading is within a figure, note, or table, respectively, on that page. Double italics indicate multiple but consecutive elements.

About the Institute

The W.E. Upjohn Institute for Employment Research is a nonprofit research organization devoted to finding and promoting solutions to employment-related problems at the national, state, and local levels. It is an activity of the W.E. Upjohn Unemployment Trustee Corporation, which was established in 1932 to administer a fund set aside by Dr. W.E. Upjohn, founder of The Upjohn Company, to seek ways to counteract the loss of employment income during economic downturns.

The Institute is funded largely by income from the W.E. Upjohn Unemployment Trust, supplemented by outside grants, contracts, and sales of publications. Activities of the Institute comprise the following elements: 1) a research program conducted by a resident staff of professional social scientists; 2) a competitive grant program, which expands and complements the internal research program by providing financial support to researchers outside the Institute; 3) a publications program, which provides the major vehicle for disseminating the research of staff and grantees, as well as other selected works in the field; and 4) an Employment Management Services division, which manages most of the publicly funded employment and training programs in the local area.

The broad objectives of the Institute's research, grant, and publication programs are to 1) promote scholarship and experimentation on issues of public and private employment and unemployment policy, and 2) make knowledge and scholarship relevant and useful to policymakers in their pursuit of solutions to employment and unemployment problems.

Current areas of concentration for these programs include causes, consequences, and measures to alleviate unemployment; social insurance and income maintenance programs; compensation; workforce quality; work arrangements; family labor issues; labor-management relations; and regional economic development and local labor markets.